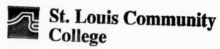

SCREENING THE PAST

SCREENING THE PAST

Film and the Representation of History

Edited by Tony Barta

Westport, Connecticut
London

Library of Congress Cataloging-in-Publication Data

Screening the past : film and the representation of history / edited
   by Tony Barta.
        p.   cm.
    Includes bibliographical references and index.
    ISBN 0-275-95402-1 (alk. paper)
    1. Motion pictures and history.   2. Historical films—History and
criticism.   I. Barta, Tony, 1942-   .
    PN1995.2.S38   1998
    791.43'658—dc21   97-37811

British Library Cataloguing in Publication Data is available.

Library of Congress Catalog Card Number: 97-37811
ISBN: 0-275-95402-1

First published in 1998

Praeger Publishers, 88 Post Road West, Westport, CT 06881
An imprint of Greenwood Publishing Group, Inc.

Printed in the United States of America

The paper used in this book complies with the
Permanent Paper Standard issued by the National
Information Standards Organization (Z39.48-1984).

10 9 8 7 6 5 4 3 2

Copyright Acknowledgments

The editor and publisher gratefully acknowledge permission to use the following material:

Excerpts from the film scripts for *Mutiny on the Bounty* (1935) and *Mutiny on the Bounty* (1962), Dialogue Continuity. Hollywood: Metro-Goldwyn-Mayer. New York State Archives, Albany, NY.

Excerpts from chapter 2 have been published in Greg Dening, *Mr. Bligh's Bad Language: Passion, Power, and Theatre on the Bounty.* Cambridge: Cambridge University Press, 1992. Reprinted courtesy of Cambridge University Press.

The cover from *Radio Times*, 15–21 June 1996, is reprinted by permission of *Radio Times*.

Chapter 8 first appeared in *Metro*, No. 100, Melbourne, Summer 1994–1995: 3–13. Reprinted by permission.

Chapter 15 is reprinted from *Common Knowledge*, Vol. 3, no. 1, Spring 1994, by permission of the author.

Excerpts from chapter 16 were first published by the journal *World Literature Today* in 1993. ©. Reprinted by permission of the editor.

Every reasonable effort has been made to trace the owners of copyright materials in this book, but in some instances this has proven impossible. The editor and publisher will be glad to receive information leading to more complete acknowledgments in subsequent printings of the book and in the meantime extend their apologies for any omissions.

Contents

Introduction

"I know, they're the ones where they write with feathers."
—Sam Goldwyn on historical films

The relationship between film and history is less cozily opposed than it used to be. It was a relatively straightforward matter some years ago for historians to criticize the misrepresentations of dramatized versions of the past: a Roman slave would not have talked like Charlton Heston's Ben Hur; the commander of a medieval army would have been rather less civilized than Eisenstein's Nevsky; a French peasant girl would scarcely have had the poise of Nathalie Baye in *The Return of Martin Guerre*. Allowances had to be made for the screen, which of course was much more the creature of historical pressures in the present than academic history was—a delusion still to be found in some corners of the academy. Commerce had to have its due: the stars were there for the box office and so were the plots. The costume department, though, should try to get things right. With "natural colour," "natural sound," and more natural acting too, our expectations rose. A muted, and therefore more vividly present, style of filming offered moments (and extended spells—in both senses) when the "realism" of artificial replication could be both admired and forgotten.

Just as cinema achieved its paradoxical invisibility, history—not uninflu-

enced by film theory and criticism—decided to become more self aware
and deconstructionist. The past was hard to access, it was in effect recreated
from fragments. Films took you there as if there was nothing simpler, every
part of the process of representation disguised. Historians needed to look
more intently at screen representation, its many historical contexts, and
their own practices as representers of the past. Professionalism demanded
reflection. Now it is acknowledged, if not widely pursued, that the presentation of history, the re-presentation of the past, have been decisively
changed by the screen media; the appetite for the moving image fed by our
everyday media encounters can be suppressed in individuals but not in the
culture as a whole. This book is an attempt to integrate the academic culture of historians—some of them screen historians—with the media realities of contemporary historical understandings.

Play on the many ways the past is "screened" (sifted, obscured, projected) gives the project a rather large brief. Absent, gone the moment it
happened, the past cannot be known, yet it permeates our consciousness
by its vivid and pervasive reproduction. Are there ways of representing the
past on the screen that also create understandings about the construction
of history? It would be odd if it were otherwise. Gore Vidal has installed
motion pictures as "the lingua franca of the twentieth century. The Tenth
Muse, as they call the movies in Italy, has driven the other nine right off
Olympus—or off the peak, anyway." His life, he says, "has paralleled,
when not intersected, the entire history of the talking picture."[1] Many of
us only feel that way.

In the essays that follow, all the authors are writing in the difficult ambience between the analytical and the absorbed. They have taken on the
extraordinary challenge of translating from one medium to another: that
imaginative staple of all art criticism which artists find so hard to imagine.
Because the medium of print does not actually shift on the page, however
much the meaning shifts in different readings, we consider the encoding of
meaning in fonts and lines of text more stable. It can be inspected and
quoted and debated with more practiced protocols. The shimmering text
of the movies is harder to be precise about in words: the translation from
a medium of light and movement to one of written speech is itself an art
that the following essays approach in quite different ways.

I have decided to let the differences—and the authors—speak for themselves. For all the variety in perspective and style, the pieces form a whole
that can be read as such from beginning to end. My major intervention has
been akin to the art dealt with in each chapter: the placing of one point of
view next to another in a sequence intended to give unity and additional
meaning. An academic editor, too, makes a montage of a book.

Every editor has very real debts. The first is to the contributors, without
whom the collective work would not exist. The second is to the publishing
house: there are now not a great number who share the idea that many

voices can be better than one. I want to thank my editors at Greenwood Press for their helpfulness and patience. The book would have been difficult to complete without support from many colleagues in Melbourne, especially Ina Bertrand and Brian McFarlane, and from my editorial assistant, Katya Johanson. The History Department at La Trobe University has facilitated the enterprise from the outset.

Through many years of teaching history and film at La Trobe I have had to share with students my regret that the relatively rare—if inspiring— writing in their specific area has made for a rather short shelf of reading. Now the leadership of Pierre Sorlin, Robert Rosenstone, and others is bringing dividends. All of us contributing to this book hope that it will soon find itself in a larger company.

NOTE

1. Gore Vidal, *Screening History* (London: André Deutsch, 1992), pp. 2,6.

SCREENING THE PAST

Screening the Past: History Since the Cinema

Tony Barta

Everyone, in the twentieth century past, has his or her first close encounter with the screen. In my memory I was very small and the screen was terrifyingly large. My father, in one of those nonchalantly confident transgressions fathers can impress us with, took me right up onto the stage of the State—or was it the Empire?—theater where the vast white expanse dwarfed both of us. It must have been in the first year of CinemaScope: I remember the slope and the curve like the inside of a giant bowl. But it wasn't the shape or the size that amazed me most. It was the holes. There seeemed to be as much absence of screen as surface and I could not think how the picture could reflect back at me with such brilliance when so much was missing.

Later, I found I had taken up the profession—the professing—of history. Most of the work had to do with other missing elements, with finding data, turning it into evidence, and finding strategies to indicate (or not indicate) how much might still be absent. The absences began to make more sense as the accomplished historians around me moved beyond our rejection of positive faith in facts into positive acceptance of difference, subjectivity, and multiple perspectives. The protocols of professional, academic history are not my focus here, however; neither do I want to labor the difference between "evidentiary history," healthily surviving its postmodern adaptations, and film as another kind of history.[1] My concern is to connect the rise of modern history with the precursors, practitioners, and successors of cinematic magic, to pause over some of the ways it works as history, and to seek signs of the transition to a postmodern consciousness in history practice after a century of film. My connections and clues will inevitably be historical, themselves a representation of a past. Just as inevitably, given my view that history on the page must seize its special advantages, they will be theoretical.

"Theory," I've only recently learned, derives from the Greek "to look at" or "to witness."[2] Faced with the huge amount of film theory that could be helpful, I've looked mainly for theory built into history, explanations of how film witnesses the past, how it helps us see history. Since I believe that history can only be "seen" as a conceptual web, as an infinitely complex set of relations which we simplify by categorizing and connecting, I think of history as a theoretical construct. We theorize because that is the only way we can see: we need other kinds of senses behind our ocular ones to trace the patterns of relations by which we make meaning—history—from the record of the past.

This kind of seeing-by-theorizing has more in common with *not* seeing, *not* believing, than with witnessing. It makes everything problematical, including the media we prefer to deal with by a *modus vivendi* of common sense. In writing and reading we come to be aware of representation, of genres, modes, and rhetoric. "Argument" and "evidence" become anything but self-evident. In film media it is the same, with the further problem of verisimilitude. We know we employ imagination to make the black marks on a white page turn into a scene, an event, or an experience. In a cinema, and often enough even watching television, we are lulled by the apparent transparency of the screen, the solidity of what is depicted. There is an effort of materialist attention and metaphorical persistence required to look at the screen as screen rather than as window. Watching a costume drama or a historical documentary we want the screen to be a window on the past. We need to sustain a different order of curiosity once we see the scope of the problems our questions raise. What, then, *is* on the screen? What do we contribute to the reality, or the history, we experience? How does a selection of projected images and sounds succeed—as most do—in projecting a whole past? When (inescapable in my historical project) did seeing become believing?

Until the century when photographic plates, then film, began to record what was before the lens, there probably never was a time when humans were sure that what they saw was really there. Or rather, "the evidence of one's own eyes" could as much be trusted to correspond with a transmaterial reality—spirit visitors, visions of other presents, pasts, and futures— as with the merely material appearance of things. Photography, initially, left little room for doubt. If a Victorian seance was going to have a spirit visitor from the Beyond, there had better be some means of making the Departed visible to light-sensitive silver as well as to the suggestible Bereaved. However, people soon learned that credulous spiritualism and skeptical (photographic) materialism were able to coexist quite comfortably, just as the current consciouness of computer manipulation of images does nothing to destroy the general credibility of news footage and advertising photography. The simultaneous flourishing must on some level be symbiotic, with doubt feeding the roots of pragmatic belief.

The other parallel development, remarkable as an amalgam of faith and scientific inquiry, indeed as such historically unique, was history. Whether popular or academic, the nineteenth-century fascination with verifiable accounts of the past was central to the positivist faith of the modern era. As print reproduction directed billions of printed words at millions of newly literate people, its illustrations of events progressed from etchings to photographs. The "mass media" arrived in time for "the masses" to have versions of the past mediated to them in apparently incontrovertible form. And when the newest media of motion pictures and voice reproduction crowned nineteenth-century belief in scientific recording of the natural world, millions of cinemagoers and phonograph listeners were set for a new era of verisimilitude, disbelief—and suspension of disbelief. Historians by then had a professional turf to protect, and even if they as yet reflected little on their own use of rhetorical arts, they could justifiably say that they were always prepared to deal with doubts about documents and arguments over interpretation. The academy was the place to slow things down: the special property of cinema was to bring truth and artifice, action and acting, documentary and drama, on to one and the same screen with not even a split second to tell them apart. Yet within a decade the new art of fragmentation and movement would compel every form of representation, from painting to academic exposition, to show its influence. Picasso's multifaceted females were a symbol of the movies; so were Wittgenstein's notes.

How the whole planet was reeducated to accept alienated images of the natural body so far from any bodily contact, of the everyday so remote from our day-to-day lives, is a history only now being explored. Many media were involved: the press, the telegraph, the telephone. The living voice now spoke directly into one's ear, but without its body. The voice was a remote yet immediate image of another life. It was present from a distance and could be recorded to remain present when the speech was past, even, indeed, when the speaker had "passed away." Everything that reason and modernity imported into the realm of positive scientific understanding expanded the range of demands on human consciousness and required a new commonsense simply to cope with the changing media environment. Reality became surreality and that became commonsense, too.[3] The positive optimism of the nineteenth-century modern was about to enter the twentieth century of postmodern doubt and insecurity.

Their minds on ingenuity rather than epochs, the Lumière brothers cranked their marvelous mechanism. Workers left the factory and the train at La Ciotât left the station. Then, on the screen, people and locomotives did it all again. Strange, this lifelike movement, lifeless and dreamlike without sound. Supposedly the brothers saw little future for their invention, after Edison's struggles and failure in the media marketplace. Perhaps amateurs would be interested in recording the world around them, or in making home movies with family actors. Out of such humdrum ambitions were the tumultuous twins "documentary" and "drama" coupled from birth. Certainly, real-life happenings were being documented on the screen. Just as certainly, they were being dramatized. Point of view, framing of shot, length of take—all constructed the record at the moment of its mere recording. The present, having been ushered by light onto a chemical film, could now simply be "developed" and cranked through again as representation, as past. How problematical was it meant to be? Not very, one suspects, and in the beginning all could celebrate the apotheosis of photography—writing with light—in the reproduction of what light shows us in nature: movement.

There are marvels here that we should review—that is, *re*-view with some of the amazement of those who first saw the brought-to-life past *re*-presented (made present again) on the screen. The dramatization devices, the new film language as Balàzs called it, had to be learned. People could quickly enter into this most natural and naturalistic medium, the one most like face-to-face communication, by employing their first-learned skills of reading expression and gesture. At the same time they had to deal with a pictorial and narrative style based on the frame, and therefore most artificial and weird. It was Griffith, according to Balàzs, who most effectively pioneered "film language" and dared to try a big close-up on a Hollywood audience. When a huge "severed" head smiled at the public for the first time, there was panic in the cinema.

The individual frames were not the only denaturalizing, renaturalizing innovation. Even more extraordinary was the shifting viewpoint of the separate shots. By simply putting one next to another an association was irresistible; since this montage always promoted a *narrative* association, an implied connection in time and space, a new storytelling time and space was created, a specifically filmic diegesis.[4] It is in this sense that Pudovkin insisted the film is not so much shot as *built*. And in the process of constructing a new diegetic approach to objects, character and action, historical reality, too, could be seen afresh. "To show something as everyone else sees it is to show nothing," deserves to be Pudovkin's most famous slogan, suitably opposed to bourgeois historiography's now notorious ambition. Historians having trumpeted their aim to show the past "as it actually was," the revolutionary Russians declared apparent realities needed to be "shot" to pieces and "built" anew before film could claim to be "showing" anything.[5]

In the four years 1914–1918, the disrupted realities of realism had become commonplace to millions. The newsreel reports from the battlefields showed faces and formations of doomed soldiers advancing into shell-fire, mud and bodies spraying, airplanes overflying the bucolic or tormented countryside, and great navies parading the power suitable to the first ever World War. Instant history on the screen foregrounded "history"—the process—as unstable and open. The fragmentation of real landscapes and real people and real powers made ideas of transforming political change imaginable. Image politics of desperately counter-fragmentary, even totalitarian unity, were the result. In the 1920s new sound technologies outstripped the movies in media politics. The microphone and the loud speaker carried the voices of party leaders into every town square. Then the movies caught up again. The next triumph of media modernism once more coincided with a high point of triumphalist history: American, Soviet, Fascist, and National Socialist achievements were projected to the world of the 1930s in ideological competition with more established varieties of imperial propaganda. The climax was again a World War. Synchronized sound and then "living" color arrived in time to make total war and unprecedended death a vivid motion picture presentation.

After Stalin and Hitler, whose persons and unexampled atrocities we still remember in the suitably stark safety of black and white, distrust of film's propaganda power contended with its documentary force. Wide-screen dramatizations of biblical times seemed safe when memories of the cruder wartime messages were fresh. Less epic dramas—screened by the conventions of the screenplay—remained as ideologically potent as before. With postwar domesticity the "returning home" genre was able to disguise the historical shift it promoted: women out of the workforce while we reintegrate the men. Movie memories now, as well as real ones, posed historical questions. Should men again have their masculinity put at risk by unemployment, as Henry Fonda refused to let happen in *The Grapes of Wrath*? Could the decency of a Jimmy Stewart not make America, and then the world, safe for democracy?

Right on cue came the shift from the heroic mode of the movies to the domestication of the moving image. Television had ambitions as grandiose as any mogul's, but they had to be realized with a new hominess. The screen was smaller, more intimate, and more insistent. The precursor of the TV set, we now sometimes forget, was less the cinema than the radio. Where sound had been, and remained, a companion inside the house (even if grandly installed, as the "radiogram," in its own piece of furniture), television demanded attention. This piece of furniture was now the one around which others were placed. When color arrived it fulfilled television's claim to be a window on the world. The set in the corner gave instant and democratizing access to statesmen, floods, famines, and, of course, wars. "Bringing the war home" meant frontline gunfire and body counts in the living room, the television permanently inciting assent to—or dissent from—national policy. Yet it always seemed undemanding. Most people rate entertainment as the primary attraction of television, and the moving, talking picture made it easy for the audiovisual stream of unconsciousness to usurp a large proportion of human capacity for conscious engagement with the world. To see without seeing is our historically peculiar vision from up close and afar.

Only rarely, within the conventions of instant-history television, do the larger historical significances become actively significant to an audience trained as passive spectators. Bill Nichols saw it happen in the case of Rodney King:

"Rodney King," as signifier for this larger array of events that so massively exceeded his own body and his own experience, bursts beyond the frame of spectacle, of sensation and banality, and viewer response run to ground. Frames collide. Excess (history itself) spills out. Response to this tape did not pour into the gutter of grounded sensation and compensatory consumption. Collective outrage demanded redress—not charity or penance. Violent response, symbolic action at its most indignant, burst beyond the frame of representation.[6]

Pathological eruptions have always been favored by social and historical analysts for the entry they open to normality. Dominating our normality is the pictorial framing of reality we have become accustomed to. Where did it come from? Neither photography nor cinema made modern times visual. The process started with the first victories of the modern. In seventeenth-century Holland, Svetlana Alpers has argued, "the visual culture was central to the life of the society. One might say that the eye was a central means of self-representation and visual experience a mode of self-consciousness. If the theater was the arena in which the England of Elizabeth most fully represented itself to itself, images played that role for the Dutch."[7] We assume that images played a role in every society, and some form of theater, too. They were combined in cinema, and in a quite transformed way in television. Television would now be nominated by most people as the system of representation most representative of our time, though elements of the still newer screen medium, the computer, already influence its way of representing ourselves to ourselves many times each minute.

Technical developments are genuinely *techno-logical*: the whole logic of apprehension, appropriation, and meaning is matched to the restless media revolution of modern times. We all sort of know this; we just hold back from dealing with it. Here also we could learn from earlier encounters. Alpers again: "It was a particular assumption of the seventeenth century that finding and making, our discovery of the world and our crafting of it, are presumed to be as one." We easily forget that the photographic realism of Vermeer and his contemporaries employed the camera obscura as a device for screening their present to themselves and mediating it as documentary and drama to us. Alpers recalls that "though the lens was long known, it had been considered distorting and deceptive. It was not until the seventeenth century that it was trusted." There is the change. "It is less the nature or use made of the camera obscura image than the trust placed in it that is of interest to us in understanding Dutch painting." This, she says, is the relevance of Kepler, who provided the scientific rationale for the belief in literal representation. "For in defining the human eye itself as mechanical maker of pictures and in defining 'to see' as 'to picture,' he provides the model we need for that particular binding of finding and making, of nature and art, that characterizes the picture in the north."[8]

From the north, three centuries later, came the new means of optical and mechanical representation that seemed to provide art with a way of picturing the actual course of reality, movement through space and time, and not just stilled moments of it. The larger course of reality, the meaning of a multitude of movements made in space and time, we call history. Could the cine-camera picture this better than the eye, become an "eyewitness" to events greater than any one pair of eyes would ever be able to see? This, once the documenting of individual actions was demonstrated, became the great promise of the new medium. Photography, the bridge between realist painting and the movies, was in its original (still) form not a particularly strong connection with the storytelling tradition of painting or the other narrative arts—drama, writing, oral accounts. Once movement was available on the screen it became the storytelling, and history-telling, medium par excellence.

Why did history as a profession hold itself aloof from this revolution? That is not hard to answer. Cinema took off not for its documenting virtues or dramatizing vices but as a business. The entertainment business that revolutionized modern media was largely Jewish, and perhaps Louis B. Mayer and Sam Goldfish (later Goldwyn) should be promoted next to the other Jewish revolutionaries, Marx, Freud, and Einstein. Neal Gabler, in *An Empire of Their Own: How the Jews Invented Hollywood*, has shown how holding on to an identity separate from America caused them to shape an America that became their country in the eyes of the world. It was nevertheless a southern gentleman, David Wark Griffith, who set the tone, and largely invented the art, of history on the screen and it was in large part his nation that Hollywood gave birth to. How much his version of American history reflected his audience, or affected its opinions, may have been less significant in the long run than his skill in making history a staple of entertainment. There was now to be little room for reflecting on the realism or verifiability of what was made and consumed largely as escapism. Anyone hoping that the newsreel would become an alternative representer of history outside the entertainment business would have been disappointed. Even Bolshevik agitprop trains mixed drama and propagandist reporting; and in the rest of the world ever grander and more fantastic picture palaces were the favored venue for seeing the "actualities" ahead of the main "feature." A country like Australia, which had been among the pioneers of both modes, and with a notably nationalist historical preoccupation, soon found that the American way would be the Australian way in both cinema style and the history featured on the screen.[9]

In the America that made modern media and that modern media made, the measure of success is consumption. Media products must appeal to the instincts of the millions needed to do the consuming. Politicians still like to invoke a heroic, simpler, more virtuous America, but they are likely to tell us in a "media event" styled as "infotainment." No television history that needs a large audience—and commercial sponsorship always needs the largest audience, or one very closely targeted—can afford to ignore the media marketplace. So academic history, with rare exceptions like *The World at War* and *The Return of Martin Guerre*, continues to have a rough time in envisaging an association with the most powerful engine of popular history in our culture.[10]

The general tendency to a world media monoculture must rank as triumph for all the prophets of modernity, not least among them Karl Marx. For a time, the epic and tragic attempt to set up an alternative road to universal modernization in the USSR produced theories of film as a practice, integrated within history as a practice, which will remain influential well beyond the collapse of the experiment and the general disillusion with modern "solutions" to historical problems. Pudovkin, Eisenstein, and Vertov worked through their kino revolution with theory arising directly from activist Marxism. The discovery that the times had right on cue delivered them a medium that could show things historically in a new way—because it was in its very mechanics analyzing and synthesizing—was only the beginning. It was also a demonstration of dialectics, a fundamentally *relational* art form, and one that could represent and again re-present the past and historical process for the working masses as no other could hope to do. To show in the realistic surfaces photographed by the camera (Pudovkin's "plastic material") the *real* historical realities—class, power, dynamic *relations*—was the challenge faced by Soviet cinema. The later edicts prescribing "Socialist Realism" were as much a betrayal of Marxist theory as everything else in the Stalin regime. It was also, in a bitter paradox Marx left himself open to, a conservative attempt to cement modernism in archaic art forms so as to stave off the postmodernism that revolutionary art had immediately begun to herald. National Socialism took an almost identical line against the "cultural Boshevism" of "decadent" (socially critical, fragmenting) art, plumping for totalitarian unification celebrated by "healthy" (conservative, representational) art. Cinema-goers got their ideological lessons through entertainment histories of increasingly epic proportions, further sweetened by the Goebbels-inspired boom in relaxing comedy and schmalz. The Nazi and Soviet reactions against modernity made sense as an authoritarian response to political and social panic about the emancipating, anything-goes attitudes symptomatic of full modernity in its postmodern guise.[11]

The home of adventurous film theory shifted to France. The country where film was invented, a refuge for modernist art and a productive environment for modern history, France also led the world in the modern sense of experiencing "history" as it happened. History—in the meaning I also sometimes employ—is as much a process, conceptually separate from a consciousness of historical process, as it is the business of interpreting the past. It is in French theorizing that the relationships between consciousness as a historically shaped present, screening as a present, and screening the past as history have received most determined and imaginative attention. Not by mere coincidence, French theorizing about history has also been the most identifiable influence in suggesting postmodern approaches to making sense of the past. Here too there are construable historical reasons to do with the shocks and transitions France has undergone that help us see how the preoccupations have opened up to each other. In film's estrangement and fragmentation of reality, in its unique replication of movement as image, and in its suturing of fragments and movements into a diegetic whole, the screen media—we can now see—are full of significances for history in every medium.

To tease out the specificities of the past gives history a difficult enough job; to slow down the past once it "hits the screen" is perhaps too much to ask. Old methods of frame analysis and new computer aids only get us part of the way there. To the alienating eye of the movie camera we have to add its unparalleled capacity to involve, and that involvement is in the complex of effects and affects achieved in the movement itself. It needed Christian Metz and then Gilles Deleuze to take up the unfinished business of montage theory for our understanding of film diegesis to advance. For historians, Metz's categories are less immediately relevant; Deleuze, on the other hand, saw in film properties that are not difficult to relate to the enterprise of any practicing historian. Two examples from many: "the movement image" and "the out of field." The former we know from the experience of being "sucked in" to the diegetic magic of the cinema screen and on a lesser, domestic scale, of being "glued to the box." "The movement image" is a densely packed concept that can help us unpack the even denser word "diegesis." Just as film "does not give us an image to which movement is added, it immediately gives us a movement-image," we know that the *movement*, together with that aural movement-image *sound*, involves us in ways very close to "real life."[12] Screen representations of real life, fantasy, future or past involve us by drawing our imaginations into an image of reality with a narrative time, space, look, and sound similar to the senses of apprehending the world we learn as very young children. We never cease to reconfirm these sense perceptions and we test them each time we follow a story (of whatever scale—advertisement, episode, or epic) on the screen. Where the involvement works, the diegetic skills of the makers are succeeding; where the involvement fails, they may be at fault or we may not be "entering in" to our part of the contract.

We should note that the contract between writer and reader is a similar one, and that there is little difference in this respect between reading a novel and a narrative history. Written history can be halted for checking, stopped and started, and should—as history—obey professional standards of reference to a consultable record. The novel can allow itself thousands of inventions, from interior psychological descriptions to historically impossible outcomes. That is the liberty of fiction. A fiction film has the same liberty, and a "true story" on the screen is as close to fiction as it is to the consultable record because so much invention is needed to create the dramatic diegesis. Almost every detail is "reconstructed" and therefore imaginatively portrayed. A hat, a shake of the head, the sound of a hawk or a handsaw—every object, gesture, or social relation has to be reinvented to represent an imagined natural world. The main difference, however, is very close to what Deleuze denotes by "the movement image." The screen present is not a picture to which movement is somehow added, and screening the past does not give us a past to which the cinema present is added. It gives us a past-image in the very present processes of film.

The diegetic present of the film, of course, has space and time contexts that have to remain active, if muted, in the imagination. It might even be said these are the most important historical elements. There are explicit depictions of time and place framed up for us, yet Liam Neeson as Michael Collins would be very easy to confuse with Liam Neeson as Schindler if we had only the sense of one star's acting within those frames. Deleuze reminds us that what is outside the frame always adds meaning to the framed action selected by the camera. The out-of-field in his discussion of framing could be a metaphor for the past, indeed the whole past-present-future continuum that is not seen in the film.[13]

Films in fact suggest quite actual relationships between what is in frame and elements outside it. As with all selection in history, the larger or alternatively constructed histories are by their nature out of frame. The greater plasticity and immediacy of the film image probably does exclude consciousness of the larger history more efficiently—but not, I think, necessarily. There are kinds of films that contrive to keep the out-of-field in the consciousness of the viewer, and even in conventional film there are styles of narrative that keep present the world beyond the screen. Though few directors comment on this explicitly (Edgar Reitz did so with reference to Gernot Roll's cinematography for *Heimat*), it would seem to be necessary to the art of directing. Without a sense of the film-outside-the-film, no film of any depth at all can be made.The most conventional narrative historiography relies on the same sense of a larger context.

Crucially, in this organization of perception there is also an inseparable dimension of time. It is true that a shot produces a mobile section of movements—"moulds" it, as both Bazin and Deleuze say, to both the space recorded and to the time. That film perspective always has this temporal dimension is crucial to its power. A film is locked to "real time" even as it bends historical time to whatever effect the filmmaker desires. Even more irresistibly when sound is added, the "viewer" has to follow the mobile section in space and time as though moving through the screen into the present the camera creates. (Though the language still privileges vision it has been compelled to incorporate hearing into "viewing." Which faculty gives the greater sense of diegetic involvement is worth checking at the cinema.)

Editing may seem to cut across these continuous properties of the shot, but of course that is not what "cutting" does. It "cuts together" different shots to expand into infinite possibilities the perspectives on space, time, and action. Many of the relations between people, spaces, and objects that create meaning are already conveyed in the shot; the montage relating one shot to another brings into the film Dreyer's fourth dimension: the zone in which the meaning being made for the viewer accummulates and works its effect. In writing, the signals of words on the page refer us into a realm of imagination not present in any of the physical properties of pages, light, or sight. In film, the more visible and audible presence of the image is popularly thought of as pre-empting the imagination. In fact this presence has the power to move our perceptions toward the most imaginative connections even as we are fully engaged with what is literally being shown. The imaginary realm in which we experience film reality is made by each of us, at the direction of the filmmakers, on the superior, interior, fully dimensional screening room of the brain.

The screening room is of course constructed and furnished by a large history of which it is unlikely to be aware: it too is out of frame. Without following Paul Virilio all the way as he extends the relation of war to cinema as "the logistics of perception," we can be reminded of the historical dimensions we are dealing with. The camera, Virilio suggests, "prefigured a growing derealization of military engagement. For in industrialized warfare, where the representation of events outstripped the presentation of facts, the image was starting to gain sway over the object, time over space." The line of aim prefigures eyeless vision from space and the numerical optics of a computer, the automation of perception. What he calls the "passive optics" of Galileo's lenses were already a revolution. "In fact, by upsetting geocentric cosmogony, this reverberation of the human look called perceptual faith into question" and then founded the new optical faith of the photograph. It was enhanced—if also questioned—by cinema, by television, then by videos, computer graphics, and "the active optics of the synthetic image."[14]

We might wonder how history as a form of inquiry could be unaffected by the change in consciousness from always seeing with one's own eyes to never seeing with one's own eyes. The military shift was certainly aligned with the shift in visual representation developed in painting and revolutionized by photography. Benjamin saw that the alienation could come from unnatural closeness as well as unnatural distance. He used the analogy of a surgeon entering the body in contrast to the distance maintained by a magical healer. "The painter maintains in his work a natural distance from reality, the cameraman penetrates deeply into its web. There is a tremendous difference between the pictures they obtain. That of the painter is a total one, that of the cameraman consists of multiple fragments which are assembled under a new law."[15] Deleuze quotes a French filmmaker, Jean Epstein, on the painter Ferdinand Leger to make the point that the evident exteriority of photography—the camera only records surfaces—is transformed by the recording of camera movement to position the spectator quite differently in the space a conventional painting or photograph might depict: "All the surfaces are divided, truncated, decomposed, broken. . . . Instead of submitting to perspective, this painter splits it, enters it . . . for the perspective of the outside he thus substitutes the perspective of the inside, a multiple perspective, shimmering, sinuous, variable and contractile," shaped by the shifting camera. I have removed from this quotation the reference to splitting into "fractions of reality"—certainly the case— "as one imagines that they are in the thousand-faceted eyes of the insect": true of Cubist painting and electronic multi-imaging alike, but not true of the classic, and developing, narrative film. The important thing, as Deleuze also sees, is not the infinitely fractionalizing potential of the screen but the fluidly organizing capability of the shot and the sequence.[16]

Film theory has always been concerned with elaborating how film art creates a sense of reality; historiography is at last beginning on the same process.[17] Historians have probably had to reflect on their distance from reality as much as any artist (pictorial or literary) and have always assembled their representations of the past from broader perspectives and interior close-ups. Only more recently, though, have they been affected by the fragmentation of modern vision so as to see their own work as having, in positive rather than negative ways, multiple perspectives, odd, accidental, and arbitrary angles.

Writers of scholarly history remain unenthusiastic about a cinematic comparison: film is still easier to see as either an authentic (recorded) past or a faked (acted) past. The stubborn argument drawing attention to the necessarily anti-historical properties of acting is hard to get round. Because acting *adds* to the historical record—new faces, behaviors, interpretations—it certainly changes perceptions of the past "dramatically." Dramatization does not need to pretend replication, however, and it is not only Brecht who reminds us that actors are interpreters of the history in which their roles are set. The more adventurous historical filmmakers, from Pabst to Peter Watkins, have had their actors act out historically shaped roles, realities, and relations, *showing* us how things were. A new and larger dramatic irony is developed as we are made aware of what it might mean to be unaware of the historical relationships within which an historical character is caught. In this kind of "alienation effect" there should be the paradox of history as well: the past we regard as strange must become familiar, as it was to people acting in it. Where there is a danger of taking actions or situations for granted, we must make them strange. Since the present in which we act is the world we take most for granted, I have always thought a priority for historians is to make our own world historical. It helps if we sometimes magnify the pixels, as it were, in our mental screens, or pause to check the suturing of fragments in our narratives and the buildup toward a closure, that most dramatizing of conventions that closes off alternative possiblities of interpretation. Without dramatic measures to distance the taken-for-granted historical present, it never becomes historical. Distance, even the least reflective historians accept, makes earlier presents historically specific, examinable . . . strange.[18]

The reality conjured up in film diegesis—what follows again explains my use of the term—cannot in fact escape being historical. Whether it plays in "the past," "the present," or "the future," it is both immediately present and narrating a completed tale. We know very well that the outcome is being withheld only from us, until the storyteller judges we are ready. In steering us through the next development, helping us to experience it, the director has the end of this present, closed off as a past, already in mind. All films move forward into the present and "back to the future" when they re-present the past. Time in the film is contained within a constructed space whose realities are those of the story—of history—not of any experience or as-it-happened reality. In its artificial, magically mobile space, the film also draws us into a uniquely synthetic expansion and contraction of time; we follow a story time absolutely unrelated to the real time of screening. If we watch a film in real time, as we might do during a flight when we do not want to "watch" the film, we can see the structure but cannot enter the film time: that happens when we hear rather than watch, as soon as we put the headset on. Only when we enter screen space does the light reflected or emitted become solid places, with real people, and only when we enter screen time does the space around us, whether cramped, convivial, or comfortable, temporararily disappear.

After just such an experience on a hot night at the local cinema—we had gone to see Jane Campion's *Portrait of a Lady*—I thought there was something I should check about my account of the past. I went down to the front and found the parting in the curtains. A friendly projectionist gave them an opening flick. My own evidence was again before my eyes: in another country, forty years later, the holes were still there. And they are still there in my understanding. All the attempts at working out from the physical properties of cinema and television into the questions of media, genre, sign, and ideology that have concerned analysts of screened representations have left me with more conceptual holes than surface. The screen in its smaller, more active forms may seem more like a mesh of connections, a net, but a unifed theory that links all the problems of processing the present as it processes the past remains as chimerical as the updated moving image.

There is no Great Net, representing a unified historical narrative, for historians in any medium. Our screening of the past, inseparable from our ways of apprehending the world, is scarcely less complex when we digitize it on the page. The choices we make are made for effect, to net our readers. They depend as much on our own historical positioning, often enough subjective, as on a search for objective coordinates in the data. Screen media have served us well if they turn us back to some lasting lessons about representing the past.

History students, often after years of university courses, never fail to be bowled over by E. H. Carr's excursus on fishing. First, many are taken in by his metaphor of the facts presented as dead catches on a kind of fishmonger's slab: the historian takes them home and cooks them in whatever manner he wishes. Wrong, says Carr. The facts are fish swimming in the vastest ocean: the historian must venture forth and decide where to cast his line. In fact the slippery, shimmering fish become facts only when the historian, or a combination of historians, makes them so. If we add a net to Carr's proto-postmodernism we see at once that it is not new as a practice, only, belatedly, as a consciousness. The first web of palm mesh dipped into a dreaming is as much a screening, an ordering in the act of appropriation, as downloading on the desktop screen from the World Wide Web. And the real dipping, with our own consciousness of screening, remains much more satisfying for historians than the pseudo-surfing of the net where every once-live thing is already caught, cooked, and mangled in megabytes of serving suggestions.[19]

Where Carr, less than four decades ago, felt no need to go further—into the relationship between medium and discourse in the serving of any history—we now have to dwell. History since the cinema cannot return to a less reflective era, before the reflections from the screen. Television has ensured that media consciousness has been through another decisive historical change, always compared in significance to the print revolution. Computer screens have taken us further again, even those of us who barely engage with their potential. We do not think about our consciousness without effort, and it is in the nature of media to pervade and to disguise their influence. In a not at all metaphorical way, it may not be very different from the house, home to both television and the personal computer. "One does not inhabit a house," it has been said, "a house inhabits you."[20] We are now inhabited by media discourses almost impossible to screen out of our present. We failed for centuries to work out how the spoken or written word created a sense of correct address, of poetry, of legend or exposition—realities we could hardly know separate from the media that communicate them.

Another failure awaits us at the other end of the media spectrum: hopes that electronic segmenting of film images can tell us how the moving image works have to be chastened by the given that anything slowed or sectioned or stilled is not the image we wanted to discuss. The coding, Deleuze should convince us, is in the movement itself. He should also convince us to persevere. However "liquid" or "gaseous" the process of perception might be, we need a semiotics of historical sense specific to different sorts of screen history if we are to understand how an historical interpretation is coded into a particular film.

A writer codes an interpretation by choosing and ordering words, just as film or television has interpretations coded into it .The actual interpretation of the code is not in the writer's or filmmaker's control. Both practice disciplines that lure them close to the presence of their subjects and seduce them into the ambition of making those subjects present to others. Historians know they approach the past with the eyes of a stranger and then try to conjure familiarity. Filmmakers expect the camera eye first of all to render the world as it naturally appears, yet they have known since the beginning that there is nothing natural in the photographed rendition the viewer translates into recognitions. An illusion so visibly made up of mechanically mobilized components saw to that. A century later historians are at last coming to grips with the realization that the past they "paint" is also a made-up one, a construct floated on the naturalizing passion of their readers.

NOTES

I have a long debt to my friends John Cashmere, Inga Clendinnen, Greg Dening, David Johanson, and Rhys Isaac for making me think about history as a discipline and for helping me sort out how evidentiary history differs from other kinds of historical storytelling. To Rhys I am especially grateful for the detailed criticism with which he nurtured the project of this chapter. Where it is still unclear, I no doubt insisted on its being so.

1. Discussing history always has some problems of usage. I will try not to confuse "history" as events and processes in the past with the broad enterprise—also called "history"—of creating understanding of the past, though I admit to seeing historical consciousness as a product of both.

2. Robyn Gardner, "Antigone's Shadow: Theory after the Holocaust," *Meridian* 2, no. 13 (October 1994): 107–123.

3. For a useful redefinition of "surreality" as each individual's commonsense perception, see Robert Solomon, *The Passions* (New York: Anchor, 1977), Ch. 3.

4. Diegesis, from the Greek to describe or narrate, is what Balàzs, Pudovkin, Eisentein, and other pioneering theorists elucidate, without giving us a term for the whole phenomenon. Metz made the word serviceable but not popular. In the interests of wider acceptance, I have adopted it to denote all the means used to create the space, time, and action of a story that readers or viewers enter. Béla Balàzs, *Theory of the Film: Character and Growth of a New Art* (New York: Dover, 1970), p. 35.

5. For introductory excerpts of important writings see Pudovkin, Vertov, Eisenstein in R. D. McCann (Ed.), *Film: A Montage of Theories* (New York: Dutton, 1966).

6. Bill Nichols, "The trials and tribulations of Rodney King," in *Blurred Boundaries: Questions of Meaning in Contemporary Culture* (Bloomington: Indiana University Press, 1994), p. 18.

7. Svetlana Alpers, *The Art of Describing: Dutch Art in the Seventeenth Century* (Chicago: University of Chicago Press, 1983), p. xxv.

8. Alpers, pp. 27–33. For a striking early appreciation of film as "representational document" see Boleslas Matuszewski's appeal in 1898 for a depository of cinematographic "witnessing," because of the "authenticity, exactitude and precision which belong to it alone." Introduction by William D. Routt. *Screening the Past: An International Electronic Journal of Visual Media and History.* (See Further Reading.)

9. See Brian MacFarlane, Geoff Mayer, and Ina Bertrand (Eds), *The Oxford Companion to Australian Film* (Melbourne: Oxford University Press, forthcoming) and Graham Shirley and Brian Adams, *Australian Cinema, The First Eighty Years* (Sydney: Angus and Robertson, 1983), esp. Chs. 3 and 4. The story of Australian cinema succumbing to American film production is certainly worth reading, together with Neal Gabler, *An Empire of Their Own: How the Jews Invented Hollywood* (New York: Crown, 1988).

10. The marketing goes beyond advertising or political conventions into large and terrible histories. See my "Consuming the Holocaust: Memory Production and Popular Film," *Contention 5*, no. 2 (Winter 1996): 161–175.

11. Clearly, I'm with Jameson on this. I can't see postmodernism as outside the emancipating, sense-making mission of modernity, though of course dialectically "transcending" it. See Frederic Jameson, *Postmoderism, or The Cultural Logic of Late Capitalism* (London: Verso, 1990). For the contemporary effect of art experimentation, see Robert Hughes, *The Shock of the New* (New York: Knopf, 1981). Bertel Ollman, *Alienation: Marx's Concept of Man in Capitalist Society* (New York:

Cambridge University Press, 1976) remains an excellent introduction to relations as the key concept of Marx's thought. On Nazi cinema see the references in Chapter 9.

12. Gilles Deleuze, *Cinema 1: The Movement Image* (London: The Athlone Press, 1986), p. 2. For Metz, see the first translation of the original essays by Michael Taylor: Christian Metz, *Film Language. A Semiotics of the Cinema* (New York: Oxford University Press, 1974). James Monaco, *How to Read a Film* (New York: Oxford University Press, 1981), pp. 186–191, provides a schema that can serve as an introduction to Metz's own more subtle text.

13. Deleuze, pp. 12–18.

14. Paul Virilio, *War and Cinema: The Logistics of Perception* (London: Verso, 1989), pp. 1–3.

15. Walter Benjamin, "The Work of Art in the Age of Mechanical Reproduction," in *Illuminations* (London: Fontana, 1982), pp. 235–236.

16. Jean Epstein, *Ecrits 1, sur le cinéma* (Paris: Seghers, 1974), p. 115; Deleuze, p. 23.

17. For the reflections of a pioneer of Reflective History, see Greg Dening, *Performances* (Melbourne: Melbourne University Press, 1996), esp. pp.103–127, "The Theatricality of History Making and the Paradoxes of Acting."

18. Australian filmmakers have produced some of the most enterprising and effective film art in this examining-estranging mode. See my "Making it Strange: Ross Gibson's *Camera Natura*, David Perry's *The Refracting Glasses*, and John Hughes's *One Way Street*" in Ken Berrymann, Wayne Levy, and John Benson (Eds), *Papers Given at the Sixth Australian History and Film Conference*, Melbourne 1994.

19. On history—long before the internet—as screening of data into meaning, see E. H. Carr, *What is History?* (Harmondsworth: Penguin, 1964).

20. Annamarie Jagose, *In Translation* (Sydney: Allen and Unwin, 1995), p. 25.

2

"Captain Bligh" as Mythic Cliché: The Films

Greg Dening

Films as cultural artifacts have a disembodied feel. Their function is to be seen, but writing the history of seeing is difficult. A film in its can is not like a book on its shelf or a manuscript in an archive. A film requires theater of some sort to be seen. Fast-forwarding, rewinding, and replaying are different experiences from rippling through the pages or rereading. At the end of the twentieth century we are all culturally postmodern. To survive culturally we must be expert readers of texts for both what they say they mean and for what we know them really to mean. Reading and living have become very close. With a film it is different. Everything is subterfuge and camouflage. Living is out of camera and off set. We see films in crowds and argue with one another over what we have seen. Maybe some time in the future I will write on *The Film* as Henri Lefevre wrote on *The Book*, and Walter Ong on *The Word*.

Not now. My concerns are more narrow. A few years ago I was ending my researches on Captain William Bligh and his famous mutiny on the *Bounty*. I had tested, as any good historian might be expected to do, the clichés we hold of the past and found those that we had of "Captain Bligh" somewhat wanting. "Captain Bligh," in our cliché of him, was violent tyranny out of control. I counted all the floggings that British naval captains inflicted on their men in the Pacific 1767–1797 and found that Bligh was the least violent of them all. Contemporaries complained not at all about his violence. They complained about his bad language. Now, that is a curious thing for sailors to complain about, I thought. So I wrote a book called *Mr Bligh's Bad Language* and worked through what the "bad language" of command might be. But that did not resolve the puzzle of the almost mythic strength of our notions of a violent "Captain Bligh."

I had decided to investigate those processes in popular culture by which myths were made, when I heard something on American Public Radio that caught my attention. It was the resignation speech of the U.S. Federal Secretary of Education, Mr. William Bennett. He had played a controversial role in President Ronald Reagan's administration and was now, in September 1988, leaving office. Mr. Bennett was a strong proponent of the notion of cultural literacy, and had voiced a fear being voiced in hundreds of places around the world, not just the United States, that children of today are culturally illiterate in their history.

Cultural literacy, for those who deplore its disappearance, is that knowledge of the past that sustains the values of the present, that knowledge that "plucks the mythic hordes of memory." Cultural literacy, in the words of the chief proponent of it, E. D. Hirsch, is "less a system of skills than a system of information," a sort of data base out of which a cultured person or a citizen is made. Dates, events, persons, achievements make up this data base, but more importantly, if less explicitly, so do interpretations of what these facts mean. Implicit in this notion of cultural literacy is a demonology of Good and Evil. The history that is meant to pull on the "mythic chords of memory" employs the past with unequivocal portraits of Good and Evil in extravagant difference. History, then, is expected to be not interpretive. In the proper sort of history moral judgments can be learned like dates.

If ever there was a demonology imbedded in our myths it is in our twentieth-century images of "Captain Bligh." He makes a comfortable sort of villain in a century in which it is the banality of evil with which we do not easily cope. We do not mythologize the banality of evil very well. The evil of those who hide their personal responsibilities behind rule and role imposed upon them comes too near to our everyday "bad faith" to let us make myths about them. "Captain Bligh," however, is easily condemned.

There should be more history in American schools, Mr. Bennett had been saying in his resignation speech, but "real history," history that children could learn. Every American child, he was saying now on Public Radio, should know, for example, why there was a mutiny on the *Bounty*. "Mr. Bennett," I wanted to shout in this my moment of relevance, "alien though I am, I am here and ready to tell every American child why there was a mutiny on the *Bounty*. I am writing a book that every American child should have." Ah, well! Even an academic historian can dream.

I cannot really say why Mr. Bennett thought every American boy and girl should know why there was a mutiny on the *Bounty*. My prejudices suggested to me that Mr. Bennett would not have been the first in President

Reagan's administration to confuse history with some product of the film industry. Charles Laughton's "Captain Bligh" and Clark Gable's "Fletcher Christian" in the 1935 Metro-Goldwyn-Mayer film, *Mutiny on the Bounty*, was a perfect example of the sort of demonology that in Mr. Bennett's eyes made for "real history." "A cardinal principle of education," Mr. Bennett used to say, "is social efficiency." "Facts, conditions, theories, activities that do not contribute rather directly to the appreciation of human betterment have no claim." "Our young must be taught the golden ideals of liberty, justice, equality, limited government, betterment of human conditions, and they should know that a large part of the world thinks and acts according to other principles." The rub, of course, is whether human betterment is advanced by learning these judgments like dates or by experiencing what is true in them or what is not. And what is the measure of "social efficiency"? How efficient is it to learn the representation without the representing? With the prejudice that demonology is destructive of the values it aims to protect, and in the hope that in describing the representing as well as the representation I would make a more creative contribution to cultural literacy, I began the last phase of my *Bounty* voyage. The Center for the Study of the Performing Arts of the New York Public Library holds part of the Metro-Goldwyn-Mayer archives. I started there. The film censors of the State of New York have collected some 55,000 scripts of films in the Cultural Archives, Albany, New York. I made inquiries there as well.[1]

There have been five *Bounty* films. The first was a 1916 Australian silent movie, *The Mutiny on the Bounty*. It is extant now only in stills. Raymond Longford, a pioneer of the Australian film industry, produced the film and shot it on location in Rotorua, New Zealand, and Norfolk Island. From the cast of characters and the reviews, it can be surmised that the film made some dramatic play on the paradox of Bligh's brutality as captain of the *Bounty* and his tenderness as father and husband within his family. "Mrs. Bligh," "Mrs. Heywood," and "Nessie Heywood" got to play their parts. The paradox touched on the dark days of Bligh's losses in his family, on Elizabeth Bligh's bewilderment, and on the Heywood women's terror at the threat of the loss of son and brother. This has not been the usual paradox played in representation of the *Bounty*. The paradox that most often came to be stressed was the apparent contradiction between the brilliance of Bligh as a seaman and his abject failure as a commander. This latter paradox, in the way of *Realpolitik*, has provided more acceptable excuses for Bligh. In any case, the critics of seventy-five years ago lauded the historical accuracy of the 1916 film, but deplored its weak human interest and lack of public appeal. Perhaps, even then, its ambiguities of human motivations were less popular than demonology.

The second *Bounty* film was another Australian version, this one released in 1933. It was Charles Chauvel's *In the Wake of the Bounty*.[2] Chauvel constructed an early drama documentary in which he mixed the story of the mutiny as narrated by Michael Byrne, the half-blind Irish fiddler, with a travelogue on Chauvel's visit to Pitcairn Island in 1932. In some desperation at a turning point in the film industry, Chauvel had been looking for an exotic location—anywhere—that had not been filmed. The North and South Pole had been "done," darkest Africa and Timbuktu as well. Chauvel's partner in his company called "Expeditionary Films" had pulled out and stayed over in Hollywood to film the lion farms of the movie studios, saying that "when everything else is exhausted, the roar of wild animals will bring them out—even on cold nights." Sound in itself was then a novelty. Chauvel decided to make a series of films on remote islands—Tristan da Cunha, Juan Fernandez, Easter Island—and stumbled on Pitcairn. He remembered that while visiting friends on a cattle station in Queensland he had spent time rooting around in dusty station ledgers that logged such agricultural data as the planting of cereal crops and the inoculation of stock. He came across another sort of log. It was Bligh's own manuscript log of the *Providence*, his second breadfruit voyage. The owners of the station, the Nutting family, were descendants of Bligh—Mrs. Lucy O'Connell Nutting subsequently donated the log of the *Providence* to the Mitchell Library, Sydney.

In the Wake of the Bounty was premiered at Prince Edward Theatre, Sydney, March 15, 1933, after some trouble with the censors about barebreasted Tahitians and a graphic flogging scene. Tasmanian-born Errol Flynn made his debut as Fletcher Christian. There are several versions of the story of how Flynn came to make his debut: his photogenic potential was noted as he displayed his torso on Bondi Beach near Sydney, says one; he was modeling men's suits in a filmed commercial, says another. A third seems attractive for its ethnographic focus. Flynn had been captaining a New Guinea coastal trader working the tobacco crops at the time, the story goes. A German anthropologist, Dr. H. F. Erbe, making an ethnographic film on headhunting on the Sepik River, featured Flynn as captain of the vessel ferrying the expedition up the river. Chauvel saw the film, recognized Flynn's photogenic, if not thespian, qualities, and offered him fifty pounds by telegram from Tahiti via Sydney and Port Moresby to play Fletcher Christian. "I was without the least idea of what I was doing, except I was supposed to be an actor," Flynn said later. "I had touched on something the world called an art form and it affected me deeply." To his delight he found that movie actors, unlike stage actors, had to learn only those lines necessary for the day's shooting. "It was a big discovery in a way," he said. Later—and through the alcoholic haze that began to envelope his life—he claimed that his family owned a sword of Fletcher Christian, which was probably not true, and that his mother was related to Edward Young, the mutineer from the West Indies who Bligh described as having a "dark and rather bad look," which we have no reason to doubt. Flynn happened to

be in Sydney for the release of *In the Wake of the Bounty*. The theater
manager offered him two pounds to appear on the stage. Flynn said he
would do anything for two pounds and appeared on the stage decked out
in a bizarre naval uniform, wearing what he claimed to be one of only two
wigs in Sydney, and looking, in his own words, like the elderly keeper of
a whorehouse on King William St. which he was prone to frequent. In any
event, the *Wake of the Bounty* never got much of a showing. MGM bought
it up to clear the ground for their 1935 version. They parceled it into two
travelogue shorts on Pitcairn and included bits of it in their trailers for
Mutiny on the Bounty.

There are three other *Bounty* films that belong more properly to modern
cultural literacy. Seen as a trio, they have each proffered a different narrative to the same events. The 1935 Charles Laughton/Clark Gable version,
with Laughton portraying a pathologically cruel Bligh and Gable a manly,
honorable Christian, displayed the classic conflict between tyranny and a
just cause. The struggle on the *Bounty* was a moral and an ideological one.
The 1962 Trevor Howard/Marlon Brando version had Brando, clearly out
of his director's control, lisping his way through the role of Christian as a
gentleman fop finding true honor in standing up against Bligh's populist
austerity. The struggle on the *Bounty* was political. In the 1984 Anthony
Hopkins/Mel Gibson version, "Mad Max" is tamed to a petulant, postur-
ing Christian with a Robinson Crusoe complex, while Bligh is a man be-
deviled by nothing so much as his own vaguely homosexual jealousies. The
struggle on the *Bounty* was psychological.

No use displaying all the inaccuracies of these version; it was their purpose to be inaccurate. They could not say what they wanted to say without
invention. The 1935 Laughton/Gable version needed the hyperbole reached
by laying at Bligh's feet every violent and unjust happening in the early
modern British navy, needed to meld Bligh and Captain Edwards into one
character, construct a Bligh who recaptures his own mutineers and brings
them back to England in his own "Pandora's Box." The 1962 Howard/
Brando version needed to invent a trigger to the whole mutiny in Bligh's
inhumane act of kicking a ladle of water out of Christian's hands as he
comforted a dying seaman maddened by drinking seawater because of
Bligh's austerities, just as it needed tons of white sand transported from
the New Jersey coast and spilled over Tahitian black beaches to make a
truly seductive Hollywood Pacific island. The 1984 Hopkins/Gibson version needed to transpose all the disciplinary issues on the *Bounty* to the
master of the ship, John Fryer, and away from Bligh, so that Bligh and
Christian could get on with teasing one another.

Authenticity in each of these movie versions was a propman's concern,
not a scriptwriter's goal. Exact re-creation of the visual environment made
a living museum for the actors' actions. What actually happened was sub-

ordinated to what it would look like if it had happened. The Campaign Books which publicity agents put into the hands of the media—with suggested headlines about the film, potted reviews, catchy phrases, and insider's information on the production—were full of the energy and cost that it took to be visually accurate. A reconstructed *"Bounty"* was the proud accomplishment of them all. The 1935 version had two reconstructed vessels. One was a full-sized replica. The other was scaled down to eighteen feet and sailed by two men below deck. The 1962 *"Bounty"* became the living museum at St. Petersburg, where the public were invited to join 200,000 visitors a year to "retrace history," "experience the romance and excitement of the south seas," "relive stark human drama," "hear the voices of Bligh and Christian," hear "decks creak in soft tropic air," hear "the sighs of mutineers in paradise." Visitors could enter the Teloptikon enshrined in a grass hut and be engulfed in the sights and sounds of the voyage of this new *"Bounty"* from the shipyards at Lunenburg, Nova Scotia, to Tahiti. "Your children's children will not see the like again. Nor will you." Realism is the wonder a viewer feels that sights and sounds can be so right. Historical accuracy is the antiquarian thrill that the buttons on an eighteenth century uniform are correct, that an eighteenth century wooden leg—for someone who in real life never had one—was authentic.

To film critics, there really has been only one *Mutiny on the Bounty* film—the 1935 Laughton/Gable version. All the other adaptations have been measured against the brilliant clarity of Charles Laughton's portrayal of "Captain Bligh" forcing impossible choices on honorable manly spirits. Each of the later versions has been declared unhistorical by the critics for omitting all that the 1935 version invented.[3]

The 1935 *Mutiny on the Bounty* came out of Metro-Goldwyn-Mayer studios. Louis Mayer of MGM was, in the phrase of a Hollywood historian, Neal Gabler, one of those "Jews who invented Hollywood." Mayer had created MGM's extraordinary success out of his chauvinistic view of American culture. He made movie versions of Norman Rockwell stills. That is, his films were full of the fantasies of stylized beauty, idealized families, and beatified mothers. Greta Garbo, Norma Shearer, Joan Crawford, Jean Harlow, Myrna Loy were some of his female stars. Mayer was not enthusiastic when Irving Thalberg, his vice-president, suggested a film about the *Bounty*. He did not want to produce a film in which mutineers were heroes. Nor did he like the notion of a film in which the women were uncivilized natives seducing good order. MGM had never made an outdoor adventure film, he protested. In any case, women chose the entertainment of their families and they would not choose violence.

Irving Thalberg had been Mayer's young genius. He had masterminded the success of MGM by providing out of its immense wealth the atmosphere in which talent could thrive. F. Scott Fitzgerald had registered his

adulation for Thalberg's genius in *The Tycoon*. Thalberg's pale intensity—
he had been a "blue baby"—haunted Hollywood with its tragic sense of
mortality. This made it difficult to play the usual cut-throat politics with
him. But in 1931 he had begun to split with Mayer. Then at thirty-two
years of age, in 1932, he had a heart attack. Mayer could not let him go.
Mayer could not let him stay. Thalberg went to Germany to convalesce
and undergo surgery on his tonsils. In Germany he saw violent anti-Semitic
demonstrations outside his hotel and discovered that his German doctor
was reluctant to operate on him, fearing the consequences should an inter-
nationally famous Jew come to harm under his knife.

Then Thalberg was back in Hollywood. These were Depression days.
Upton Sinclair and the "leftist" scriptwriters were forming unions and writing scripts that disputed the unquestioning conservative politics of the film
industry. There was a widespread questioning of the pristine American values that MGM had so consciously instilled. Thalberg, out of his German
experience, feared fascism, but to him communism among the left scriptwriters was an even greater threat. In the internal politics of MGM, David
Selznick had begun to take Thalberg's place. Left without easy access to
the stars of MGM studios, Thalberg established a special unit of his own.
He began a series of expensive, special, and masterful films—*The Barretts
of Wimpole Street, Ruggles of Red Gap, Les Miserables*. His chief coup,
in his own mind, was in bringing the sophistication and class of British
acting to Hollywood, principally in the figure of Charles Laughton. Thalberg's anglophilia was part studio politics and part cultural cringe. But his
sense of a world in tension between fascism and communism was to give
a decisively strong political dimension to the sort of representation *Mutiny
on the Bounty* came to be.

Against Mayer's fears about how women would receive the film, Thalberg had no scruples. "It doesn't matter that there are no women in the
cast. People are fascinated by cruelty and that's why the Mutiny will have
appeal." And in any case there were more than male sexual fantasies to
titillate. The critics' first judgment on *Mutiny on the Bounty* was that it
was "no woman's picture." A second viewing, however, suggested to them
that more footage in the film was devoted to Clark Gable's "gams" and
Franchot Tone's "manly stems" than was ever given to Marlene Dietrich's
legs. Women's sexual fantasies at this time might not yet have been mar-
keted with anything more than a wink and a nudge, but the managers of
Loew's theaters all over the United States remarked that the proportion of
women among the hundreds of thousands who saw the film in its first week
of release was high. They thought they knew why that was so.

Thalberg's explicit answer to Mayer's fears about the socially destabilizing effect of a film idealizing mutineers is not recorded. His real answer
was to make a film in which the hero was not the mutineers at all, but the
British Navy, and a British Navy that was a weapon of freedom in a threat-

ened world. The fade-in Foreword and the fade-out ending made that
meaning of the film quite clear. The fade-in Foreword scrolled before the
audience read:

In December, 1787, HMS *Bounty* lay in Portsmouth Harbour on the eve of departure for Tahiti in the unchartered waters of the Great South Sea.
    The *Bounty*'s mission was to procure breadfruit trees for transplanting to the
West Indies as cheap food for slaves.
    Neither ship nor breadfruit reached the West Indies. Mutiny prevented it—mu-
tiny against the abuse of harsh eighteenth century sea law. But this mutiny, famous
in history and legend, helped bring about a new discipline, based upon mutual
respect between officers and men, by which Britain's sea power is maintained and
security for all who pass upon the seas.

    What did it matter that the whole British fleet mutinied just ten years
after the *Bounty* and thirty-six men were hanged? What did it matter that
flogging went on in the navy for forty more years? Thalberg's message was
that the act of mutiny, wrong in itself, had good effects. The reason was
that institutions of power are ultimately responsive to men of good will.
    This didactic message of *Mutiny on the Bounty* was played out in the
final scenes. The writers, Charles Nordhoff and Norman Hall, from whose
trilogy on the *Bounty* the script of the film had been taken, had invented
a character, "Roger Byam." Byam was their narrator. In all the things he
did and which were done to him, Byam was Peter Heywood of the real
Bounty. The film script dispensed with a narrator but kept "Roger Byam"
as a midshipman, played by Franchot Tone. The film ends with Byam making an impassioned speech to the officers of the courtmartial, just before
being condemned to death. Bligh is made to be present at the courtmartial,
as he had also been made to be captain of the Pandora. Franchot Tone
played the whole scene in one long filming. It was one of those famous
Hollywood "Cut it. Can it" feats. The whole film crew stood around and
applauded.

Captain Bligh you've told your story of mutiny on the *Bounty*, how men plotted
against you. Seized your ship, cast you adrift in an open boat. A great venture in
science brought to nothing, two British ships lost.
    But there's another story, Captain Bligh, of ten coconuts and two cheeses. The
story of a man who robbed his seamen, cursed them, flogged them, not to punish
them, but to break their spirit. A story of greed and tyranny and anger against it!
Of what it cost! One man, My Lord, would not endure such tyranny. That's why
you hounded him, that's why you hate him, hate his friends. And that's why you're
beaten. Fletcher Christian is still free.
    But Christian lost, too, My Lord. God knows he's judged himself more harshly
than you could judge him. I say to his father, he was my friend. No finer man ever
lived. I don't try to justify his crime, his mutiny. But I condemn the tyranny that

drove him to it. I don't speak for myself alone, nor for the men you've condemned. I speak in their names, in Fletcher Christian's name, for all men at sea. These men don't ask for comfort, they don't ask for safety! If they could speak to you they'd say: let us choose to do our duty willingly, not the choice of a slave, but the choice of free Englishmen.

They ask only the freedom that England expects for every man. Oh, if one man among you believed that. One man! He could command the fleets of England, he could sweep the seas for England. If he called his men to their duty, not by flogging their backs, but by lifting up their hearts! Their hearts . . . that's all.

Lord Hood then condemns the mutineers to death. As the court disperses, Hood passes Bligh and refuses to shake his hand. Hood says: "I must admire your seamanship and courage, but . . ."

The scene changes to St. James's Palace where Sir Joseph Banks is pleading for the life of Byam before King George. "We do not exaggerate when we say that a new understanding between officers and men has come to the Fleet. By returning Byam to duty, your Majesty will confirm that understanding, and not for today only, but for all time to come."

Then the cameras move to a naval vessel. Roger Byam, now pardoned, is coming aboard as midshipman to one of the ships whose captain, Colpoys, had earlier condemned him to death.

Abbreviations for the filming instructions in the script should be read in the following way: CS = Close Shot; o.s. = off screen; b.g. = back ground; LAP = Overlap; ELS = Extreme Long Shot; MLS = Medium Long Shot.

Colpoys: Very glad to have you with us, lad.

Byam: Thank you, sir.

CS—Edwards and Byam—they shake hands and speak—Edwards exits left—Officer enters—shakes hands with Byam—then exits right—CAMERA MOVES up on Byam—he looks o.s.—smiles—turns to b.g.

LAP Dissolve into

Edwards: May I, Byam?

Byam: Of course.

Edwards: We're off for the Mediterranean, lad. We'll sweep the seas for England.

ELS—Ships of the British Fleet moving forward—
MLS—Shooting up to the sails of the ship—the British flag waving—superimposed title:

THE END

FADE OUT

The significance of these scenes did not escape the critics. Richard Watts writing for the *New York Herald Tribune*, scoffed at "Hollywood's romantic crush on Empire" and deplored its servile politeness and "cringe in the presence of foreigners." He looked forward to the sequel, "Mutiny on the Pinafore." No doubt Mayer escaped his dilemma and Thalberg plucked "mythic chords of memory" in such dissolves and fade-outs. "Captain Bligh" had become a metonymy of the right sort of institutional evil against which one can rebel.

Without laboring this point by introducing an elaborate aside, let me briefly consider another mutiny film, *The Caine Mutiny*, made in 1954. It also resolved a number of Mayer's dilemmas about idealizing mutineers but in a significantly different way. *The Caine Mutiny* was directed by Edward Dmytryk, one of the Hollywood Ten. As one of the "Ten" he had been exposed to the vitriol of the McCarthy hearings and had been imprisoned for contempt of Congress after refusing to give the hearing information on writers with communist leanings in Hollywood. In 1954, Dmytryk had just been allowed to work again after his imprisonment, recantation, and naming names. The "Captain Bligh" of the Caine Mutiny was Captain Queeg (Humphrey Bogart), a weak, pathetic, and paranoid character. And the "Fletcher Christian" was Lieutenant Keefer (Fred McMurray). Keefer was written into the script as an intellectual by Hollywood standards, and it was he who persuaded the innocent Lt. Steve Maryk (Van Johnson) to depose Queeg. It was Maryk, not Keefer, who was subsequently courtmartialed, but was freed when Queeg was humiliated in court by a young Jewish lawyer, Greenwald (played by Jose Ferrer), who hated what he was forced to do in destroying Queeg. Keefer in the end has a cocktail thrown in his face for his cunning cowardice and is accused by Greenwald of being the true cause of the mutiny. There were no heroic mutineers in *The Caine Mutiny*. The message was that legitimate professional authority in a weak Queeg was calling for help. It was betrayed by self-interested liberals who had no loyalties to institutions. Keefer could have been a hero like "Roger Byam" had he made his deferences to the institution's hegemony, had he scotched his own cynicism and been more trusting of power's good will.

In the Laughton/Gable *Mutiny on the Bounty*, Bligh's pathological cruelty made room for a hero. But the real hero finally was not an individual, it was an institution. Authoritarian and unbending as it was, the institution of the navy was portrayed as listening to committed men of good will—but only to committed men. Relativism, the agreement that things can be changed, comes in institutions only after an absolute submission. Then the mimesis of these responsive and commonsensical institutions makes you feel warm all over. Fade Out.

There were others reluctant to be involved in the filming of *Mutiny on the Bounty*. Clark Gable was even more reluctant than Louis Mayer. "I'm a realistic kind of actor," he complained. "I've never played a costume picture in my life. Now you want me to wear a pigtail and velvet kneepants and shoes with silver buckles. The audience will laugh me off the screen. And I'll be damned if I'll shave off my moustache because the British navy didn't allow them. This moustache has been damned lucky for me." Gable had other problems, too. He felt his accent would be flat against Laughton's. And he was uncertain how he would play the gentleman against Laughton's performance of violence. His macho father had always said that he would become a sissy if he became an actor. His problem was how he could be Good against violent Evil without being feminine—and to do it in kneepants that showed how bandied his legs really were.

Gable need not have worried. His "gams" were seen as manly rather than bandy. His patent virility overrode his deficiencies in the techniques of acting. The tinge of rascal in his gentlemanly role made his Christian an American hero. Wallace Beery had been considered for the role of Bligh but had been rejected because he was "too American." It is significant that none of the American versions of the *Mutiny on the Bounty* could cope with an American actor as Bligh. The "mythic chords of memory" were plucked by older, more colonial demonologies. Gable's Christian, full of sexuality, had a chauvinist dimension as well.

Laughton was not reluctant to play the role of Bligh, but once begun he was stricken with self-doubts. All the scenes of the film involving the cast were shot on Catalina Island off the California coast. The logistical feats accomplished during these eighty-eight days of filming became, like the price paid for masterpieces in an art gallery, a sign of the film's greatness. Five old sailing ships were assembled there as well as the reproductions of the *Bounty*. Speedboats and seaplanes ferried visitors and supplies to the encampment. The filming took on a life of its own, as the crew and cast managed the peaks and troughs of intense activity and vacuous boredom. The very first day of shooting exploded in a savage dispute between Gable and Laughton. Laughton had begun to play his Bligh with arrogant dismissiveness, looking off screen and not at Gable. Gable thought Laughton's acting was a kind of soliloquy, complete with claptrap in which he was being reduced to an extra. Gable also punched a make-up man for some comment made while powdering his face. Meanwhile, Laughton was beginning to feel physically ill with the loathsomeness of the character he was creating. By telephone and seaplane visits, Thalberg managed to quieten Laughton's and Gable's rivalries and promote their self-confidence, only to find the actors turning their venom on the director, Frank Lloyd, who wanted to make the *Bounty* ship—or so they thought—the star of the movie.

Laughton's "Bligh" dominated the sets of the movie. Soon, comics in nightclubs and on radio began to play the ironies of his chilling phrases. "Mr. Christian, come here!" became one of those catch phrases, raising a sort of nervous laughter at the sentiments and an appreciation of the realism of the caricature. The audiences could laugh off the seriousness of their engagement in the poetics of *Mutiny on the Bounty* in a caricature of a caricature, in a mimicry of Laughton mimicking Bligh. Those who filmed the *Mutiny on the Bounty* were dominated by something other than the figure of Bligh. They were awed by Laughton's cultural literacy. They savored his historical diligence, but more, the historical continuities that he was able to establish with Bligh. Laughton told of going to Gieves, the military tailors on Saville Row, London, with inquiries about eighteenth-century naval uniforms. He was told by the clerk assisting him that, if he would wait, they would check Mr. Bligh's measurements from an account on the last uniform Bligh had ordered. Laughton himself lost fifty-five pounds in some historical awe at his discovery. Then when the propmen went looking for something as arcane and foreign to their experience as a Book of Common Prayer, they were staggered to find that Laughton not only knew of it but could recite passages from it because of his brief experience in the navy. Of an evening on Catalina he would read plays or declaim Shakespeare. Laughton had been educated by the Jesuits at Stonyhurst, and been strongly affected by their long theatrical tradition. His theatrical ambitions had disturbed his parents and undermined their ambitions for him as hotel clerk and manager. He came to Catalina Island with an educated touch of class that mesmerized those around him.

Frank Lloyd, the director, had been shrewdly entrepreneurial about *Mutiny on the Bounty*. He had seen the potential of Charles Nordhoff and James Norman Hall's fictional trilogy, *Mutiny on the Bounty, Men Against the Sea*, and *Pitcairn Island*. He had bought the film rights for $12,500 and had offered them to Irving Thalberg on condition that he direct the film. The *Bounty* trilogy had been a publishing triumph. An estimated twenty-five million people read the books even before seeing the film. It was serialized in the *Saturday Evening Post*. There seems to have been hardly a secondhand bookshop anywhere in the world where one could not buy copies. Nordhoff and Hall had made their names as writers by writing a history of the Lafayette Escadrille, the volunteer American squadron flying for France in the First World War. They had been flyers in that squadron. They had persuaded publishers to advance funds for them to do a tour of the Pacific, following Robert Louis Stephenson's example. Settled in Tahiti, they were distracted from their broader project by the *Bounty*. "Rare primeval stuff of which romance is made," they wrote.

Thalberg gave one of the most prominent scriptwriters in Hollywood, Carey Wilson, responsibility for the script, but took it away from him when he discovered Wilson moonlighting for Sam Goldwyn and working on two scripts at the same time. Talbot Jennings finished it, with large input from

Thalberg himself. Lloyd's preoccupation was always with the representation of the realism of the ship and the exotic background of Tahiti. Thalberg's preoccupation was managing the dramatic intensity of the passions of the mutiny.

To effect his realism, Lloyd took the reconstructed *Bounty* and Pandora to Tahiti with sixty technicians, nine camera outfits, and a hundred tons of equipment. At Tahiti he engaged 2,500 "semi-savage natives" as extras. He supplied them with every spear and club that Hollywood prop warehouses could provide. He came like Bligh, prepared to barter for their labor. Bligh had adzes, shirts, and beads. Lloyd had bird-cages, snakes-in-a-box, harmonicas, mirrors, pocket knives, wrist watches, celluloid dolls, straw hats, bracelets, necklaces, earrings, and Spanish combs. Unfortunately, nature's own realism played its part. The first 80,000 feet of scenic and sound film were destroyed by mildew and had to be done again. Lloyd's own efforts to transplant fullgrown breadfruit trees back to Catalina Island failed against the social realism of California plant quarantine laws. He had to be content with paper mache copies made frenetically as the customs officers destroyed the trees. Lloyd's true love was the *Bounty* itself and the portrayal on it of the rhythms of naval life. Ten athletes from California college football teams and the recent Los Angeles Olympic Games were trained in seamanship and clambered the *Bounty*'s rigging with speed and dexterity.

Historicity, however, needed something more. No director, after all, could be totally unaware of how realism is invented. Lloyd needed an authenticating experience. Representation through intimacy, one is tempted to call it—the cultural literacy that comes from knowing something happened in the past because one has touched a thing or a document that has survived. Lloyd's authenticating experience came in a strange place. He was sitting in the Blue Lagoon Cafe in Papeete, bemoaning with Norman Hall that he had looked the world over for Bligh's logs and had not found them. A little white-haired lady at the next table overheard him and said, "I know where they are." That lady is a figure of some reverence in Pacific History circles. She was Ida Leeson, librarian of the Mitchell Library, Sydney, New South Wales. She was new in her position and was making the library one of the great repositories of material connected with William Bligh. Not that seeing the copies of Bligh's logs made any difference to Lloyd's representation. Seeing them, however, made him confident that what he was doing was true.

Thalberg's interventions concerned the dramatic realism of the representation of the mutiny. He was concerned with the poetics of the portrayal of the "true" Bligh, and how something made "true" by extravagant caricature could be believable. He made Bligh's pathological and inhuman cruelty believable by inventing two clowns, Smith, the cook (Herbert Mundin) and "Bacchus" or Thomas Huggan, the surgeon (Dudley Digges). The cook's continual dilemma in getting rid of the slops against the wind underscored the ambivalences of Bligh's language and the absurdity of his rages. Bachhus's ever-changing story of how he got his wooden leg offered his peccadilloes as the human foil to Bligh's righteous evil. The cook, "Bacchus," and Bligh all made one another believable.

Not many Hollywood films are reflective on their own poetics. But there seemed to be an almost missionary zeal in proving the film's historical authenticity. The Campaign Books were full of the film's accuracies and of efforts to make it factual. The producers went so far as to produce a Teachers' Manual for distribution through U.S. high schools. It is an interesting primer in the sort of cultural literacy Hollywood thought it was promoting. Dr. William Lewis of Weegahie High School, Newark, New Jersey, helped produce it and was invited to observe some of the filming. The manual begins with the protest that there is "nothing in it of dogmatic theory, but merely helpful suggestions which may serve the dual purpose of aiding the teacher and of enlarging the literary knowledge of the student." It suggests that students use as texts the Nordhoff and Hall trilogy, Sir John Barrow's *Mutiny on the Bounty* (available in World Classics in 1928), Owen Rutter's *Trial of the Bounty Mutineers* (1931), Lord Byron's *The Island*. The manual suggests to the teacher that the questionnaires requiring answers from students are designed to help generate impressions of the film, to alert them to indicators of judgment, tastes, and emotional development, and to act as an introduction to training in story and setting.

Students, in one set of questions, were asked to describe the themes of the film and its leading characters in a sentence. They were asked to describe the most dramatic scene, the scenes they liked best, the "scene [that] best displays the art of the motion picture," who of the players acted the best, whether the mutiny was justified. Ah, yes! and "Did you like the ending? Give reasons." The questions, not to put too great an emphasis on Hollywood's short-term educational ambitions, were small exercises in cultural literacy, small lessons in discovering the cultural operators in narrative forms. What were—to ask a question that can only have surmise for an answer—the cultural functions of the ending? Surmise: the warm optimism that came from Roger Byam's reinstatement, the ultimate goodwill of institutions of power, the inspiration that came from true justice being done and righteous patriotism expressed find rooms in the "memory palace" of the public mind. The hegemony of common sense makes the narrative naturally believable, even mythic.

The second set of questions in the Teacher's Manual concerned critical skills in interpretation. Students were asked, "In what way does the film differ from Nordhoff and Hall? In what respect does Nordhoff and Hall differ from actual history?" Students were invited to make living museums of themselves as press-ganged sailors or as Bligh himself or as a native of Tahiti or as a seaman of the *Pandora*, and to record their experiences. They were asked as well to put themselves at various points of moral dilemma in the narrative—would they have gone with Bligh in the launch or stayed on the *Bounty?*—would they have waited at Tahiti or gone with Christian? The thrust of these questions was to stress familiarity rather than difference. And where authenticity of the narrative was explicitly questioned—in the first question about the differing histories of the mutiny—it is interesting to follow the answers in the crib. Facticity and difference in the answer are subordinated entirely to the effectiveness in expressing the meaning of the narrative.

So when the students had read the fiction of Nordhoff and Hall, the histories of Barrow and Rutter, and seen the film, they inevitably would have discovered that much of what Nordhoff and Hall had described as the cruelty of other British naval captains and all of what Captain Edwards had done on the *Pandora* had been made to be Bligh's responsibility in the film. There was an "obvious reason" for this, the crib answer said: "The actions of Captain Courtney and Edwards were typical of the class of ship commanders to which Bligh belonged. The transference of these actions to Bligh allowed a closeknit, strong and more comprehensive study of Bligh's character and thus the exclusion of characters, who, having little or no part in the actual story, might have possibly confused the issue." Ambivalence, multivalency, alternate interpretation does tend to create a different sort of cultural literacy than demonology.

Audience response when the film was released in November 1935 was extraordinary. In an unprecedented move, all of Loew's theaters showed only this film. Record attendances were reported from every city where it was shown. Within six weeks 600,000 people had seen it. The Capitol Theater in New York, with its 5400 seats always filled, held the film for an unheard-of four weeks, and only ended its showing when Harpo Marx made unpleasant scenes about the delay of the premieres of *A Night at the Opera*. Five hundred stores around the Capitol reported sales up by 40 percent. With the Depression as daily context, the headlines about the film stressed the extravagance of its cost, the size of its returns, the consequences of its success—employment, sales, relief to the needy from MGM's American Christmas and Relief Fund. Hopefulness in bad times was as much the film's contribution to cultural literacy as its demonology.

"No woman's picture," "hard-boiled," "strong meat" were among the critics' responses. There was some complaint that all the "flogging and torture stuff" made the film 131 minutes long and posed theater managers with problems in serving peanuts and popcorn. Doyens among the critics— Joseph Alsop and Otis Ferguson—thought the film brilliant. Laughton was overpowering, the "ship a living thing." The only sour note came from

Richard Watts of the *New York Herald Tribune*, who, on a second viewing, remarked that much of the film was "slightly embarrassing nonsense." *Variety* offered a reflection on the sort of cultural literacy with which the film would be seen: "The Polynesians are considered members of the white race by many experts, but whether they are so held by the majority of laymen is questionable. And Gable's and Tone's girlfriends are very much Polynesian in appearance. But it is all done so neatly the kicks won't be numerous." Gable had sailed into New York for the premiere after a much publicized and lubricous cruise of South America. There was much smirking condescension in the reviews as they remarked on how this "no woman's picture" roused female sexuality. Gable's "gams" and Tone's "manly stems" were seen as much a triumph of theatricality as the use of "unspoiled girls rather than Hollywood temptresses."

We have no "cultural-literacy-meter" to measure the various poetics of representation in the 1935 *Mutiny on the Bounty*. What "mythic chords of memory," we might have asked, does lubricity play? What poetic did "gams" and "unspoiled" girls contribute to the narrative and its reading? The images of mind of the millions who saw the film in its immediate cultural context are gone. Our own images are cluttered with sixty years of experience in-between. Let me be modest, then, in my certainties, and merely list what I think was there to be read: A sense that the extravagant violence of authority excused rebellion but did not legitimate it; a sense that institutions of power were ultimately goodwilled and responded to the ideals of men committed to them; a sense that the historical narrative is not divorced from the total ambience of its representation—that its meaning can be found as much in its cost of production as in its plots; a sense that historicity is more a matter of visual consistency than interpretation. Above all, in this period of a technological revolution in representation through sound film, there was a growing confidence in the realism of illusions. Five old hulks in a bay of Catalina Island could be the British fleet at Portsmouth. Tahitians at Matavai on Tahiti could appear to converse with "Fletcher Christian" at "Matavai" on Catalina. A set on a bobbing barge in an open sea could be the deck of the *Bounty* so long as the light and the camera angles were right. Illusions make things true; truth does not dispel illusion.

There seems common agreement that the 1962 film *Mutiny on the Bounty* was the beginning of the end of Marlon Brando as an actor. The whole venture was grossly decadent—from its $27 million cost, the sensual wallowing of the whole crew for months at Tahiti, Brando's use of his $6 million to buy a Tahitian island (Tetiaroa, to which Millward, Burkitt, and Churchill had deserted), his marriage to the Tahitian "unspoiled girl" (actually Mexican) who had played Franchot Tone's girlfriend in the 1935 version, Brando's unprofessional behavior in the filming, the near obscene cultural arrogance in changing Tahitian landscape, diverting rivers, making black sands white, the presumption of the filmmakers that their own sexual fantasies of the Tahitians was the reality. The lowest of many low points in the film undoubtedly came when, to depict the irrational conflict between Bligh and Christian, Christian was ordered to copulate with the "King's daughter" so that Bligh could get his breadfruit. A smirking Brando reports his obedience, peeling a banana, with "Rule Britannia" playing in the background.

To do him justice, Brando never wanted to do the film. It was the producer's decadence and greed that made him accept Brando's near-impossible terms. Certainly Brando did not want to do the adventure film constructed by Eric Ambler's script. Brando wanted to do a film with what his more sardonic critics called "more philosophy" in it. Brando did not even want to be Fletcher Christian. He wanted to be John Adams, the final survivor of all the mutineers on Pitcairn Island. The "philosophy" he wanted to present was not that of heroic mutiny against outrageous tyranny, but the mystery of violence in human nature. Even when the mutineers had a chance to make an island paradise on Pitcairn, they were self-destructive. Brando wanted to show "man's inhumanity to man." "I wanted to draw a parallel with what's happening in Africa today," he said.

In the end, all was total disaster. Brando's liberalism did not fare well at all. The film, wrote the *New York Times* critic, was full of "hoarse platitudes of witless optimism until at last it is swamped with sentimental bilge." The script, taken again out of Nordhoff and Hall, was finally credited to Charles Lederer, but not before it had gone successively through the hands of Eric Ambler, William L. Driscoll, Border Chase, John Gay, and Ben Hecht. An extravagant $327,000 was spent on the script alone. Brando, in response to criticism of his behavior on the set in constantly muffing his lines, claimed that there were scenes for which he had seen eleven different scripts.

Brando made a study of the *Bounty*. It was part of his acting technique to read himself into the context of a part. One press release said he had read a million words on the mutiny. He grasped at what he saw out of his reading to be the essential conflict between Bligh and Christian. Bligh was not a gentleman, and Christian was. Bligh was uneducated. Christian had all the superior knowledge of his class. For Brando, a Restoration dandy was the "ideal type" of gentleman. He proceeded to make Christian a wealthy, irresponsible fop, constantly making a fool of Bligh. Trevor Howard played Bligh much less psychopathologically than had Laughton. The conflict on the deck of the *Bounty* was class warfare.

Aaron Rosenberg, the producer, chose Carol Reed as director. Reed's strengths were other than in creating the spectacular. He crafted spare, intense films such as *The Third Man*. Reed was also British. He did not cope easily with Brando's indiscipline. There is more than a hint in the constant conflict on the sets that Brando's caricature of an English gentleman put an edge on relationships both with Reed and with Trevor Howard and Richard Harris, who played the part of John Mills, seen in the film as instigator of the mutiny. Brando's preposterous accent, among other things, picked at the scabs of old cultural wounds. In the 1962 *Mutiny on the Bounty* there was no accommodation given to the ultimate propriety of the British navy. Forces of cultural literacy which made it impossible to have an American actor play Captain Bligh were also at work on the film sets. The British actors had to wonder whether Christian's conflict with Bligh was not also Brando's conflict with their Britishness.

One whole season of filming on Tahiti in 1960 was botched. The final script came long after the crew had established themselves at Tahiti. The rainy season interrupted filming. Reed's health was ruined. He could not guarantee that the film, whose costs were now rising catastrophically, would be completed on schedule. MGM replaced him with the seventy-year-old Lewis Milestone. Milestone, in filming a second season at Tahiti, did no better than Reed. Three men were killed in accidents. The reconstructed *"Bounty,"* overloaded with filming equipment, was dangerous. The farce was being touched with tragedy. Milestone, demeaned by Brando's behavior in countermanding his direction, also quit. Brando, still hankering to make the whole film turn on Pitcairn, was secretly given charge of the scripts and direction of the final scenes.

These last scenes have come to be seen as among the most bizarre of movie history. Brando as Christian is dying on the cliffs of Pitcairn, having heroically tried to stop the others from burning the *Bounty*. (The real Christian, it might be remembered, was murdered by Tahitian slaves some four years after the landing at Pitcairn.) Brando is lying on 200 pounds of ice so that he can "method" the tremors of death. The cold, however, makes him forget his Tahitian lines. The crew write them in crayon on Maimiti's forehead when she leans over him as he dies.

Abbreviations for the filming instructions should be read in the following way: MCS = Medium Close Shot; o.s. = off screen; f.g. = foreground; CS = Close Shot; CU = Close Up; MCU = Medium Close Up.

MCS—Mills and Williams—Camera shooting past Young and Brown as they rise into scene, Brown holding Young back—Minarii enters left, pushing Williams and Mills back—Brown pulls Young o.s. right—CAMERA TRUCKS in as other natives enter f.g., pushing Williams and Mills away—natives exit f.g.—CONTINUES TRUCKING in—Williams tries to explain—

> *Young*: . . . scum!
>
> *Brown*: Ned. Ned, stop!
>
> *Williams*: No—I'll swear that I gave him bad for good. I never done out anybody in my whole life before.

CS—Christian, as Brown strokes his brow—Camera shooting past latter in left
f.g. and Young in right f.g.—Brown hold Christian down as he tries to sit up—

> *Christian*: Brown—wh-what's happened. Brown?
>
> *Brown*: We're on the beach, Mr. Christian. There was an accident. You've
> been burned and you must lie still.
>
> *Christian*: Was I hurt badly?
>
> *Brown*: Not too bad. You're going to be all right, but—but it's important
> that you stay as—as still as possible.
>
> *Christian*: The *Bounty*?
>
> *Brown*: It's hopeless.
>
> *Christian*: It's gone. The sextant—did we—did we—Have we lost it?
>
> *Brown*: No, I have it here, . . .

MCS—Mills, McCoy, and Birkett, as Mills comes forward—CAMERA TRUCKS
back

> *Brown (o.s.)*: . . . Mr. Christian
>
> *Christian (o.s.)*: Hide it, Brown. Hide it quickly.

MLS—Camera shooting past Christian, Brown, and Young, to Mills as he comes
forward—CAMERA PANS down and TRUCKS in as he kneels before Christian—
crew in b.g.

> *Christian*: So, it was your work. The burning, was it? You filth!

MCS—Mills—Camera shooting past Christian in f.g. and past Brown, and
Young at right

> *Mills*: I have no want in me to harm you. For the love of God, believe, I
> regret what has happened to you. We all do. But each man has to follow
> his own belief, no matter what.

CU—Christian

> *Mills (o.s.)*: You've said this many times, after the mutiny. What I did—what
> I thought I had to do— . . .

MCU—Mills

> *Mills*: . . . I burned the *Bounty* for the good of all. It wasn't in bad faith. It
> was just bad luck.

Ext. Shore—Night—CU—Christian

> *Christian*: For the good of all, Mills? Mmm?

MCU—Mills

> *Mills*: Yes, sir.

CU—Christian

> *Christian*: But why did you have to burn the *Bounty*? You'd no reason to fear me.

MCU—Mills

> *Mills*: We were afraid, Mr. Christian. We were afraid you were going to take us to London by force.

CU—Christian

> *Christian*: Oh, God—
>
> *Mills (o.s.)*: We're sick and sorry for what's happened to you. We'll never forget what you've done for us.
>
> *Christian*: It's all right, Mills. It wasn't your fault. Bligh left his mark on all of us.

MCU—Mills

> *Mills*: Goodbye, Mr. Christian. May God have mercy on you.

CU—Christian reacts—lifts his head slightly—

> *Christian*: Uhh—Am I—am-m I—am I dying, Brown?

MCU—Brown and Young

> *Brown*: Yes, Mr. Christian.

CU—Christian

> *Christian*: What a useless way to die.

CU—Young

> *Young*: It's not useless, Fletcher. I swear it. Maybe we'll get to London, or maybe not. But the Blighs will lose. We'll tell our story somehow, to someone.

CU—Christian

> *Young (o.s.)*: It only needs one of us to survive.

CS—Mills—looks to b.g., then rises—CAMERA PANS up—he exits right as Maimiti runs forward, looking down to o.s. Christian
CU—Christian reacts
CS—Maimiti—CAMERA PANS down as she kneels—pours some medicine
CU—Christian

> *Christian*: Never mind that, Maimiti. We haven't much time.

CS—Maimiti
CS—Christian—shivers

> *Christian*: Please—Please know that—that I—I loved you—more than I knew.

MCU—Maimiti

> *Christian (o.s.)*: And—if I'd only had had time to—. . . .

CU—Christian—dies—Maimiti sobs o.s.

> *Christian*: . . . to—

CS—Maimiti, her hands covering her face as she sobs—Camera shooting past Christian in f.g., as she embraces him—CAMERA PANS down—PANS her up, as she looks at him—CAMERA TRUCKS right past them to *Bounty* as it sinks—

> *Maimiti*: Oh, Fletcher—(in Tahitian)

> > FADE OUT

Historicity did not loom large in the claims for the 1962 version of *Mutiny on the Bounty*. Instead the Campaign Books suggested headlines such as: "*Bounty* Blockbuster with Style," "$20 Million Mutiny Film Topnotch Excitement," "Brilliant—That's the Word for Brando." A fishing sequence filmed with a thousand islanders as extras on Bora Bora near Tahiti roused

the strongest claims for primitive realism. Historical realism was left for
the post-film experience of the Living Museum of the *Bounty* at St. Petersburg. The 1935 Campaign Book had been full of suggestions as to how a
wider audience could be made to be engaged in the film's historicity—ship
model contests ("a million stores cooperate"), Sea Scouts' knot-tying com-
petitions, navigation displays in museums, logbooks for sale, Sailors'
Chanty Centers, *Bounty* cut-outs, striped sweaters in a seaman's mode, love
songs of Tahiti. By 1962, the targets of the publicity men had changed. In
that year, the Campaign Books were featuring sarongs modeled by Tavita
(this film's "unspoiled girl"), table decorations of coconuts and melons (or
grapes and plums as substitute), raw fish recipes, hair and skin care from
the Pacific islands, poi as a gourmet dish, Tahitian drums and songs, and
travel tours. Perhaps advertising agents are not as expert ethnographers of
our symbolic nature as their fees claim them to be, but it is clear that they
must have believed that the 1962 Mutiny film tapped a different form of
cultural literacy. They must have thought the body, social standing, the
present would spring to mind in a reading of the film, not institutions, not
social change, not the past.

Seven successive scriptwriters were, in any case, likely to leave historicity
in some sort of limbo. The final script ruthlessly subordinated time, space,
action, event, and agency on the *Bounty* to making mutiny by a decadent
fop halfway credible. So out of the "natural" logic that Bligh was preoccupied with the breadfruit, that the breadfruit needed more water than the
Bounty carried, that men would go crazy with thirst as they were brutally
ordered to work the ship without water, that someone would drink seawater in these circumstances, that a gentleman like Christian would finally
have to choose between breadfruit and a seaman's life—comes the mutiny.
Mutiny finally happens when Bligh kicks a ladle of water from Christian's
hands as he helps a dying, mad Williams. "You snob," Bligh calls Christian,
as he does this last unforgivable act. He had been taunted by Christian's
aristocratic condescension into absolute inhumanity.

Charles Lederer, who was responsible for the final script, said it was a
"most rewarding creative experience." He had read a hundred books on
the *Bounty* to get it right. What he had right, no doubt, was his sense of
cultural literacy. His script was not of what happened on the *Bounty*, but
what would have happened if all the common expectancies of cultural literacy were true. The "natural" logic of the events is the reading to which
cultural literacy responds. The "mythic chords of memory" in this case are
all the vague cultural memories that men will go mad drinking seawater,
that madness creates responsibilities in other higher-than-institutional loyalties. The cultural literacy that Lederer taps says that it does not matter
that there was no ladle kicked out of anybody's hands, there would have
been a mutiny if there had been.

William Bligh was always convinced that Tahiti was the cause of his mutiny. When the mutineers who had been captured by the *Pandora* were tried and three of them hanged, Bligh defended his opinion about the cause of his mutiny by quoting a former shipmate of Christian's as saying, "He was one of the most foolish young men I ever knew in regard to the sex." Tahiti was, at the end of the eighteenth century, a license for much ribald imagination and invention. It prompted a considerable literature of the "knowing" type and soft-porn descriptions of Tahitian native life. To his contemporaries, there was not much doubt about Christian's heterosexual propensities. But at the end of the twentieth century that clarity has become blurred. In 1984, Robert Bolt went not to the Nordhoff and Hall trilogy which an estimated twenty-three million people had read even before the Laughton/Gable film, but to Richard Hough's splendid history, *Captain Bligh and Mr. Christian* (1972). As befits the psychological interests of our time, Hough went to a suggestion by Madge Darby, an amateur historian of New South Wales, that if we wanted to understand Bligh's and Christian's conflict, we should think of what a heterosexual splurge on Tahiti would have done to a homosexual love affair on the *Bounty* between Bligh and Christian. She had no evidence for her suggestion other than that Christian had said, "I am in hell, Mr. Bligh, I am in hell," in the middle of the mutiny, and had whispered some secret to Peter Heywood to take home to his family. Considering that at this time about three sailors a year were hanged for sodomy and hundreds more a year were flogged for the less lethal charge of "uncleanness," it is not a matter that would have been passed over lightly by contemporaries. I have to say, however, that there is little that I have read through thirty years of engagement with the *Bounty* that suggests that it is likely that there was a homosexual relationship between Bligh and Christian, or that no one would have known about it if there was one.

There was an intensity about Bligh's and Christian's relationship that might have been homoerotic rather than homosexual. Some of those who had sailed with Bligh and Christian before the *Bounty* remarked on Bligh's partiality to Christian and were at a loss to explain it. It is clear that on the *Bounty* relations deteriorated after an incident at the Cape of Good Hope, when Christian borrowed money from Bligh and Bligh was able to force an early repayment by selling the "IOU" to his merchant relatives in England. Christian's impoverished family would have been saddled with the debt, which Christian had probably planned on redeeming after the *Bounty* voyage, when he had been paid. I cannot say whether the homosexual slant on Hough's story made Mel Gibson reluctant to accept the role of Christian. But Gibson, like Gable and Brando, was a reluctant Christian. When I asked the man who helped cast Gibson how Mad Max could have been persuaded to accept the role, I was told a story. They wanted Gibson, I was told, because he was halfway physically similar to the original Christian—shortish, 5'9", olive complexion, strongly built. So

they pursued him to a lunch at Claridge's in London. They put it to him
that he visit the Christian family home of Moreland Close in the Lakes
District of England. There in the lead guttering was supposedly an imprint
of Fletcher's foot put there by him in about 1783. If Gibson's foot fitted,
would he take the part? It did, and he did.

Robert Bolt's screen play for the 1984 Hopkins/Gibson *Mutiny on the
Bounty* is the most accomplished of them all. The opening credits with
Vangelis's haunting music makes for a "sound and light" experience that
sets a mood of mystification. Bolt uses the courtmartial of Bligh for the
loss of his ship as the baseline of his narrative structure. That courtmartial—not the courtmartial of the mutineers—was much more formalistic
than Bolt suggests. The public reaction—and the Admiralty's—against
Bligh was much later. In this early courtmartial he was much more the
hero. Hopkins gives a splendid nuanced performance as Bligh. Gibson is
stilted and subdued. The supposed homosexual tension between Bligh and
Christian is displayed by innuendo rather than explicitly dramatized. That,
among other things, makes the theater of the 1984 version a class above
the 1935 and 1962 versions.

These many years my contribution to cultural literacy has been to teach
the history of the *Bounty* to undergraduates in their senior years.[4] I have
always put it to them that history is something we make rather than something we learn. I have always been confident that out of events and people
apparently so trivial and unimportant as the *Bounty* they would discover
questions large enough for them to answer as well as the creativity to find
the mode of their answering them. Of course, as their teacher I am not
innocent. I want to persuade them to certain things. I want to persuade
them that any question worth asking about the past is ultimately about the
present. I want to persuade them that any history they make will be fiction—not fantasy, fiction, something sculpted to its expressive purpose. I
want them to be ethnographic—to describe with the carefulness and realism of a poem what they observe of the past in the signs that the past has
left. It is my hope that they make themselves culturally literate in giving
ear to the questions women and men around them are asking about themselves, and that they find in their history-making the capacity to represent
human agency in the way in which it happens, mysteriously combining the
totally particular and the universal.

My students respond enthusiastically to this patently presentist, relativist
notion of history. It seems "soft," no hard facts to learn. It warms their
prejudice that history is just opinion, one as good as another. There is some
alarm among them in the beginning at how empty their minds are of questions and the awful realization that if they look at their navel too long all
they will see is a bellybutton. There is also a growing chagrin at how hard
one must work at being creative and how elusive the past is.

It is not until my students have begun to produce their various historical fictions on the *Bounty* that I show them the Laughton/Gable, the Brando/ Howard, and the Hopkins/Gibson films. The films inevitably make them angry and scornful. They see the films as irresponsible, negligent of the rights of a historical past to be properly represented. They laugh at how obviously the films fail to cope with either the differences between the present and the past or with the differences between cultures. They discover that their own presentism, relativism, and fictions have responsibilities. I call that cultural literacy. I find it is acquired somewhere between theater and living.

NOTES

1. Moving uncomfortably into a field of research that was not my own, I embraced Michael Rogin, *Ronald Reagan the Movie and Other Episodes in Political Demonology* (Berkeley: University of California Press, 1987) and Neal Gabler, *An Empire of Their Own: How the Jews Invented Hollywood* (New York: Crown, 1988) with enthusiasm because they began to teach me how to "read" a film historically. Then I blessed two sorts of people I thought I would never bless—film censors and studio publicity agents. The New York film censors demanded, like the Royal Chancellors of old as censors of the theater, the script of every film shown in New York. That made a marvelous collection in the Albany Cultural Archives. The studio publicity agents were the wink-wink cultural anthropologists of popular culture as they tried to calculate what the public wanted to learn of the making of the film and collected the public response to their showing. The scripts, "Mutiny on the *Bounty*" (1935) and (1962) Dialogue Continuity. Hollywood: Metro-Goldwyn-Mayer. Copy: Albany, New York State Archives, were of great help, though, of course, I did not peruse all the versions that preceded the final scripts.

The Campaign Book 1935 (*Mutiny on the Bounty Campaign Book*. New York: Public Library, Center for the Study of Performing Arts. ZAN-T8, reel 35, NC 199–202) and the Press Books 1935 and 1962 ("*Mutiny on the Bounty 1935 Pressbook*." New York: New York Public Library, Center for the Study of Performing Arts. MFL x NC 1561 and "*Mutiny on the Bounty 1962 Press Book*." New York: New York Public Library, Center for the Study of Performing Arts. ZAN-T8, Reel 35. NC 199–202) were my real encounter with the films as a total cultural experience.

2. Such information as I have about the 1916 and 1932 Australian films on the *Bounty* comes from Charles Chauvel, *In the Wake of 'The Bounty': To Tahiti and Pitcairn Island* (Sydney: Endeavour Press, 1933); Stuart Cunningham, *Featuring Australia: The Cinema of Charles Chauvel* (Sydney: Allen and Unwin, 1991); Errol Flynn, *My Wicked, Wicked Ways* (New York: G. P. Putnam, 1959); Michael Freedland, *Errol Flynn* (London: Arthur Baker, 1978); Andrew Pike and Ross Cooper, *Australian Film 1900–1937* (Melbourne: Oxford University Press, 1980); Peter Valenti, *Errol Flynn* (Westport, Conn.: Greenwood Press, 1984).

3. There is a plethora of biographies and reminiscences surrounding the production and the stars of both the 1935 and 1962 versions of "Mutiny on the *Bounty*." They stand somewhere between hagiography and scatology. My selection out of them was these:

1935: Paul L. Briand, *In Search of Paradise. The Nordhoff-Hall Story* (New York: Duell, Sloan and Pearce, 1966); George Carpozi, *Clark Gable* (New York: Pyramid, 1961); Bosley Crowther, *Hollywood Raja: The Life and Times of Louis B. Mayer* (New York: Henry Holt and Co., 1960); Kathleen Gable, *Clark Gable: A Personal Portrait* (Englewood Cliffs, N.J.: Prentice-Hall, 1961); Jean Garceau, *"Dear Mr. G—": The Biography of Clark Gable* (Boston: Little, Brown, 1961); James Norman Hall, *My Island Home* (Boston: Little, Brown, 1916 [1952]); Warren G. Harris, *Gable and Lombard* (New York: Simon and Schuster, 1974); Charles Higham, *Charles Laughton: An Intimate Biography* (Garden City, N.Y.: Doubleday, 1976); Rene Jordan, *Clark Gable: A Pyramid Illustrated History of the Movies* (New York: Pyramid, 1973); Elsa Lanchester, *Charles Laughton and I* (New York: Harcourt, 1938); Samuel Marx, *Mayer and Thalberg: The Make Believe Saints* (New York: Random House, 1975); Robert Roulston, *James Norman Hall* (Boston: Twayne, 1978); Kurt Singer, *The Charles Laughton Story* (London: Robert Hale, 1954); Bob Thomas, *Thalberg: Life and Legend* (Garden City, N.Y.: Doubleday, 1969); Lyn Tornabene, *Long Live the King: A Biography of Clark Gable* (New York: G. P. Putnam, 1976); Jane Ellen Wayne, *Gable's Women* (Englewood Cliffs, N.J.: Prentice-Hall, 1987).

1962: Anna Kashfi Brando and E. P. Stein, *Brando for Breakfast* (New York: Crown, 1979); Gary Carey, *Brando* (New York: Simon and Schuster, 1973); François Guerif, *Marlon Brando* (Paris: Collection Tetes d'Affiches, 1977); Charles Higham, *Brando: The Unauthorized Biography* (New York: New America Library 1987); Rene Jordan, *Marlon Brando* (London: W. H. Allen, 1975); Metro-Goldwyn-Mayer, *M.G.M. Presents Mutiny on the Bounty* (London: Arcola Picture, 1962); Bob Thomas, *Brando. Portrait of a Rebel and an Artist* (London: W. H. Allen, 1975).

4. Mr. William Bennett is perhaps a walk-on "extra" to my theater of the *Bounty*. His ideas on history and his plans for it in American education can be found in William J. Bennett, *James Madison High School* (1987);*What Works. Research about Teaching and Learning* (1987); *American Education. Making it Work. Report to the President* (1988) all published in Washington by the U.S. Department of Education; and *Our Children and Our Country* (New York: Simon and Schuster, 1988).

3

Re-screening the Past: Subversion Narratives and the Politics of History

Daniel J. Walkowitz

"When History is Up For Grabs" headlined an op-ed piece in the December 28, 1995, *New York Times*, the newspaper generally acknowledged to be the U.S. "paper of record."[1] From his present title as chairman of Prison Fellowship Ministries, the author, Charles W. Colson, might have seemed an unlikely source for such a concern—except that the subject of Colson's essay was the release of Oliver Stone's new Hollywood blockbuster, *Nixon*. Colson, who had found God while a felon sentenced for his part in the Watergate conspiracy, had been Richard Nixon's close personal aide in the White House and had remained his lifelong friend.

Never acknowledging that his own historical legacy is tied to Nixon's, Colson emphasises broader concerns. The perspective, practices, and complicity of the filmmaker with the historical profession threatens, in Colson's words, to "turn individual mistakes and weaknesses into a sweeping indictment of the country's history." Nothing less than "the very character of America," he insists, is at issue. Citing the judgment of his "old adversary" Bob Woodward of the *Washington Post*, "half the movie is based on facts. The other half ranges from sound speculation to borderline slander." Stone's failure is not simply his representation of Nixon, but the broader critique of American history embedded in it. Again, in Colson's words: "The 'deeper truth' that Oliver Stone talks about appears to be that America is rotten to the core, festering since the founders." "This," continues Colson, "is not merely historical revisionism. It is deconstructionism applied to American democracy. Mr. Stone's free play of facts and fantasy is employed to fashion his own private, politicized vision of American history."

These are no small matters; media representations of the past provide a major and powerful source of historical information today. Moreover, Colson, displaying his penchant for the subversion narrative best associated with his mentor, worries that gullible "young people who don't know the facts" and who can be seduced by imaginative media "where falsehoods and distortions work their greatest harm," "will have their imaginations primed with the image of a half-crazed Nixon casting a dark shadow over two centuries of American history."

And can historians (presumably, to Colson, Stone is not one) be relied on to counter this pernicious storytelling? *Au contraire.* Continuing the subversion narrative, the historical profession, descending into the infernal fires of revisionism, deconstruction, relativism, and left-wing political correctness, has been taken over by "radical subjectivism." Colson's subversion narrative replicates Richard Nixon's own formative political strategy. Nixon, you may recall, rose to political prominence as a "premature" McCarthyite on the coattails of Whittaker Chambers's controversial 1946 House Un-American Activities Committee testimony against Alger Hiss. Chambers was a reborn ex-Communist, and now Colson casts in that role none less than the renowned Marxist historian turned neo-conservative Eugene Genovese. As Colson writes:

[Stone] is unlikely to be called into account by most historians, because our academic history departments have themselves caved into deconstruction. A text is whatever the reader makes of it we are told; claims to objective truths are power plays. As the historian Eugene Genovese has said, observing this trend, "We are being told that since objectivity rests only with a God who does not exist, we should scorn it as the ideology of oppressors."

In the United States, Colson's editorial is of a piece with the [multi]"cultural wars"—multiple both in the sense that they are multifaceted and that they pit a conception of conflictual diversity against one of consensual pluralism.[2] An insurgent New Right and Christian Coalition wage this war against humanities programming which they see dominated by a historical profession that, in their view, is incapable of telling right from wrong and is committed to a wrongly critical history. It is important to remember, however, that this is hardly a new critique: Spiro Agnew, Nixon's Vice President (one forgets that both executives resigned in that administration from two different scandals), complained in 1969 of "nabobs of negativism." And the historical trajectory from Agnew to Colson reminds us that this is a deeply political, longstanding and frustrated conservative complaint. Theirs is a political and social movement which celebrates heterosexuality and an imagined or idealized nuclear family. In a racialized and gendered script, neo-conservatives and the Christian Coalition see social welfare, abortion rights, and homosexuality as immoral and anti-Christian, and affirmative action as unfair.

Yet their view of the historical profession as the enemy is not without foundation. With the rise of the New Social History in the 1960s, the historical profession *has* made racial minorities, women, and the study of sexuality legitimate, significant, and integral parts of the historical experience, and the integration of these subjects into a new historical canon has made history and the humanities exhibitions that reflect this subject-shift a natural enemy to the New Right. Moreover, preliminary but widespread evidence suggests that Colson's concerns reflect debates recurring worldwide. Indeed, I believe it is possible to see Colson's concerns with "truth," "facts," and untrustworthy historians as part of a global crisis in and of history.[3]

Colson connects three issues which I think reflect this crisis over history today and complicate the public's response to the narrower New Right political agenda. In addition, they are issues for which historians bear some responsibility. First is an objectivity crisis created by the postmodern linguistic turn and anxiety over "truth." Second is the difficulty establishing the identity of the historian in historical work in the public arena. Third is the distrust, if not rejection, of contemporary historians by many who dominate the political culture. In sum, Colson argues that the problem for the public today is one of contemporary historical practice, who is authorized to do it, and its inability to rely on the historical profession.

But the debate over *Nixon* is but one of a series of public debates in the United States during the last three years that have called the historical project into question. Two other controversies in particular, a rancorous dispute over the "*Enola Gay* Exhibition" at the National Air and Space Museum of the Smithsonian Institution, and a to-do over the National Standards for U.S. History produced by the National Center for History in the Schools, raise most of the same questions. In all three cases, critics presented historians as professionals who had lost their bearings, and had become untrustworthy if not irresponsible.

My concern here is not whether the history in these projects was "good" or "problematic"; rather, I am more interested in how historians were located in public discourses about the history in these forms of production. I want to look at the history of history in these discussions. These subjects provide, I believe, a way of asking what it means to "think like a historian," how to engage the place of public memory in historical presentation, and how to construct "ourselves" when some of those selves are at variance with "others." Then, I wish to ask why the present debate is occurring at this historical moment, and borrowing from an old comrade, what is to be done.

The profound skepticism about *Nixon* and Oliver Stone builds both on the reaction to his earlier film, *JFK*, and to a rising neo-conservative polemic about the politicalization of the humanities and the historical profession. During this period, the *Enola Gay* Exhibition and the publication of the History Standards were prime neo-conservative texts on which they built their case.

Briefly, funded by the National Endowment for the Humanities (ironically by Lynne Chaney, who would later lead the attack against them), the Standards were guidelines for teaching American history in primary and secondary schools. In the protracted controversy over the Standards, the dominant press accounts presented the picture painted by outraged politicians: the motif suggested universal public opposition, ideologue historians, and "subjective" (meaning irresponsible or bad) history.[4] Neo-conservatives attacked the report empirically (the "facts" game) and conceptually: opponents counted the number of times certain figures appeared, complaining, for instance, that too many were female, black, or Native American, and criticized its overall message as negative, as weighted toward criticisms of McCarthyism or the Ku Klux Klan rather than toward appreciation of leaders such as George Washington or Abraham Lincoln. Lost in all the press accounts of the controversy, however, was public support for the Standards in the form of 30,000 orders, and its adoption to date by at least five states as the basis for curriculum revision.[5] Indeed, there are several claims to the public voice, if not several public voices, but they have unequal access to power with which to authorize their view of the public, their claim to speak for it. Historians may have their journals, but neo-cons have Congress, and it is the latter's story that has fashioned the prevailing media account.

The controversy over the proposed Smithsonian exhibition of the *Enola Gay*, "The Last Act: The Atom Bomb and the End of World War II," exposed the media's reliance once again on the neo-conservative subversion narrative. Writing in the *American Journalism Review*, Tony Capaccio and Uday Mohan note that "the controversy was largely fueled by media accounts that uncritically accepted the conventional rationale for the bomb, ignored contrary historical evidence, and reinforced the charge [by some veterans' groups, air force personnel, and politicians] that the planned exhibit was a pro-Japanese, anti-American tract."[6] Congressional voices decried efforts by "revisionists" to subvert our past, while historians and curators moved into liberal mode, trying to re-"balance" accounts with greater emphasis on Pearl Harbor, Japanese atrocities, and so forth. But to opponents, the issue was *not* "balance" or "complexity," but "truth," which in this case meant nothing less than a vindication of use of the bomb and, more generally, the past as they "knew" it from memory and childhood school lessons. Two weeks after the American Legion called for its cancellation, the Smithsonian acted. On January 30, 1995, the National

Air and Space Museum, billed as "the world's most popular museum," announced that it would replace the exhibition it had been planning for six years with a small commemorative display that would avoid controversy and "interpretation."[7]

The Smithsonian's action threatens to become accepted procedure and raises fundamental questions about control of historical interpretation and the identity of the historian. Not surprisingly, then, in response to the debate over the Standards and the *Enola Gay* (and there has been a consistent run of similar controversies since[8]) historians have focused on the role of memory and on historians' relationship to publics whose stories these exhibitions tell. Major blocks of recent 1995 journal issues recount symposia on these matters and reflect the historians' considerable anxiety about its continuing role. The December 1995 issue of the *Journal of American History* presents a roundtable in which a dozen historians agonize in more than 120 pages over "History and the Public: What Can We Handle?" Not to be outdone, the *Journal of Social History* published an entire supplementary special issue on "Social History and the American Political Climate—Problems and Strategies" in winter 1995. And in its December 1995 issue, *The Public Historian* published a symposium on Disney and the Historians (Walt Disney corporation has proposed Historical Disneyland theme parks), asking "Where Do We Go From Here?"[9]

These questions need to be asked. But implicit in them is another set of questions: Who *is* the historian? What is the role of the public? What, indeed, is history, and what is its "factuality" or relation to "truth"? And finally, who "owns" history in public, often "heritage," venues created to "honor" supra-historical commemorative issues? Put in alternative perspectives: how do we "honor" memory which engages its corollaries—forgetting and nostalgia?

History and memory (as well as nostalgia and heritage) are often antithetical—we remember part of history, but it is their complicated relationship that is at the heart of the historical project, both in reconstructing the past and in the meanings people draw from it. For as Michael Kammen has observed, "Nostalgia, with its wistful memories, is essentially history without guilt. Heritage is something that suffuses us with pride rather than shame."[10]

As a "fictional" genre, the film *Nixon* makes these connections between the politics of history and memory explicit, building on the anger resonant in the culture war cases. The *New York Times*, for instance, opened its discussion of the film with a long essay by Richard Reeves, a former *Times* reporter who had written a book about Kennedy and was completing one on Nixon. Appearing on the front page of the Sunday "Arts & Leisure" section, a bullet drew readers to its salient question: "How far can one go with the defense 'Hey, it's only a movie.' "[11]

But, in fact, Stone wants his film to be taken seriously as a historical work. And I believe it should be, not the least because its wide distribution gives it a central place in the public history of the era. To counter the broad criticism of his earlier film *JFK* for its reliance on Jim Garrison's conspiracy theory about the assassination, Stone has also gone to great lengths to provide "legitimizing" scholarly apparati for *Nixon*. The film opens with what Reeves characterizes as a disclaimer, but what I see as the meta-commentary on sources historians typically place in footnotes and an introduction:

This film is an attempt to understand the truth of Richard Nixon, 37th President of the United States. It is based on numerous public sources and on an incomplete historical record. In consideration of length, events and characters have been condensed, and some scenes among protagonists have been hypothesized or condensed.

Inventing characters is a complicated and dicey historical discussion for another occasion, although I hasten to add that I supervised the translation of my book on nineteenth-century workers into a docudrama—that is, a fiction film—funded by the National Endowment for the Humanities as a historical account of the nineteenth-century urban industrial experience. It is, I have written, entirely fictional and all "true"; that is, from the evidence available to me, it accurately portrays my conception of that past.

But my program was but a blip in the endless run of television pabulum, although I did have to add a scholarly Roman Catholic priest to my advisory board to fend off attacks from the local public television executives who worried that my advisory board was "too left wing." (They never bothered to question the priest's political leanings, which were little different from those of the other board members.) Stone, however, has a very public presence, writes about a widely contested public figure with whom many in the present feel invested, and offers a highly controversial interpretation: in particular, his conspiratorial notion that Nixon was prisoner to a "system" ruled by a conspiracy of oil barons, militarists, and right-wing anti-Castro fanatics. This view, it should be noted, is not far from Eisenhower's warning in his farewell address of the growing domination of the military-industrial complex. Stone invents a shadowy Texas oil baron in *Nixon* and regularly inserts pregnant comments from Nixon about the Bay of Pigs. Again, while Stone finds evidence to justify this "invention," critics complain he simply adopts the mantle of the historian to give credibility to his artistic flights of fancy.[12]

Stone's efforts to counter skepticism of *Nixon* as "serious history" only begins with the opening statement of method for viewers. Simultaneous with release of the film, he published a co-edited book on the subject. The centerpiece of the nearly 600-page volume is an annotated version of the film script, complete with 168 footnotes and a bibliography. In addition, the book begins with thirteen short scholarly and journalistic essays, ranging from personal accounts of Nixon's "secrets" by film advisers (and subjects) such as John Dean to analyses of his self-conscious effort to shape his own historical image by Wisconsin professor of history Stanley I. Kutler. The volume concludes with over two hundred pages of Watergate documents and excerpts from the White House tapes.[13]

To these critics, the film's political view is unbalanced and excessively psychologizing. (I, incidentally, agree with this latter complaint, and would suggest it is a risk of biographical accounts, especially those from the subject's point of view. In the film, Nixon is often portrayed with a drink in his hand, and as compensating for inferiority bred by a strict, evangelical mother and lower-middle-class roots.) For historians, however, the most serious complaint about *Nixon* is that Stone has subordinated rigorous historical method to personal conspiratorial views rooted in his infatuation with 1960s New Left hostility to "the system."

Ironically, Stone's effort to overwhelm doubters with evidence plays into his opponents' hand, for it makes the same error as do many historians and, following us, the public. The issue is not how many facts one can muster; it is in the nature of evidence, the problematic and shadowy character of the fact itself. It is hardly surprising that the Society of American Historians produces as its contribution to media history a volume by some of our most able craftpersons that simply evaluates the factual accuracy or thematic value of some of Hollywood's classic American historical films (*Patton, Gandhi, JFK, A Man for all Seasons*, etc.). More to the point, I think, would be, first, to dissolve the implied distinction between "fact" and "fiction," docudramas and documentaries. Second, we need to interrogate the constructed nature of all images, all narratives, and focus on the argument in the assemblage, not on whether or not the shoes are "authentic."

There may be little Stone can do to counter the prevalent public view that he is a crank and a historical misanthrope. He has become a standing joke for editorial writers and cultural pundits. Late-night television comics and op-eds parody historical heroes as if portrayed by Oliver Stone (i.e., Jay Leno's *Tonight Show* skit on Oliver Stone's version of Abraham Lincoln: "I'll call myself 'Honest Abe.' That'll sell, and then I can do whatever I want.")[14] Meanwhile, against "The Stoning of Stone," as another critic has summed up his reception, Stone presses his case for "truth" in *Nixon*, even into the reaches of cyberspace. Thus, a 66-second statement from Stone on the problem of negotiating "truth" in *Nixon* with Anthony Hopkins, the actor as interpreter, can be downloaded from the Buena Vista World Wide Web site (it is also available with video). Listen to how Stone begins: "I just deal with what I see as the truth, and if it's not the truth, I want to discuss it and raise it with the actor." The segment, while hardly profound, nevertheless demonstrates the reach of contemporary debates, the means available to discuss it, and something of how the historian as interpreter appears throughout production processes in public history.

Much as Colson's conspiracy narrative resonates with public anxiety about the reliability of historians today, the central theme of Nixon's life and his recording of it (or more to the point, construction and erasure of it) make the effort to tell his story paradigmatic of the crisis in public history (or history in the public) today. Nixon's crucial missing 18½ minutes of White House tape, his career-long use of McCarthyite conspiratorial scripts, his well-documented and deep involvement as Vice President and later President with CIA and FBI plots against Cuba and domestic dissidents, and his moniker as "tricky Dick," are at the heart of his career. Like many politicians increasingly since, he also slaved to construct a public historical image for historians. How, then, does the historian step back from constructed "facts" and tell the story about a conspiratorial personality who engaged in conspiracies when the record is deliberately elided, obfuscated, and manipulated by the historical actors? And how do you do so without seeming yourself to be conspiratorial?

Stone's almost obsessive need to win public approval seems not unlike the plaintive cries heard today from many historical quarters where authors bemoan small audiences and public disapproval. Why does no one listen to us? Is it because we are boring? Indeed, we often are. Or, are we lost in theory? Actually, compared to other social sciences and cultural critics, historians have tended to be anti-theoretical. Are we no longer able to tell stories? In fact, I think calls for the return of a master narrative are just that: making the master (the white male) the story once again. However legitimate these complaints, though, issues of style should not be allowed to obscure what are at least as much issues about conception, argument, and ideology—about, in a word, politics. The past as understood by many historians today some in the public find disquieting and historians may have to learn to live with their disapproval. Seeking love is for the therapist's couch, not the historian's workshop. Moreover, it is not merely a chimera, it is undesirable. Comfortable minds breed bad history. Rather, the furor should stir the blood, warm the heart, and quicken the need to take to battle. The uproar means someone is watching, that someone cares. Engagement is also the first stage in historical thinking. The key, of course, is still to be taken seriously so that someone *does* engage, and the risk for Stone (and for historians as subjects of the culture wars) is not controversy but marginality, of being placed outside the cultural ken.

The second heartening point for Stone (and all of us) is to realize that this criticism is not new to historians. History has been up for grabs before and often, but profound changes in the profession and political economy have deepened the contemporary crisis. Well before World War II, historians such as Charles Beard and artists such as Diego Rivera had their work censored for unpopular interpretive positions. Similarly, in the Great Depression, groups like the Film and Photo League offered contested filmic representations of strikes and protest that countered those of the newsreel that ran in the cinema palaces. Thus, as Raphael Samuel and Michael Kammen, and other historians have documented, history has always been contested, but some views have been more easily heard.[15]

Until the last third of the century, whiggish and triumphal consensual views dominated textbooks, classrooms, museum exhibitions, and cinema emporiums. We live in a post-colonial moment with the legacy of colonial narratives. The rapid expansion of higher education in the postwar years, however, brought fundamental changes to the profile of the historian and her and his interests. In the United States, the history graduate student was increasingly likely to be a Jew, another immigrant, and/or a woman. There were few racial minorities, but their history was also central to the problem of otherness that animated these new historians. By the 1960s, reflecting their own class and ethnic backgrounds, this generation pioneered a resistance to consensus historical accounts in New Left and the New Social History. Committed to writing history from the bottom up, the New Left brought a new conception of the past to the New Social History's methodological concerns. In this new conception, workers, ethnics, women, African Americans, and indigenous native peoples were present and involved in the making of the past.

The rapid expansion of public sites for historical work in the 1970s brought the differences between earlier consensual views and those of the New Left into sharp relief. New relationships between producers of historical writing to state funding and civic consumption placed historians with this broadened conception in intensified tension with the memories and views of dominant political groups. During the 1970s, the tensions remained muted. Programming remained in its infancy and opponents to it were fettered by Democratic Congresses. But the Reagan, Thatcher, fill-in-the-blank political and cultural counterrevolution unleashed festering antagonisms from frustrated conservatives and a politics of resentment from middle-income whites who understood their economic fragility as part of the privileging of minorities, women, and labor in Great Society social policy and in historical accounts.[16]

Today, the crisis in history, all the talk about "truth," "facts," and the profession's descent into "radical subjectivity" reflects a broader political and economic crisis in late capitalist societies. Disorder and instability have created a search for authority: for Facts, Objectivity, Order. Global and political restructuring, ethnic chauvinism, and resurgent nationalism have created a widespread political cynicism and a thirst for political and social security. They have also become meta-languages for class and racial bias, as for instance, in the language of the middle-classness, the restructuring of welfare, and the attack on immigrant "ethnics." Under euphemisms such as "downsizing," corporations have begun to undermine the job security and economic base from which the professional-managerial class had always believed itself immune. The diminution of the two-parent family has also destabilized traditional familial expectations. The welfare state has been eviscerated or under attack in North America, Europe, and Eastern Europe. Competing nationalisms have divided neighbors throughout the former Soviet bloc, while the promises of the much heralded "free market" have as often given way to anxiety, corruption, crime, and destitution.

Historians' flirtation with if not embrace of postmodernism gives them some responsibility for the crisis in history. The focus on multiple voices and unstable texts in the postmodern move or linguistic turn undermines the public's yearning for stability. Indeed, I think critics and the press have misread its corollary, what Peter Novack has called the "Objectivity Crisis," to suggest that the postmodern historian make no truth claims. Most, I believe, would emphasize the multiplicity and contested nature of historical voices, focusing on narratives as constructed interpretations by historical actors and analysts. Actually, the press and politicians may fear most the idea that people might question *their* authority. In practice, particular versions of the past, both in the past and in the present, are authorized simply by those with greater access to power, but that does not make them "truer."

But the need to anchor ourselves in a usable past has made the character of history and the role of the historian central to the "culture wars" and the search for authority. For societies have traditionally looked to historians as authorities they could trust to provide a narrative of the past on which people could build usable national and personal identities. Many historians' abiding concern with the race, class, gender trinity (among whom I count myself), make them an unsatisfactory source for whiggish older accounts, but the historians' postmodern move has further destabilized the authority of both the historian and the text, and contributed to public anxiety.

Complicating the traditional relationship of the public to the historian is the fact that this political crisis occurs in conjunction with the revolution in media information systems. As George Orwell once wrote, Richard Nixon articulated, and the public realizes, that to control the past is to control the future.[17] And in the widespread expansion of history into the public, the future is now. History already is written in a steady stream of videos, exhibitions, policy analyses, and so forth, and in an extraordinary array of venues. New computer-based technologies have already begun to give Everyman (and Woman) the potential to produce history in countless spaces—private, public, and cyber. And we ain't seen nothing yet. Thus, the ascendance of new interactive public media and venues for the presentation of history, and its coincidence with a current crisis of authority in both "post-socialist" (or, do recent reversions in some East European countries suggest "pre-socialist"?) and late capitalist societies, have conspired to make this, I believe, a critical moment for historians.

Two aspects about how we work as historians shape this emerging crisis for our craft as it enters the twenty-first century. First, writing history is always a political act. Historians choose subjects because they engage issues that matter to them, issues about which they wish to inform others. Second, historical writing must involve critical thinking (indeed, the term is a redundancy, to be thinking we must have a critical distance from our subject). Historical presentation, like all thinking, must be an active act, not congratulatory or comfortable, but disruptive and engaged. Surprised or confounded, history should evoke the listener, reader, or viewer to exclaim "I didn't know that" or "I wonder about that?"

Increasingly, the problem before today, however, is that history in the public world engages audience memories framed by traditional expectations about sites, holidays, and events that they seek to memorialize. What, then, is the historian's responsibility to public memories; and how to engage the public in narrative that runs counter to deeply held beliefs and needs?

These questions will become increasingly central to historical work in the twenty-first century as the role of public venues in shaping historical consciousness increases geometrically. Filmic representations such as *Nixon* are major elements in this growth, but they are only a part. Cities around the world have mounted or redeveloped museums to tell their history; New Zealand and the United States both have forthcoming dictionaries of national biography; federal agencies increasingly ask historians to preserve, chronicle, and analyze their histories. But historical presentation in the twenty-first century seems likely to be even less tied to the academic classroom and the printed monograph; it is also more likely to be interactive, written with computer text and graphics programs, and as inclined to appear in cineplexes and cyberspace as in classrooms. How will the historian "write" in these formats? It will not merely be a book on a wall or in film; that ignores the potential and problems in the different media. Moreover, as we work collaboratively with curators, cinematographers, biographers, how do we understand, explain, and defend what it means to "think like a historian"? What role will historians have in these complicated modes of production?

A recent encounter brought home to me that the public is not as unilaterally skeptical, confused, or single-minded about history as neoconservatives would have us believe. I found myself on a checkout line at a bookstore in Lower Manhattan one snowy Saturday morning, preparing to buy my copy of *Nixon*. In front of me, a young girl of about 10 or 11 years tugged on her father's sleeve, imploring him to let her buy a book she tried to shove at him. It was, I believe, a medieval adventure. "It's historical fiction," she explained to him somewhat plaintively, implying, I thought, that it was not a frivolous purchase. The father glanced at me with a small smile and the hint of a shrug. But seeing an opening to satisfy my own curiosity, I turned to the girl and asked her, "What is historical fiction?"

She was taken aback briefly, but only briefly. She was, after all, a New York kid. Public interventions were not out of the ordinary. And her father *was* there. Turning to look from him to me, I could see her mind calculate for an instant whether my question was an imposition or an opportunity. Clearly deciding it was the latter, an opportunity to demonstrate that she was the smartest kid in the class, she explained as if it were perfectly clear: "It just means that what happened, actually happened, just not to these people."

"Precisely right," I thought to myself. And looking at the nearly 600-page opus under my arm, I wondered where and why the message had gone wrong. A schoolgirl had no trouble seeing the history *in* fiction; somehow this understanding had been imparted without jeopardizing the nation's history. Indeed, this young person's response suggested, one, that at some point as children learned "history," this understanding receded and was displaced by a crude empiricism—history as facts—and two, that the contemporary issue is not postmodernism or radical subjectivity. The issue is politics. Historians have become out of step with political and social elites; or, equally to the point, the reverse: elites no longer can count on historians to authorize their version of the past.

Indeed, the historical profession has fundamentally changed since mid-century, and the meaning of this change is most apparent now in societies that have had a backlash and find older elite cultures (male, white, and Eurocentric) in power: Thatcherism in England and Reaganism (the New Right) in the United States are but two examples.

If postmodernism is part of the problem, however, it may also be part of the solution. Professional historians and the historical public culture we have helped create remain too wedded to empirical, positivist narrative strategies from the nineteenth century. Postmodern narratives that destabilize texts and authority and de-center the study of how the past is made from privileged, white male elites will not please such folks, especially as they seek to hold on to their authority. Multiple voices and broken time also reflect how the past and present engage one another, how people through the struggle over memory experience the presentness of the past. Barbara Abrash's and my 1990 film *Perestroika from Below* and 1994 *History Workshop* article suggests how one can intercut archival film, reflective oral history, and contemporary events with layers of music and narration in what we call "postmodern filmmaking." The Australian filmmakers Ross Gibson and John Hughes (in, respectively, *Camera Natura* and *One Way Street*) and Barbara Abrash, in her experimental documentary *Margaret Sanger*, as I have written previously, can be seen as part of the beginning of a genre that can be called postmodern. And, *Nixon*, for all its problems, brilliantly uses black and white footage, exaggerated images, and flashbacks in a comparable way to create a powerful historical commentary on memory, personality, and policy in history. In the film, for instance, Nixon's present is seen through his imaginings and experiences of the past, and we are not sure which is the case.[18]

New technologies and public venues demand that as historians of and for the twenty-first century we retool ourselves and radically revise how we train students, define our roles, and create new narrative strategies. It is professionally irresponsible to dismiss something as "only a film," or museum. Yet, new sites and technologies do not make for new history. As much film has simply used history as backdrop and transferred books or slide shows to film, most CDs are merely texts in bytes. Clearview Press advertises over 190 video and CD-ROM titles—the French Revolution CD-ROM, the Wild West CD-ROMs, Imperialism CD-ROM—none with authors.[19] In a three-page spread on nine new products, the February 1996 issue of *The Computer Shopper* headlines "Virtual Time Machines: History on CD-ROM." "Forget the boring tomes of yesteryear. Learning about history on CD-ROM is not only interesting, it's actually fun."[20]

These efforts are the products of electronic publishing houses, in which, to date, professional historians have been little involved. Nor is it clear that they want more than our imprimatur. The brief promos selling these works, however, leave this historian breathless and quivering. Still, giving students access to vast archival repositories on disks has the democratic potential to allow them to create their own histories. Historians such as Roy Rosenzweig and Steve Brier of the American Social History Project have even created a CD-ROM version of their pioneer textbook *We Who Built America*. And Art Speigelman's CD-ROM study of his cartoon series on the holocaust, *Maus*, begins to realize the interactive capacity of the format. Speigelman intercuts the oral history debates between himself and his father which shaped the construction of each frame and episode in the series.[21]

In conclusion, the historical profession must recognize that history is being written everywhere, by everyone, and that such work cannot be dismissed. Rather, we must ask what is to be the role of the professional? What does it mean to think like a historian, and how do we transmit this to the public? The October 1995 issue the American Historical Association's newsletter *Perspectives* did just that, asking the question of a dozen historians. There was little agreement, but as one historian, David Trask, noted, the public and students tend to think it is "one damn thing after another." Against this notion, Trask and many other respondents generally seem to agree that the concept and verisimilitude are crucial. I would, in fact, agree, and blur the difference between fiction film and documentary; both are constructed "fictions," and both are documents of a past time. In this regard, *Nixon* is a terrific example, in part just because 18½ minutes of his recorded life is missing. The subversion narrative can so easily construct Stone as a paranoid in part because he is writing about a paranoid in an instance where evidence suggests public paranoia is justifiable.

Thinking historically, however, demands a critical stance, one shrouded in the instability of sources and multiplicity of voices. The past, like the present, is contested, and history writing is an active engagement with the social construction of the past. And training to do so properly involves establishing the broad context (not the fractured balkanization of "events"), including the historiographic context, in which an event takes place.

But while historians are everywhere, not all pass through graduate schools. How do we hold them and ourselves accountable? Can the "untutored" or the private sector produce good history for hire? Ken Burns, for example, *is* a historian of the Civil War. The issue is whether his history is any damn good. What is central is not eleven hours of facts; it is his conception. It is not enough for him to deny responsibility for the work as history and claim he is a filmmaker, a poet, or a songwriter—all positions he has adopted. Indeed, he is all of the above, and if we have problems with his "conception," meter, or key, we have the obligation to say so and/ or tell the story ourselves. We must become the filmmaker-historian, archivist-historian, curator-historian. These were never opposites, and it is a luxury of the past to think so. The future of history is not in the academy, though that is a good place to study how to do it. The doing is everywhere: library, studio, editing room, museum, halls of congress, the streets. Our training and identity as historians must adapt to the task, moving from sole reliance on the modes and practices brought forward from the nineteenth century to the modes, technologies, and venues of the twenty-first. We cannot expect audiences to understand the instability of texts and "facts" until we explain to them that we do not mean to say we obfuscate or lie. We must make it clear that we say that which we believe to be true, as best we can tell.

The present "crisis" makes clear that we must confront the politics of history and act politically. To do otherwise is to put our head in the sand. We must accept that we will have losses, upheaval, and public disquiet. In the task I wish to conclude with a series of guidelines.

1. Relate to the public and its memories through the history of memory. Allow for counter-narratives to your/our own story, but remember that history is about power in discourse, about which stories get organized and authorized.

2. As the historian Michael Wallace has noted, historians can, nay, should, participate in commercialized histories such as those organized by the Disney Corporation, but they should not kid themselves and *insist on public accountability*. At the same time, all doing such work must take responsibility as historians. It is also not enough to claim to do it and not

do one's homework, or to write off the need for care as "well, it's only a film" or "poetry."

3. As the historian Tom Bender reminds us, the gatekeepers are not even-handed or equal in power; evidence is not privileged by academic creden-tials, but public historians must "maintain the integrity of intellectual standards" everywhere—in films, galleries, books.[22]

4. The historian of the twenty-first century will need to be postmodern, public, and self-consciously political. But the exploration with new media and narrative strategies should not obscure that objectivity or "truth-telling" remain unobtainable yet firm goals in an imperfect world. But com-peting truth claims are judged for their evidence and coherence daily in public and professional courts, and historians must begin to weigh in with their evidence and verdicts.

5. Finally, we must become storytellers again. Academic historians tend to speak only to themselves, too often exhibiting disdain for the point of view of the public. The views of such elitist ostrich professionals deserve public suspicion and derision. At the same time, the academic profession must not fear public ostracism, real or imagined. We should write acces-sible, engaging stories, but not presume we will be loved for them. As historians we should not seek to create comfortable minds, nor should we fear criticism. Rather, we should stand ready to relish the struggle, for that is where history is made.

NOTES

As always, my thinking on these matters is especially indebted to my regular conversations with Barbara Abrash.

1. Charles W. Colson, "When History Is Up for Grabs," *New York Times*, December 28, 1995: A21.

2. There are many commentaries on the "culture wars" and the historical pro-fesssion. See, for example, Richard Jensen, "The Culture Wars, 1965–1995: A His-torian's Map," *Journal of Social History* 29 Supplement (1995): 17–37; and Gary B. Nash, "The History Standards Controversy and Social History," *Journal of So-cial History* 29 Supplement (1995): 39–49; and on its relevance to England, see John K. Walton, "The Lion and the Newt: A British View of American Conser-vatives' Fear of Social History," *Journal of Social History* 29 Supplement (1995): 73–84. There are also recent extended symposia on the subject in major journals. See, for example, "Symposia: Disney and the Historians—Where Do We Go From Here?" *Public Historian* 17, no. 4 (Fall 1995): 43–89; and "History and the Public: What Can We Handle? A Round Table About History after the *Enola Gay* Con-troversy," *Journal of American History* 82, no. 3 (December 1995): 1029–1144. The latter, reflecting the historians' commitment to "evidence" and "facts," includes reprints of some relevant documents.

3. Walton, "The Lion and the Newt," reminds us of the possibilities and lim-

itations of such comparisons. Local context matters, but many of the concerns and ecomonic shifts are transnational.

4. Lynne Chaney's views are cited by Jensen, "The Culture Wars," p. 23.

5. Gary Nash, "National Center for History in the Schools to Revise History Standards," *Perspectives*, American Historical Association Newsletter, 33, no. 9 (December 1995): 32, 34.

6. Tony Capaccio and Uday Mohan, "Missing the Target," *American Journalism Review* (July/August 1995): 19–26.

7. David Thelen, "History After the *Enola Gay* Controversy: An Introduction," *Journal of American History*, p. 1029.

8. The Library of Congress, for instance, canceled (and after considerable protest, reinstated) an exhibition on Freud when some protesting women, in the name of feminism, insisted that Freud's theories were discredited. A month later, in December 1995, the Library of Congress also canceled an exhibition on slavery, "Big of the Big House," because employees complained that it was an uncritical allegory about themselves. The next month, the Museum of the City of New York fired the historian who had raised the money for an exhibition on the Irish-American experience in New York when she insisted on final authority over its content. And, most recently, post-modernism itself has been the focus of a hoax pulled by a contributor to the Spring 1996 issue of *Social Text*: he argued that publication of his jargon-ridden spoof proved that the entire enterprise of "cultural studies" (the umbrella under which he placed deconstruction and post-modern criticism) was bankrupt.

9. *Public Historian* 17, no. 4 (Fall 1995): 43–89.

10. Michael Kammen, *Mystic Chords of Memory: The Transformation of Tradition in American Culture* (New York: Knopf, 1991): 688.

11. In fact, in the article we learn that Oliver Stone did not say this; rather, Reeves characterizes Stone's refusal to take responsibility if an audience misinterprets his meaning as an " 'it's only a movie' defense." Richard Reeves, "Nixon Revisited by Way of the Creative Camera," *New York Times*, December 17, 1995: H1, 41.

12. Walter Goodman, "With Fact in Service to Drama," *New York Times*, January 3, 1996: C9, C15.

13. Eric Hamburg, ed., *Nixon: An Oliver Stone Film* (New York: Cinergi Productions 1995).

14. Lincoln Skit, "The Tonight Show," late December 1995. There was also a parody op-ed in the *Times* of late December or early January 1996 of another politician as seen by Stone.

15. Raphael Samuel, *Theatres of Memory* (London, 1995); Kammen, *Mystic Chords of Memory*; Nash, in *Perspectives*, December 1995.

16. A more conservative version of this account can be found in Jensen, "The Culture Wars."

17. Orwell and Nixon are cited in Stanley I. Kutler, "Richard Nixon: Man and Monument," in Hamburg, ed., *Nixon*, pp. 43–49.

18. Barbara Abrash and Daniel J. Walkowitz, "Sub/versions of History: a Meditation on Film and Historical Narrative," *History Workshop Journal* 38 (1994): 203–214.

19. *Social Studies* (Chicago: Clearview Inc. 1996).

20. Stephen A. Booth, "Virtual Time Machines," *The Computer Shopper* (February 1996): 200–202.

21. Art Speigelman, *Maus* CD-ROM (New York: Voyager, Inc., 1995).

22. Thomas Bender, Nancy Cott, Eric Foner, and Robin D. G. Kelley, "A Conversation with Eric Foner," *Culturefront* 4, no 3 (Winter 1995/96): 17–24, 74–75.

4

"Smart Jews": From *The Caine Mutiny* to *Schindler's List* and Beyond

Sander L. Gilman

One of the most pervasive myths in modern Western thought concerns the superior intelligence of the Jews. Jews are, according to this legend (often repeated by Jews themselves) smarter, more astute, and more adaptive than non-Jews. This is an important theme in American as well as European culture and it reflects the attention to the relationship between "race" and "intelligence" that has haunted racial thinking since the nineteenth century. The recent appearance in the United States of Richard J. Herrnstein and Charles Murray's book *The Bell Curve: Intelligence and Class Structure in American Life* has again drawn attention to the debate about the relationship between inheritance and intelligence, a debate which in the American context is usually read as a comment on "race" (read: blackness) and *lower* intelligence.[1] Yet there are two ends to Herrnstein and Murray's "bell curve," each of them thin and rare. As rare as is the lowest end of the curve, those of lowest intelligence, according to the classic argument, it is equally true that the upper end of the curve is also rare. It is fascinating that little or no attention is given in the analysis of such studies to the "normal" center. The thin ends define the problem—the "normal" center is understood as the model of intelligence and therefore also the model of virtue. It is erroneously assumed in these investigations that only the deviant, following the model of the pathological in medicine, can provide insight into the normal. And thus the center—the two standard deviations from the norm in this model—is invisible. It remains the implicit site of virtue though (or because) of its "average" intelligence. It is true that Herrnstein and Murray devote only one page to the highest group in terms of intelligence—"Ashkenasic Jews of European origins" who "test higher than any other ethnic group." Based on this model that equates intelligence with virtue, we would come to expect that the higher the intelligence, the greater the protection against criminality, the greater the virtue of the group. According to Herrnstein and Murray, "Jews in America and Britain have an overall IQ mean somewhere between a half and a full standard deviation above the mean, with the source of the difference concentrated in the verbal component."[2] Such test scores, however, are not sufficient for them to establish the superior intelligence of the Jews; they also rely on "analyses of occupational and scientific attainment by Jews, which constantly show their disproportionate level of success, usually by orders of magnitude, in various inventories of scientific and artistic achievement." Jews are not only smart but they are creative—and following Max Weber's reading of American-Protestant culture—this is a sign of their virtue, for worldly success is a sign of a virtuous life. Such an image in American popular "scientific" culture has a direct relationship to the image of the intelligent or successful Jew in the mass media from the 1940s to the present. However, it is always shown as more complex and more difficult than the deceptively simple presentation in Herrnstein and Murray's text.

If Jewish superior intelligence is understood as having meaning in American popular culture, it is a compensation for the physical weakness of the Jew that has remained a theme in American culture. Recently, an African-American author noted: "Another classmate said that while black people were gifted in sports and music, Jews had provided the world with intellectual genius. As proof, he ticked off three names: Freud, Einstein, Marx. I got very angry. For a long time I wondered whether the Jews were really chosen by God, as one of my Jewish classmates suggested. The argument seemed watertight. Wherever Jews were given the chance they have shown themselves to be smarter than anyone else. *Look how well we've done in America and everywhere else we've gone. Look at the Jews. Look.*"[3] This is a version of the myth of economic superiority as a sign of Jewish superior intelligence, but it also obscures the argument about compensation. If, in such a view, music and sports are compensatory to a lack of intelligence among Blacks, Jewish intelligence is compensatory to Jewish physical inferiority. Such images haunt the representation of the Jew in Hollywood— remember Jose Ferrer as Barney Greenglass, Humphrey Bogart's lawyer, in *The Caine Mutiny* (1952), his "Jewish" body dominated by the other military figures in the film.[4] The relationship between "mind" and "body" in such views is extraordinarily powerful.

The representation of smart Jews in American cinema during the post-Shoah period had been relatively rare until recently. In the movies and, by extension, in television, Jews had been represented as victims, as "sensitive," as "ethnic minorities," but rarely as Jews of exceptional intelligence. Of the trilogy of "smart Jews," "Marx, Freud, and Einstein," evoked in European writing on Jewish superior intelligence, Marx rarely appears in American popular culture, but Einstein and Freud do. (One might note that Moses, Jesus, Einstein, and Freud are the first four "Jews" listed in a recent tabulation of "the most influential Jews of all time." Marx shows up as number seven and Spinoza in tenth place.[5]) Einstein is the essential smart Jew in American popular culture. But his appearance in Stephen Herek's comedy *Bill & Ted's Excellent Adventure* (1989) or as the feature figure, played by Walter Matthau in Fred Schepisi's film *IQ* (1994), is as a comic figure. He is asexual and only marginally aware of the realities about him. In the latter film, he serves as a matchmaker between his "too-smart" niece (played by Meg Ryan) and her proletarian boyfriend (played by Tim Robbins). Einstein, no matter what his actual reputation in late twentieth century biographies as a lover, never gets the girl in American popular film. Likewise, Freud seems to be ubiquitous in modern American culture, from the sensitive Freud (played by Montgomery Clift in the 1962 film biography) to the appearance of a spectral Freud in Joshua Brand and John Falsey's television drama *Northern Exposure* in 1993. Freud dots the landscape of mass culture. Unlike Einstein, he is rarely a comic figure in the presentation of his "insight" but (even with the traditional association of Freud with sexuality) he is never a sensual figure.

The compensatory function of high intelligence in American mass and popular culture is clear when the theme of the work is love and sex. Thus in the representation of mixed couples, the continuation of the image of the *Mischling*, the Jewish partner is always smarter and better educated. Perhaps this should be called "*Annie Hall* syndrome," since the relationship between Woody Allen and Diane Keaton in that film of 1977 set the pattern for the self-conscious exposure of failed intermarriage as the marrying down in intellect.[6] Recently, in the television series *Chicago Hope*, Aaron Shutt (played by Adam Arkin) is a neurosurgeon who was married to a blonde, Catholic wife who is a nurse. All such relationships fail. Indeed, Miles Silverberg (played by Grant Shaud), the Harvard educated producer on CBS's *Murphy Brown*, articulates the ineffectual Jewish intellectual who seems to have no specific sexuality at all. As in all of these characters, Silverberg is permitted to articulate his "Jewish" identity and his Jewish superior intelligence as part of the construction of the gender of his character.

In the mass media, however, there seem to be no "dumb" Jewish women. Even if the image is not of Jewish superior intelligence but of the "maternal" woman (such as Molly Goldberg), she is never represented in the same way as Diane Keaton. Yet the image of Jewish superior intelligence is always linked to some type of dysfunction, and this cuts across gender. Gender seems to be the significant variable when one speaks of "smart Jewish

[male] doctors" and "dumb gentile [female] nurses," but in Barbra Streisand's *Prince of Tides* (1992), it is the Jewish woman who is the stereo-
typically intelligent, educated, slightly neurotic New York psychiatrist.
Thus gender is dependent on the category of "race," that is, "Jewishness"
defines gender. In Streisand's world, it is the model of Jewish identity that
defines the gendering of the image. Barbra Streisand's character Susan
Loewenstein in *Prince of Tides* is a head-smart Jewish female psychother-
apist, but her personal (and professional) life is a mess. She sleeps with her
analysand, a problem that even the reviewers saw as reflecting on her role
as a therapist in light of the discussion of sexual exploitation in therapy
during the 1980s and 1990s.[7] Thus Barbra Streisand's *Yentl* (1983) provides a further example of the problems seen in the presentation of Jewish
superior intelligence on the screen. In order to fulfill her role as a "smart
Jew" in I. B. Singer's fiction of the Eastern European shtetl, the protagonist
must disguise herself as a man. Such figures of the smart Jew run parallel
to Barbra Streisand's early role as a bright, social activist in Sidney Pollack's
The Way We Were (1973), in which she plays her intelligence off against
Robert Redford's "All-American" good looks. But there, too, unhappiness
and the lack of personal fulfilment result from being too smart. You can't
be happy and too smart—especially if you are Jewish.

In spite of the fact that all smart Jews are alike (at least in the mass
media), the case of *Yentl* provides a model that implies the damaged masculinity of the "smart Jew." Yentl is a woman masquerading as a man,
whose Jewish superior intelligence can only be articulated in her masked
state. In speaking about the constructed category of "the Jew" throughout
this study, I have gendered him male, as does the literature discussing him.[8]
Thus Miles Storfer in his 1990 study of Jews and their accomplishments
compiles lists of accomplished Jews that are exclusively male and stresses,
in his discussion of postwar American tests, that it was Jewish males that
outperformed all other groups including Jewish "girls." Needless to say
Storfer's idealized account of Jewish Talmudic education is implicitly gendered, as only boys were permitted to study under the circumstances described by him.[9] Yentl reappears in the guise of science!

The inarticulated anxiety about Jewish visibility and Jewish racial difference has dominated Jewish male representation in the media. "Jewish superior intelligence" must be understood as an aspect of the question of
Jewish visibility in post-Shoah America. The casting of Paul Newman (blue
eyes, Jewish father, raised as a Christian Scientist) as the Jewish hero of
the film based on Leon Uris's novel *Exodus* (1960) was one of the anom-
alies of this anxiety about the implied difference of the Jewish body. How
could Jews be "racially" different if they looked like Paul Newman! Indeed,
in Robert Mandel's *School Ties* (1992) the theme of "passing" works only
because of the sports activities of Brandon Frasier. He is not quite able to
"pass" in the snooty (and anti-Semitic) private school that he attends. Yet

in *School Ties* the character is not only athletic but also smart and compassionate. His athlete's body is not sufficient, within the narrative of the film, to enable him to be accepted, to pass successfully.

The ghost of the "smart Jew" haunts the representation of the Jew even into the 1990s. In Robert Benton's *Nobody's Fool* (1995), based on a novel by Richard Russo, the following scene with the working class protagonist, played by Paul Newman, takes place in a bar:

> *Lawyer*: "Don't blame me, these aren't my holidays. I'm a Jew."
>
> *Sully (played by Paul Newman)*: "You're a Jew? I never knew you were a Jew." [beat] "How come you ain't smart?"

Being smart and being Jewish are linked, even in the world of Paul Newman, the exemplary "Jewish" figure of the age of the "tough Jew." The image of the "tough Jew" and the "smart Jew" merges during the 1990s. Simon Louvish, the Anglophone Israeli/British novelist, has one of his characters in *The Silencer* (1993), his novel about the charge of dual loyalties among American Jews, sketch the following history of modern Jewish identity formation in Israel:

> When we met, when was it, 'sixty-nine? You'd just started on your work for the paper, and I was demobilized from the army magazine and was taken on as a reporter. The first years of the Occupation. The heyday of Golda Meir. "Who are these Palestinians? I've never met any." A neat and closed orthodoxy. Now it's all blowing in the wind. The great victory of 1967. The ship was sailing. The Americans came on board. Everybody admired us, except the Third World, that bunch of wogs, who cared? Everybody deserves an imperial hubris. Ours just happened to last half an hour. The warning signs of arrogance and presumption. The Yom Kippur War. Menachem Begin. Lebanon. No more invincibility. And then to twist the knife, *intifada*. Some people just can't take it, Joe. They want that half-hour back, to stretch for ever. They want the smart Jew, who pisses on everyone.[10]

Louvish's novel is the novel of American-Israeli identity formation as seen from a British perspective. His history, however, collapses the image of the "smart Jew" with that of the "tough" Jew. Here the transvaluation of the Diaspora "smart" Jew into the aggressive, powerful body of the Israeli as colonial aggressor (following a European model) provides a new reading of the "smart" Jew, a Paul Newman figure who thinks he can think, but, of course, really lacks any insight or intellectual acuity. This view was seconded by Ehud Barak, the retired Chief of Staff of the Israeli Defence Forces in 1995. Quoted in an essay in The *New York Times* on the "Israeli deglamorizing of the military," Barak championed the concept of "a smaller and more clever I.D.F."[11] As the "tough Jew" is seen in Israel and the United States to be more and more problematic, the desire for the "smart" or the "clever" Jew returns, at least subliminally.

By the 1990s Jewishness and Judaism, Jewish identity and the different body of the "smart Jew," come to be interchangeable categories. With Gary David Goldberg's *Brooklyn Bridge* in 1991 (who based the show's premise on his own childhood in Bensonhurst and whose protagonist eventually gets into the Bronx High School of Science) and *Northern Exposure* that appeared a year earlier, being Jewish is now something that can be represented in American culture—but only as it equates to being smart. Thus Joel Fleischman (played by Rob Morrow), the protagonist of Joshua Brand and John Falsey's *Northern Exposure*, is brought to the wilds of Alaska (in the pilot for the series) because the inhabitants of Cecily, Alaska, want a "smart Jew Doctor," since Jews are smarter than other people. And as doctor, it is implied, they are also more virtuous. This hint at a "biological" model for the smart Jew vanishes quickly (and is made to seem an anomaly of the racial bias of the quirky character, the multimillionaire ex-astronaut, Maurice Minniefield [played by Barry Corbin], who uttered it). Yet it is an echo of the view that permeates American popular culture in the 1990s: Jews are smarter than everyone else because—they are Jews! And yet the unhappy and ultimately unsuccessful attempt of Joel Fleischman to enter into the world of Cecily, to achieve happiness and fulfilment with the gentile bush pilot from Grosse Point, Maggie O'Connell (played by Janine Turner), is the overarching plot of the series until his character vanishes back to New York City in the winter of 1995. In this long, protracted withdrawal from the series, Fleischman proves his virtue by allowing himself to be physically and spiritually tested in the Alaskan outback, showing that he is now morally prepared to return to (his natural space?) New York City.

In the course of the series Joel Fleischman's Jewishness is transformed into Joel's highly ambivalent relationship to his Judaism. Thus in one episode the same ex-astronaut, in order to keep his "Jew Doctor" happy, arranges to comb the wilds of Alaska for ten adult male Jews so that Joel can say the prayer for the dead for his uncle. The show ends with Joel abandoning his search for a *religious* community and saying "Kaddish," the prayer for the dead, in the church cum community center of Cecily, Alaska, with the inhabitants of the town, people of all "races" and "religions," his new congregation. The counter moment in this series is the episode in 1991 when the French-Canadian owner of the local bar/restaurant Holling Vincouer (played by John Cullum) decides that he must have himself circumcised in order to please his 18–year-old sweetheart Shelly (played by Cynthia Geary). Circumcision here is divorced from ritual practice but associated with personal virtue. Jewish difference becomes masculine difference and virtue. Yet throughout the series it is Joel's physical insufficiency, his lack of hardiness (unlike that of Holling Vincouer who fights off a bear singlehanded) that is paralleled to his status as a "smart Jew," as a Jewish physician. Like the war films of the 1940s and 1950s (such as *The Young Lions* [1958]), the Jew's presence is marked here as a sign of the plurality of American culture. Also in those films his physical insufficiency and his religious identity seemed to be linked. They are, of course, but only through the vehicle of the reverse movement of the post-Shoah construction of Jewish religious identity out of the ashes of a secularized racism.

This brings us to my friend Jo Miller's three firm rules of contemporary American mass media in representing American Jews as "smart":

1. All Jews are smart or at least clever.

2. All Jews are from New York.

3. Unless they are from Los Angeles, in which case they are movie producers (who must nevertheless speak with New York accents to demonstrate their New York-Jewish roots).

It is clear that the "Jews" in American cinema after the Shoah are "smart," but this is not always a virtue. Indeed it often comes to be tied in complex ways to the victim status of Jews within popular myth after the Shoah. Certainly this is the image parodied in Mel Brooks's *Blazing Saddles* (1974).

If the Jews are smart but victims, it is also the case that the "Germans" are also represented as smart—yet with quite a different twist. For their genius is that of the demented, evil intelligence—Moriarity to the Jew's Sherlock Holmes. This is the other side of the image of the scientist as intellectual. Thus Orson Welles in *The Stranger* (1946), Sam Jaffe as "the professor" in *The Asphalt Jungle* (1950), Peter Sellers as Dr. Merkwuerdigliebe in Stanley Kubrick's *Dr. Strangelove* (1964), Hardy Krüger in *Flight of the Phoenix* (1965), or, indeed, Walter Slezak or George Sanders in any of their fiendish Nazi incarnations in the "B" movies made before 1945, are "evil." The evil "German" scientist is in many ways the extension of the idea of Jewish superior intelligence, now associated (as it was in the nineteenth-century literary stereotype) with the German scientist. Jews, if they are not victims, can be the equivalent of the "evil" German. Such an image of the smart yet destructive Jew can be found in Frederick Wiseman's character as a nihilist-anarchist in *Viva Zapata!* (1952), leading the Mexican children of nature to their doom, apparently for the sheer pleasure of it.

Thus multiple versions of the myth of the "smart Jew" are to be found within the contemporary popular culture that spans the world of Herrnstein and Murray's *Bell Curve*. The myth of Jewish intellectual accomplishments stands in contrast to German-American, African-American, and

Italo-American expectations, but also the myth of Jewish intellectual superiority as compensating for the imagined weaknesses of the Jewish body. Framing *The Bell Curve*, they show how alive and real the myth of Jewish superior intelligence, and its relationship to images of virtue, remains in a wide range of contexts.

The representation of Jewish superior intelligence in the mass media became a major theme of the mid-1990s with the appearance in 1993 of Steven Spielberg's *Schindler's List* and in 1994 of Robert Redford's *Quiz Show*. These films (and the texts that parallel them) present the question of Jewish superior intelligence as a moral moment in cultural representation. The question of whether or not "being smart" is also being virtuous is posed in both of these films and both present a rather striking answer—in their own complicated way—to the myth of Jewish selection and the meaning attributed to the Shoah in many of the popular cultural discussion of Jewish superior intelligence.

One can begin with the Australian author Thomas Keneally's novel *Schindler's Ark* (1982) (released in the United States as *Schindler's List*). The culture bias in the studies of Jewish superior intelligence by American Jews or Jews living in America (such as Patai, Weyl, and MacDonald) can be judged from the relatively plaintive work by Bill Rubinstein, Professor of Social and Economic History at Deakin University in Australia and a leading historian of Jewish life in Australia.[12] He lists Jewish geniuses from music, science, and other realms of culture throughout Europe and North America. But then Rubinstein comments on the absence of Jewish superior intelligence in Israel, which, given this catalogue approach has produced virtually no genius in the realm of culture. His one exception is S. A. Agnon. Israel, with its mass of Jews and its absence of Jewish superior intelligence, provides only prologue to his real complaint—the lack of Jewish intellectuals in Australian life. He can mention two, the writer Pinchas Goldhar and the architect Harry Seidler. For Rubinstein "there is something clearly missing—a spark of genuine greatness, an absence of originality, style and excellence in all but the rarest cases." Unlike America, Rubinstein comments, "there is much less in the way of engagement with secular intellectual or cultural life." Jews in Australia become "professionals (especially lawyers and doctors) or businessmen" rather than "academics, scientists, or intellectuals and artists." At the antipodes, the view looks very different. It is talent that seems to be missing for the Jews, while the mere inclusion of the Jews in the professions, so vital to the eugenic and sociobiological argument, marks the absence of Jewish superior intelligence.

Given this reading of the absence of Jewish superior intelligence in Australia by Rubinstein, it is fascinating to read an Australian author looking at this phenomenon as one located within the world of Central European Jewry. Keneally's understanding of the location and meaning of the idea of Jewish superior intelligence is framed by his sense of its exotic and particular location and its origin. Steven Spielberg recasts this primarily "outsider" perspective in terms of an American reading of Jewish superior intelligence and its implications within the reception of the Shoah. (One might note that Spielberg made number 94 in Michael Shapiro's *The Jewish 100: A Ranking of the Most Influential Jews of All Time.*)

Keneally's historical narrative in fictive guise focuses primarily on the figure of Oskar Schindler, the non-Jewish entrepreneur whose actions rescued the workers assigned to his factory in occupied Poland. The central theme of the novel is "virtue," as Keneally explains in the introduction.[13] And it is this virtue that becomes the central theme all the way through Steven Spielberg's Academy Award-winning movie of 1993. It is a "strange virtue," according to Keneally, in that it is inexplicable at the beginning of Keneally's narrative.[14] Keneally begins his novel with a historical preface in which he sets the stage for his own discovery of the story of Schindler and his own rationale for writing this tale. Spielberg begins at the historical beginning of Schindler's tale—in Cracow during the German occupation— and provides flashbacks to show how "ordinary" Schindler's life really was. And in these flashbacks, all of which are part of Keneally's narrative, Schindler's ordinariness is contrasted to the idea of Jewish superior intelligence. Keneally observes that during his childhood Schindler went to school with the sons of his next door neighbor in Zwittau, the liberal rabbi Felix Kantor, a modern Jew who wrote "articles not only for the Jewish journals in Prague and Brno, but for the dailies as well."[15] Kantor's views were that "we are secular scholars as well as sensible interpreters of the Talmud. We belong both to the twentieth century and to an ancient tribal race. We are neither offensive nor offended against." He is an intellectual who sees himself as part of two intellectual cultures, and even more he is the father of "smart Jews." His children "become two of the rare Jewish professors at the German University of Prague." Schindler, too, according to Keneally, is "like the Kantor boys . . . a prodigy."[16] But his genius lay in the fact that he owned the only red Galloni motorbike in all of Czechoslovakia. This irony—comparing the image of Jewish superior intelligence with the acquisitive abilities of the teenage Oskar Schindler—begins the tale. The novel and the movie present the story of the shaping of a "virtuous" man. The narratives serve to illustrate what this virtue was, how it evolved, and why it occurred. And it is contrasted positively with Jewish superior intelligence throughout. For Schindler survives; the Kantors move in 1934 to Belgium and vanish.

In the course of the film and the novel Oskar Schindler eventually and remarkably comes to represent the possessor of virtue—true virtue—while the Jews in the camp seem to possess only the qualities of victimhood and, a few of them, the product of perpetual victimhood, Jewish superior intelligence. Indeed, the central pairing of the natty Schindler (played by Liam Neeson) and his bookkeeper, Itzhak Stern (played by Ben Kingsley, physically reprising his role as Gandhi [1982] for which he prepared by losing twenty pounds) in both the book and the movie provides the contrast between an evolving sense of virtue on the one hand and the receding of the importance of intelligence on the other. Stern is a "Polish Jew," the bookkeeper in a fabric firm.[17] He is initially introduced into the narrative and the film to resolve a problem. German soldiers had entered the firm and "bought" bolts of fabric with worthless Bavarian notes and World War One occupation money. How was the firm, now under "Aryan" management, to deal with this act without offending the German authorities and without compromising the firm's profit? Stern suggests a Solomonic solution—he burns the offending (non) money and writes off the losses to "free samples." Thus the reader or the viewer is introduced to Stern, whose audience in the novel and the film "liked Stern's dry, effective style with the legal evidence."[18] It was smart and direct.

For the observer, Itzhak Stern's physicality defines him: "He was so thin, and there was a scholarly dryness to him. He had the manners of a Talmudic scholar, but also of a European intellectual." When he is introduced he has a dreadful cold and we see him "blowing his nose and coughing harshly." In "the accountant's lean features" one saw "the complexities of Cracow itself, the parochial canniness of a small city."[19] It is "canniness" rather than Jewish superior intelligence that Stern represents, but it is a "canniness" of Cracow, not of the Jews—at least initially. But Keneally moves from that generalizing moment—small town craftiness—to understanding this as a reflex of Jewish experience. And he must, as he reads this as a quality of Stern's physiognomy—of Ben Kingsley's emaciated face.

Here the evocation of Gandhi in the film with the casting of Kingsley and the emphasis on Stern's protruding ears should be mentioned. If Gandhi's emaciated body is the reflection of his revolt against colonialism, the Jew's body is a reflex of his Jewish nature in the film. This is mirrored in Stern's ears. There is an old trope in European culture about the Jew's ears. It can be found in the anti-Semitic literature of the fin de siècle; but it is also a major sub-theme of one of the great works of world literature, Heinrich Mann's *Man of Straw* (1918).[20] In that novel, Mann's self-serving convert, Jadassohn (Judas's son?) "looked so Jewish" because of his "huge, red, prominent ears," which he eventually has cosmetically reduced. And while Jadassohn is only "witty," other Jews in the novel are "too clever."[21] Stern's image in the film picks up on the visible contrast between the huge, dominant, masculine body of Schindler and the diminutive body of the Jew.

Itzhak Stern, like the Jews of Cracow (but not like the other inhabitants of that small city), simply expects the Germans to disrupt their lives, even to "sporadically slaughter" them, according to Keneally. But they assumed "the situation would settle; the race would survive by petitioning, by buying off the authorities—it was the old method, it had been working since the Roman Empire, it would work again. In the end the civil authorities needed

Jews, especially in a nation where they were one in every eleven."[22] Here the problem of "canniness" as a reflex of historical experience is highlighted. So much for the "cleverness" of the Jews. For—in retrospect—we and Keneally know that such an assumption was inherently false. The Germans did not "need" the Jews—indeed, they wished to destroy the Jews root and branch. The Jewish superior intelligence that understands the situation of the Jews proves to be not even "canniness" but simply blindness.

In the novel, Stern is confronted with Oskar Schindler and sees in him part of the age-old plan to rescue the Jews. Stern needs Schindler, for "in men like Stern [there was] an ancestral gift for sniffing out the just Goy, who could be a buffer or partial refuge against the savageries of others." Ignoring the image of the "sniffing" Jew and the "just Goy" (read: dog and master), it is clear the Keneally sees in Stern an inherent "canniness" that enables him to recognize a useful tool—Stern is not a virtuous man. Yet when Stern is confronted by Schindler, he recognizes him as different: "*This isn't a manageable German.*"[23] Stern's Jewish superior intelligence meets its match, for Schindler does not easily fit into the mold of the "righteous" or even the "malleable" gentile. He is as different from the other gentiles as he is from the Jews. His absence of intelligence is in point of fact a sign of his potential virtue.

For this "just Goy" was dumb, while Stern was smart (like Rabbi Kantor): "Stern spoke softly, learnedly. He had published articles in journals of comparative religion. Oskar, who wrongly fancied himself a philosopher, had found an expert. The scholar himself, Stern, whom some thought a pedant, found Oskar's understanding shallow, a mind genial by nature but without much conceptual deftness."[24] Stern, like Kantor, is an intellectual. He publishes learned articles that show him to be one. Oskar is a braggart, whose intellectual ability is merely "shallow" and "genial." In the course of the narrative, Stern finds a like-minded Jew in the figure of the "young and black-bearded" Rabbi Menasha Levartov with whom he could discuss: "Stern, when it came to comparative religion, got greater pleasure out of talking to Levartov than he could even have received from bluff Oskar Schindler, who nevertheless had a fatal weakness for discoursing on the same subject."[25] Intellectual pursuits are not the strength of Schindler, but virtue is—and Keneally as well as Spielberg set these against one another as antitheses.

Schindler is a seductive speaker. He has a "rowdy sense of humor" and exudes an "easy magnetic charm." His language is certainly unintellectual—evidently even in discussing comparative religion. The Jews, such as Stern, "could never make a straight statement or request unless it arrived smuggled under a baggage of talk of the Babylonian Talmud and purification rites," according to Schindler. And this difference of intellect is inscribed on their bodies. Unlike the "ascetic" Stern, Oskar is "big, sensual." Stern is "clearheaded," and yet that "clearheadedness" is valueless without Schindler's virtue. As it becomes clear that intelligence will not rescue the Jews, the need is for virtue. Virtue and intelligence come to be reinforced as antithetical qualities. One of the intellect and the other of the emotions. Neither Stern nor his friend Rabbi Levartov is rescued by Jewish superior intelligence. Stern is rescued from deportation to the death camps by Schindler, and Levartov's life is spared by the misfiring of the camp commandant Amon Goeth's gun. He then is rescued by Schindler. Schindler's virtue saves the Jews, even though retrospectively "some say, and there is some truth to it, that Emalia and Brinnlitz [Schindler's factories] succeeded in their eccentric way because of the acumen of men like Stern . . ." Stern's intelligence in the management of the company becomes the vehicle through which Schindler's virtue can act. Thus Stern comes to be "the only father confessor Oskar had, and Stern's suggestions had a great authority with him." And yet it is Schindler's virtue that gives meaning to Stern's "canniness."[26]

In the novel and the film it is the smart Jew who comes to be the object needing to be rescued. Intelligence, especially when it is connected with the supposed superiority of the intellectual, is clearly a negative quality in this world. Stern's "canniness" recognizes that the "just Goy" is necessary to rescue the Jews and that his own intelligence should be harnessed to this vehicle for that rescue. Yet this is Jewish "canniness," the learned protection of 2000 years of persecution. The other side of the coin is the assumption that intellectual ability, as measured by Western standards, would serve to provide the Jews with any form of protection. Keneally and Spielberg present this in a case study of Jewish superior intelligence. The case is that of Diana Reiter, the architectural engineer who demanded of a noncommissioned officer that the foundations of the concentration camp building whose construction she was supervising be torn down and rebuilt "correctly." Her argument attracts the attention of camp commandant Amon Goeth. She approaches him with "the bogus elegance with which her middle-class parents has raised her, the European manners they had imbued her with, sending her—when the honest Poles wouldn't take her in their universities—off to Vienna or Milan to give her a profession and a heightened protective coloration."[27] Here is the case study of Jewish superior intelligence. The Jew as professional, as certified by the institutions of Western culture as a member of the elite. She has not recognized the most evident truth—that European anti-Semitism does not provide any such space for the Jew. The Jew always remains the Jew, and her intelligence remains dangerous.

When Spielberg has his writers restructure this scene in the film, he adds a line. Kneeling before a German solider, his pistol drawn, Elina Lowensohn, the actress who plays Diana Reiter, looks up at the camera—standing in the place of Amon Goeth—and states that "it will take more than this . . ." More than this to—to show that I am wrong, to destroy Jewish superior intelligence. Not at all. Spielberg's change reads this scene as showing that it will take more than killing a single Jew to kill "the Jews." Reiter's death is thus transformed from a comment on the futility of Western acculturation as protective coloration for the Jew (or specifically the Jewish woman as intellectual) to a meta-commentary on the Shoah. Thus the engineer's complaint that the foundations of the concentration camp barracks will subside because they are poorly built becomes in the film a symbolic statement that building the edifice of the Thousand Year Reich on the murder of the Jews assures its destruction. Such a view certainly represents a desire on Spielberg's part to give meaning to the death of the Jews, who through their martyrdom bring down the kingdom of evil. This is, of course, wishful thinking. Since no meaning greater than their actual murder can actually be assigned to the destruction of the Jews, no reading of their death, no matter how symbolic, can be understood as providing meaning for it. In no case, except retrospectively, can the intelligence of the Jews give symbolic meaning to the Shoah.

In the novel it is the intelligence of the Jew—not the Jew's canniness, but her command of the discourse of the intellectual, that marks the Jew as dangerous. "She went on arguing the case, and Amon nodded and presumed she must be lying. It was a first principle that you never listened to a Jewish specialist. Jewish specialists were in the mold of Marx, whose theories were aimed at the integrity of the government, and of Freud, who had assaulted the integrity of the Aryan mind." He orders her shot. And Keneally draws the appropriate lesson: "Miss Diana Reiter could not save herself with all her professional skill." Jewish superior intelligence is a negative in this world; only "prompt and anonymous labor" seemed to count toward anything. And that too comes to be understood as false reasoning. For it is not even work that could save the Jews. The SS understood that "the Jewish child is a cultural time bomb, the Jewish woman a biology of treasons, the Jewish male a more incontrovertible enemy than any Russian could hope to be." Only total destruction can be the answer.[28]

Genius plays no role in Keneally and Spielberg's image of the concentration camps and the Shoah: "While the pistol-waving Amon Goeth believes he maintains Plaszow by his special administrative genius, it is as much the bloody-mouthed prisoners who keep it running."[29] Genius has no place in the structuring of such a world. Virtue, the special realm of Oskar Schindler by the close of the novel and the film, turns the myth of Jewish superior intelligence into the reverse. The Jews are saved by their stupidity. Schindler manages to sabotage his own factory's war effort and lay the blame on "the stupidity of you damned people!" at least in the presence of the armament inspectors. "I wish they were intelligent enough to sabotage a machine. Then at least I'd have their goddamned hides! But what can you do with these people? They're an utter waste of time." Indeed, there is only one mention of "smart Jews" in the novel, and it comes at its very end.

"Smart Jews" are those such as the man in the horsecar to Dachau, who hangs the bodies of the dead from horse hooks to give more space to the living. Here intelligence and death are linked—intelligence cannot save lives, only virtue can.[30]

The Shoah is thus the space that gives the lie to Jewish superior intelligence—not intelligence but virtue is the way to survive, and survival is the proof of goodness. Schindler's virtue dominates the tale. The rescued Jews (and Schindler's own survival) become proof of what truly has value in this representation of the Shoah. Thus the tale of Schindler is the tale of survival and virtue; the tales of Stern and Reiter are of the uselessness of Jewish superior intelligence unless it is connected to the virtuous act of the non-Jew. Only that gives meaning to Jewish superior intelligence in any of its forms.

It is a fortuitous association that Ralph Fiennes (who played the camp commandant Amon Goeth in *Schindler's List*) and Rob Morrow (Joel Fleischman in *Northern Exposure*) come to reprise versions of their characters in Robert Redford's 1994 film *Quiz Show*. This film illustrates quite a different tale of intelligence and virtue—for virtue is missing from the tale completely, and its vanishing marks the dismissal of what passes (according to the film) for intelligence in the 1950s—the rote memorization of facts and their instant recall. The Redford film is the tale of the quiz show scandals of the 1950s and of the two central participants: the lower-class Jewish war veteran Herb Stempel (played by John Turturro), the quiz-show contestant who blew the whistle on the show "Twenty-One" in 1959 before a congressional committee. He reveals that he was bested in a fixed contest by the upper-class, gentile, academic Charles Van Doren (played by Ralph Fiennes), son of critic Mark Van Doren. Here Fiennes plays the Aryan as intellectual rather than as madman. But here, too, race is inscribed into the film in direct and unmistakable ways. The conflict between Van Doren, according to one newspaper account "the apparent embodiment of e.e. cumming's line 'more brave than me, more blond than you,' "[31] and the dark, working-class Stempel is described within Paul Attanasio's screen-play as the working out of post-Shoah anti-Semitism, a sort of retrospective *Gentlemen's Agreement* with Gregory Peck's role as a gentile assuming the social identity of a Jew now taken by a "real" Jew.

The problems of race, of anti-Semitism and its internalization within the Jewish characters are thematized. Here both Jews and gentiles are shown to be neither smart nor virtuous, because the claim about innate intellectual ability comes to be a charade, a simulacrum of real intelligence. It is the IQ test writ large on the television screens of the day. Memorize masses of meaningless material and you are a master of the medium. Yet Stempel's hidden secret is not that he threw the final match to Van Doren—he rages that he knew the answer (What film had won the Academy Award for best picture in 1955? The answer: "Marty") and was made to look foolish because of the commonness of this information. Rather, in the course of the film, Stempel is revealed to have been given answers all along, not just forced to throw the last match. Here he is revealed not to be much like Ernest Borgnine in "Marty," a true working class hero. His intelligence, like that of Van Doren, is not only compromised—but in the scenes where Van Doren rattles off information to the producers, Stempel is shown in comparison to be slightly less clever and certainly less attractive than Van Doren.

In the film, all is corruption and even the theme of class versus race—of the upper-class gentile beating the working-class Jew—comes to be revealed as part of the game. For neither Stempel nor Van Doren is virtuous. It is the figure of Richard N. Goodwin (played by Rob Morrow) who recognizes the fix. Goodwin, whose Jewish identity is submerged in his desire to belong, to play the game, is shown to be the only character to have virtue. He is accused by his wife as having been seduced by Van Doren when he gives him a chance to "come clean." Goodwin is an example of real Jewish superior intelligence, a top-of-the-class graduate of Harvard Law School, whose confusion is between virtue and status. He eventually chooses virtue, and "intelligence" in the world of *Quiz Show* is revealed to be specious. The seduction of the truly smart Jew does not take place. Goodwin is tested—like Joel Fleischman—and is able to return to his world a better (and smarter) Jew. The smart Jew is also the confused Jew—confused at least on his identity and his loyalty—his virtue is tested but he perseveres. Unlike Stempel, Goodwin is the upper-class, educated American Jew who seems not to need to use his Jewish identity to establish his victim status. Both the working-class Jew and the upper-class gentile are revealed to be cheats. But the upwardly mobile Jew becomes the hero because of his tested virtue. He is not the parvenu, but rather the virtuous American. Here the theme of virtue is manifest.

Sections from Richard Goodwin's memoir *Remembering America* served as a basis for the film script.[32] Goodwin's account of his life, "a voice from the sixties" (the subtitle of the memoir) begins with his sense of the "anti-Semitism of Maryland," which he first experienced when his father moved to Washington at the end of the depression. His account of his iridescent anger at being called a "Jew Boy" frames his sense of his own accomplishment when he completes Tufts University and eventually is admitted to Harvard.[33] A member of the *Harvard Law Review* staff, and eventually its editor, Goodwin graduates first in his class at Harvard and goes on to clerk for Justice Felix Frankfurter at the Supreme Court. Frankfurter becomes his idol, "an incarnation of the American dream. Born to Jewish parents in Vienna, Austria, he had arrived in New York at the age of twelve, unable to speak a word of English. A few years later he had plunged into the melting pot of City College and then gone to Harvard Law School, graduating with the highest honors."[34] Not a parvenu, certainly not Monroe

Stahr, Frankfurter comes to represent the conservative, Republican establishment within Goodwin's text, even in regard to Goodwin's own relationship to politics during the Kennedy-Johnson era.

After his year of clerking for Frankfurter, Goodwin goes to the House
Subcommittee on Legislative Oversight and begins his investigation of those
"national heroes, living exemplars of American genius," the winners of the
quiz shows. The key to the success of the quiz shows like "The $64,000
Question" was the relationship between money and the "hitherto secluded
brilliance of fellow citizens."[35] Central to this most American of undertak-
ings was the figure of Charles Van Doren, according to signs at the Columbia University campus where he taught "the smartest man in the world."[36]
He was the American answer to the "soviet Sputnik," according to Goodwin. He was a "touch of class."[37] "Gifted with an extraordinarily retentive
memory, widely read," Van Doren was prepared for this role by "a century
of breeding."[38] His nemesis, the man he had defeated to become champion
on "Twenty-One," was the "dark, Semitic" Herb Stempel. "He had come
from a working-class background, a family in the anonymous lower reaches
of the social-structure, whose otherwise unremarked history had contained
some dormant code of DNA gifting Stempel with a remarkably spacious
memory, which he had furnished with an extraordinary collection of information."[39] Intelligence, for Goodwin, but less so for Redford, is inscribed in the genes. Van Doren's "century of breeding" presents a brilliant
though shallow intellectual; two thousand years of Jewish persecution provides Stempel with a recessive store of Jewish superior intelligence that
appears in his generation. Both come to be parodies of the image of the
"intellectual," but Van Doren's life descends into this role; Stempel's life is
raised up into the realm of the pseudo-intellectual. He went from being an
"unknown, unappreciated, unprivileged young man" to an "instant celeb-
rity."[40] And he was targeted to be defeated by someone "who, in Stempel's
lucid, fevered imagination, had everything—privilege, breeding, aristocratic
birth and manner—who seemed to possess every advantage that life had
so cruelly and capriciously denied him."[41] Goodwin's identification with
Van Doren, evident in the film, haunts his text. He is certainly not Stempel;
yet he could indeed see himself as Van Doren as seen through Stempel's
eyes. Yet there is an aspect of the loss of virtue in *Quiz Show* that is
underplayed in Goodwin's account, one that appears in a text which certainly served as one of the intertexts for Goodwin's retrospective narrative.

The anxiety about Jewish superior intelligence in modern culture is
rooted in the general fear of the Jew as the embodiment of the different.
As Jean-Joseph Goux has observed about the Shoah: "The fatal inclination
of such an aesthetic fiction of the political . . . is towards the elimination
of all that seems misshapen, strange, unhealthy, and heterogeneous to the
beautifully organized totality of the community—the extermination of the
Jews."[42] The Shoah was to no small degree the result of the anxiety about

German heterogeneity, and no small part of that anxiety is expressed in the myth of Jewish superior intelligence. The continuation of this myth into the latter half of the twentieth century is the perpetuation of the anxiety about Jewish difference among American Jews. What is a Jew? Is Jewish difference absolute—in which case the image of the Jews as American is in doubt—or are all the qualities of Jewish difference able to be copied by others? Is virtue guaranteed by one or the other? The continuation of these models of argument that began in the nineteenth century and continue into the late twentieth century is a sign that there is little chance of the myth of Jewish difference, as represented by Jewish superior intelligence, vanishing. The Jews—with or without their own state, with or without their being anchored in the Diaspora, have little likelihood of becoming anything like a "normal" minority. For the qualities ascribed to the Jews are qualities projected onto them by the cultures in which they live and have been internalized by them as if they are part of their own reality—as indeed, these qualities soon become. Are "the Jews" smarter than everyone else? Are "the Jews" different from everyone else? Only if the cultures in which they dwell desires them to be. And that is the hidden truth of both ends of *The Bell Curve*.

NOTES

1. Richard J. Herrnstein and Charles Murray, *The Bell Curve: Intelligence and Class Structure in American Life* (New York: Free Press, 1994). The comments on Jewish superior intelligence are to be found on page 275. On this comparison see Seymour B. Sarason, "Jewishness, Blackishness, and the Nature-Nurture Controversy," *American Psychologist* 28 (1973): 962–971.

2. Herrnstein and Murray, *The Bell Curve*, p. 275.

3. Joe Wood, "What I Learned about Jews," *New York Times Magazine* (April 10, 1994): 42–45, here, 44.

4. On American films and the Jews see David Desser and Lester D. Friedman (eds), *American-Jewish Filmmakers: Traditions and Trends* (Urbana: University of Illinois Press, 1993); Lester D. Friedman, *Hollywood's Image of the Jew* (New York: Ungar, 1982), as well as his *The Jewish Image in American Film* (Secaucus, N.J.: Citadel Press, 1987); Lester D. Friedman (ed.), *Unspeakable Images: Ethnicity and the American Cinema* (Urbana: University of Illinois Press, 1991); Sarah Blacher Cohen (ed.), *From Hester Street to Hollywood: The Jewish-American Stage and Screen* (Bloomington: Indiana University Press, 1983); Judith E. Doneson, *The Holocaust in American Film* (Philadelphia: Jewish Publication Society, 1987); Patricia Erens, *The Jew in American Cinema* (Bloomington: Indiana University Press, 1984); Matthew Stevens, *Jewish Film Directory: A Guide to More than 1200 Films of Jewish Interest from 32 Countries Over 85 Years* (Westport, Conn.: Greenwood Press, 1992). See also Regine Mihal Friedman, *L'image et son Juif: le Juif dans le cinema nazi* (Paris: Payot, 1983); Dietmar Pertsch, *Jüdische Lebenswelten in Spielfilmen und Fernsehspielen: Filme zur Geschichte der Juden von ihren Anfängen bis zur Emanzipation 1871* (Tubingen: M. Niemeyer, 1992).

5. Michael Shapiro (ed.), *The Jewish 100: A Ranking of the Most Influential Jews of All Time* (New York: Carol Publications Group, 1994). The list is as follows:

Moses—Jesus of Nazareth—Albert Einstein—Sigmund Freud—Abraham—Saul of Tarsus (Saint Paul)—Karl Marx—Theodor Herzl—Mary—Baruch de Spinoza—David—Anne Frank—The Prophets—Judas Iscariot—Gustav Mahler—Maimonides—Niels Bohr—Moses Mendelssohn—Paul Ehrlich—Rashi—Benjamin Disraeli—Franz Kafka—David Ben-Gurion—Hillel—John Von Neumann—Simon Bar Kokhba—Marcel Proust—Mayer Rothschild—Solomon—Heinrich Heine—Selman Waksman—Giacomo Meyerbeer—Isaac Luria—Gregory Pincus—Leon Trotsky—David Ricardo—Alfred Dreyfus—Leo Szilard—Mark Rothko—Ferdinand Cohn—Samuel Gompers—Gertrude Stein—Albert Michelson—Philo Judaeus—Golda Meir—The Vilna Gaon—Henri Bergson—The Baal Shem Tov—Felix Mendelsohn—Louis B. Mayer—Judah Halevy—Haym Salomon—Johanan ben Zakkai—Arnold Schoenberg—Emile Durkheim—Betty Friedan—David Sarnoff—Lorenzo Da Ponte—Julius Rosenwald—Casmir Funk—George Gershwin—Chaim Weizmann—Franz Boas—Sabbatai Zevi—Leonard Bernstein—Flavius Josephus—Walter Benjamin—Louis Brandeis—Emile Berliner—Sarah Bernhardt—Levi Strauss—Nahmanides—Menachem Begin—Anna Freud—Queen Ester—Martin Buber—Jonas Salk—Jerome Robbins—Henry Kissinger—Wilhelm Steinitz—Arthur Miller—Daniel Mendoza—Stephen Sondheim—Emma Goldman—Sir Moses Montefiore—Jerome Kern—Boris Pasternak—Harry Houdini—Edward Bernays—Leopold Auer—Groucho Marx—Man Ray—Henrietta Szold—Benny Goodman—Steven Spielberg—Marc Chagall—Bob Dylan—Sandy Koufax—Bernard Berenson—Jerry Siegel and Joe Shuster. The last two are the creators of "Superman"!

6. Eric Lax, *Woody Allen: A Biography* (New York: Knopf; distributed by Random House, 1991).

7. See the discussion in Clifford Pugh, "Psyched Up," *Houston Post* (March 10, 1992), and "Psychiatrists Analyze Dr. Lowenstein," *New York Times* (January 19, 1992).

8. Parallel questions have been raised concerning the role that gender has in defining genius. See Christine Battersby, *Gender and Genius: Towards a Feminist Aesthetics* (Bloomington: Indiana University Press, 1990).

9. Miles D. Storfer, *Intelligence and Giftedness: The Constitutions of Heredity and Early Environment* (San Francisco: Jossey-Bass, 1990), pp. 315, 326–328.

10. Simon Louvish, *The Silencer: Another Levantine Tale* (New York: Interlink, 1993), p. 75.

11. Clyde Haberman, "Israelis Deglamourize the Military," *New York Times* (May 31, 1995): A9.

12. Bill Rubinstein, "Genes and Genius," *Generation* 3 (1993): 12–24. I want to thank John Efron for this citation. Needless to say, not everyone agrees with Rubinstein.

13. All references to the novel are to Thomas Keneally, *Schindler's List* (New York: Touchstone, 1993), here p. 14. See also Frank Manchel, "A Reel Witness: Steven Spielberg's Representation of the Holocaust in *Schindler's List*," *Journal of Modern History* 67 (1995): 83–100; Simon Louvish, "Witness," *Sight and Sound* 4 (1994): 12–15; Mordecai Richler, "Why I Hate *Schindler's List*," *Saturday Night* 109 (1994): 34, 68; Michael André Bernstein, "The *Schindler's List* Effect," *The American Scholar* 63 (1994): 429–432; Tim O'Hearn, "*Schindler's Ark* and *Schindler's List*—One for the Price of Two," *Commonwealth Novel in English* 5 (1992):

9–15; Michael Hollington, "The Ned Kelly of Cracow: Keneally's *Schindler's Ark*," *Meanjin* 42 (1983): 42–46.

14. Keneally, *Schindler's List*, p. 14.

15. Ibid., p. 34.

16. Ibid., p. 4.

17. Ibid., p. 44.

18. Ibid.

19. Ibid., pp. 43–44.

20. Heinrich Mann, *Man of Straw*, no trans. (London: Penguin, 1984). *Der Untertan* was first published by Kurt Wolff in Berlin in 1918.

21. Mann, *Man of Straw*: 57, 86–87.

22. Keneally, *Schindler's List*, p. 45.

23. Ibid., pp. 44, 46.

24. Ibid., p. 48.

25. Ibid., p. 207.

26. Ibid., pp. 18, 19, 68, 77, 135, 221, 293, 392.

27. Ibid., p. 167.

28. Ibid., pp. 167–169, 174.

29. Ibid., p. 224.

30. Ibid., pp. 340–354.

31. "The Enigma of 'Quiz Show': No Crowds," *New York Times* (February 12, 1995): H19.

32. Richard N. Goodwin, *Remembering America: A Voice from the Sixties* (New York: Perennial Library, 1989).

33. Ibid., p. 15.

34. Ibid., p. 27.

35. Ibid., p. 44.

36. Ibid., p. 45.

37. Ibid., p. 48.

38. Ibid.

39. Ibid., p. 49.

40. Ibid., p. 50.

41. Ibid.

42. Jean-Joseph Goux, "Politics and Modern Art: Heidegger's Dilemma," *Diacritics* 19 (1989): 10–24, here p. 19.

5

"A Stab in the Back on a Sunday Morning": The Melodramatic Imagination and Pearl Harbor

Geoff Mayer

> Well you may crow Mr. Tojo! You've done a good job of stabbing in the back. You've darkened our cities, you've destroyed our property, you've spilled our blood. Our faith tells us, to all this treachery there can be one answer, a time-honoured answer: "For all they that live by the sword shall perish with the sword."
>
> —The narrator in *December 7th* (1942)

Melodrama has enjoyed a certain degree of rehabilitation since the 1970s, although its status as either a cinematic genre and/or a dramatic mode emanating from the late eighteenth century theatrical form is not yet totally clear. Peter Brooks published *The Melodramatic Imagination* nearly twenty years ago; if largely neglected for the first ten years, it now could be said to have acquired an aura of orthodoxy.[1] Melodrama, Brooks argues, is the "principal mode for uncovering, demonstrating, and making operative the essential moral universe in a post-sacred era "and as" a central fact of the modern sensibility."[2] The narrative voice of melodrama is not content to "describe and record gesture" but applies constant pressure to the surface so that it will yield its "full potentialities as 'parable.' "[3] For Brooks, the primal scene is a necessary element in the operation of a melodramatic imagination based on polarizing the world into moral absolutes. Within these Manichean parameters of the melodramatic imagination, the Japanese attack on Pearl Harbor on December 7, 1941, was the primal scene, the traumatic violation of innocence. Consequently, the presentation of World War II by both President Roosevelt and the American film industry was predicated on an interplay of melodramatic signs concerned with betrayal, resurrection and retribution.

Melodrama is not perceived in this chapter as a recurring set of themes or icons.[4] It is an aesthetic and cultural system that attempts to make sense out of the "reality," a system that draws upon the represented world to transfer meaning from one context, the "surface world," to another context, the underlying moral universe. The genius in Peter Brooks's study resides in his title. It is the "imagination" provoked by melodrama that permeates both culture and aesthetic form. Polarization is a central device in melodrama, as it is a world of absolutes and the "melodramatic," the hyperbolic, excessive presentation is a consequence of the desire to locate and articulate what Brooks calls the "moral occult" or moral universe in a post-sacred era that is the domain of operative spiritual values. The primal scene is the pivotal moment as it represents the traumatic violation of innocence. It is, in effect, the overt expression of the Manichean. Brooks does not consider its psychoanalytic origins in great detail, but he makes it clear that the dramatic legacy of the traumatic violation of innocence in melodrama parallels, in a different field of human experience, Freud's description of the traumatic aftermath for the infant who witnessed sexual intercourse between his parents.[5] In both cases the "primal scene" produces anxiety which is expressed through a system of metaphors.[6]

The enormity of the primal scene is in evil's moment of spectacular power, where it creates a "moment of intense, originary trauma that leaves virtue stunned and humiliated."[7] Such a moment, with similar effects on the American people, was the surprise attack on Pearl Harbor by the Japanese on December 7, 1941.

On November 26, 1941, a Japanese task force left the Kurile Islands with the intention of decimating the American military forces on Oahu, the most populous island in Hawaii. The specific target was the naval base at Pearl Harbor, which the Japanese believed to be the major obstacle to their southern expansion through Asia. On the morning of December 7, the force reached a position some 220 miles north of Pearl Harbor and by 7a.m. the first wave were headed for "Battleship Row" where America's naval might was anchored. Only the aircraft carriers *Lexington* and *Enterprise* were out of port. The United States suffered damage to eighteen vessels, including eight battleships, three light cruisers, three destroyers, and four auxiliary aircraft. Nearly two-thirds of the naval aircraft were destroyed. Hickam, Wheeler, Ewa, and Kaneothe airfields were severely damaged, as were the installations on Ford Island in the middle of Pearl Harbor. Casualties for the day totaled 2,403 Americans killed or missing, with a further 1,178 wounded. The Japanese, on the other hand, lost only five midget submarines, a large submarine, and twenty-nine planes out of an attacking force of three hundred and sixty aircraft. Sixty-four Japanese were dead or missing.

The Japanese plan to attack Pearl Harbor was conceived by the Commander-in-Chief of the Japanese Combined Fleet, Admiral Isokuru Yamamoto, in early January 1941, although its first official appearance was in the *Practical Plan of Operations* published in September, and it was not until the end of October that the Naval General Staff accepted Yamamoto's scheme. Yamamoto, however, insisted that the final diplomatic note be delivered before the first shot was fired, as he maintained that there was a significant difference between "a strategic surprise attack" and a "political sneak attack."[8] The final note was to be presented three hours before the attack, but this was later reduced to one hour. However, a directive was issued prohibiting the use of a typist and, following other administrative mishaps, the note was finally delivered fifty-five minutes after the initial attack. This, according to Gordon Prange, was of little significance, as the Japanese government never intended that the "timing make any material difference; it was strictly a formalistic bow toward the conventions. Tokyo had left no margin for error."[9]

For the American people the attack without warning meant more than the omission of "a formalistic bow toward the conventions"; it was a "deep emotional experience, indeed a traumatic shock."[10] Gordon Prange describes its effect as a "mind staggering mixture of surprise, awe, mystification, grief, humiliation, and above all, cataclysmic fury."[11] Two factors in particular generated this response. First was the awareness that the detailed preparations for the assault were carried out simultaneously with the expression of peaceful intentions from Ambassador Nomura and Special Envoy Kurusu in Washington. The use of direct action without a formal declaration of war was the second factor, and an intense sense of indignation was felt throughout the United States as "December 7th" emerged as a significant moral sign. The Japanese attack effectively destroyed the choices facing the American people. Prior to the attack it was possible to propose a range of options with regard to the war in Europe and China. Pearl Harbor removed the doubt and hesitancy and encouraged a singleness of purpose, as the opening lines of Roosevelt's Address to the Congress the day after the attack made clear: "Yesterday, December 7th, 1941—a date which will live in infamy—the United States of America was suddenly and deliberately attacked by naval and air forces of the Empire of Japan."[12] The phrase "a date which will live in infamy" was an inspired opening, as it captures the essence of the melodramatic imagination. Roosevelt immediately polarized guilt and responsibility for the attack by emphasizing the fact that not only was the United States at peace with Japan but also, "at the solicitation of Japan, . . . still in conversation with its Government and its Emperor looking toward the maintenance of peace in the Pacific. . . . It will be recorded that the distance of Hawaii from Japan makes it obvious that the attack was planned many days or even weeks ago. During the intervening time the Japanese Government has deliberately sought to deceive the United States by false statements and expressions of hope for continued peace."[13] Each subsequent address reiterated the "violation of innocence" pattern, explaining the attack in terms of Japanese betrayal. The effect was to position "December 7th" as the primal scene in an unfinished melodrama.

There is no such thing as security for any Nation—or any individual—in a world ruled by the principles of gangsterism.

There is no such thing as [an] impregnable defense against powerful aggressors who sneak up in the dark and strike without warning. . . .

We may acknowledge that our enemies have performed a brilliant feat of deception, perfectly timed and executed with great skill. It was a thoroughly dishonourable deed. . . . [14]

Throughout each address the United States was presented as interested only in peace and, consequently, "innocent" of complicity in the disaster at Pearl Harbor. Roosevelt stressed that during the negotiations prior to December 7 the "Japanese Government repeatedly offered qualified statements of peaceful intention" but "it became very clear, as each proposal was explored, that Japan did not intend to modify in any way her greedy designs upon the whole Pacific world."[15] The response must be equally uncompromising. "There never has been—there never can be—successful compromise between good and evil. Only total victory can reward the champions of tolerance and decency, and freedom and faith."[16]

American films, not surprisingly, adopted this structure and carefully utilized selected passages from Roosevelt's December 8 Address to Congress. The ethical sign "December 7th" performed the function of the primal scene. For example, both *Wake Island* (released August 12, 1942) and *Air Force* (March 20, 1943) include actual radio reports of the Kurusu/Nomura/Hull negotiations to establish the immoral nature of the enemy and their betrayal of "innocence." "December 7th" generally required no explanation—it represented betrayal and violation without any accompanying material. In *Air Force*, for example, the crew of a plane flying from San Francisco to Hawaii listens to the news that "Japan's intentions are wholly peaceful." This is followed by an insert of the navigator's hand writing "Position at 0224, December 7th," although the significance of the date, at this stage in the film, is appreciated only by the audience.

A newspaper headline in *Across the Pacific* (August 18, 1942) similarly emphasizes Japanese duplicity: "Hirohito Reply to Roosevelt Will Insure Peace . . . Say Nomura and Kurusu." A subheading reinforces the point: "Special Envoy Kurusu Assures Tokyo Peace Efforts Will Succeed." However, a camera movement from the headline to the date of the newspaper—December 7, of course—exposes the true situation to the audience.

Salute the Marines (August 2, 1943) and *Spy Ship* (June 4, 1942) also employ newspaper headlines and the latter graphically combines this device with the face of the Japanese villain sarcastically expressing his regret ("so sorry"), superimposed over actual footage of the destruction in Pearl Harbor. The assimilation of melodrama with "reality" was also evident in *Man from Frisco* and *Betrayal from the East*, which use radio reports of the Nomura/Kurusu negotiations with Washington.

It is not just the mention of "December 7th" nor the use of Roosevelt's reaction but its placement in the narrative sequence as each film reinforces the presentation of an "innocent" America. For example, in *So Proudly We Sail* (June 22, 1943), an American convoy carrying a group of nurses crosses the Pacific in December 1941 unaware of the Japanese plans. Relaxing on a warm, sunny day on the deck of the ship, Lieutenant Joan O'Doul (Paulette Goddard) interrupts her letter writing to ask, "What's the date?" The first reply to her question presents the nurses as "innocence," the sign of Virtue: "Sunday. We had chapel." O'Doul's reaction to the date perpetuates the convention that the United States was blissfully unaware of the Japanese preparations for war ("Thanks, I'll just head it eighteen shopping days to Christmas"). The audience is reminded of the significance of December 7th by the sudden arrival of heavy black clouds accompanied by an ominous musical chord on the soundtrack. Similarly the written prologue in *Somewhere I'll Find You* (August 6, 1942) immediately establishes the moral context of the story: "October 2, 1941. When we still had 83 shopping days until Christmas . . . and 63 days until Pearl Harbor."

The immediate significance of the "December 7th" in these films was to establish a sense of blame and the need for retribution. In *Bombardier* (May 13, 1943) when one of the trainee airmen bursts into the military chapel with the news of Pearl Harbor, the rest of the group are occupied with prayers. In the next scene the leader walks up to a calendar on the wall and points to the date ("December 7, 1941") and tells his men: "Gentlemen, there's a date we will always remember, [pause] and they'll never forget!"

The presentation of the Pearl Harbor attack within the context of the melodramatic "violation of innocence" was evident not only in these feature films but also in the documentary *December 7th*, supervised by John Ford. The project was intended as a "factual" account of the Japanese attack, and was initiated by William J. "Wild Bill" Donovan, head of the recently formed Office of Strategic Services.[17] Donovan assigned Commander John Ford's Field Photographic unit and Ford selected cinematographer Gregg Toland to direct the film. Toland and the special effects man Ray Kellogg began work on the project in January 1942. They flew out to Hawaii and assembled film of the attack, shot by navy photographers, and

footage of the salvage operations. This was combined with a recreation of
the attack utilizing miniatures, rear-screen and process photography, and
simulated "interviews" with civilian personnel on Hawaii.

The Navy, however, opposed the production of the film and eventually
confiscated all the work prints and it was only resurrected twelve months
later, in a shortened form, after Ford edited the negative. What was initially
planned as an eighty-five minute film was reduced to the twenty-minute
version which won an Academy award in 1943.[18] A thirty-minute version
now available reveals a similar pattern to the feature films. At the start of
the film "Uncle Sam" is shown asleep as the narrator evokes the Japanese
plans:

"Warned of the fire licking across the ocean from without. Warned of
the dangers that were threatening within. Tired from wrangling with con-
science and fatigued after a long dark night full of disturbing events that
indeed the year 1941 was. He slept in the early Sabbath calm. Safe and
secure behind its military ramparts . . ." This opening, similar to the scene
cited above in *So Proudly We Sail*, together with other films such as *Gua-
dalcanal Diary* and *Standby for Action*, correlate with the structure noted
by Brooks in nineteenth-century theatrical melodrama, where the play "typically opens with a presentation of virtue and innocence, or perhaps more
accurately, virtue *as* innocence."

We see virtue, momentarily, in a state of taking pleasure in itself, aided by those
who recognize and support it. . . . And there swiftly supervenes a threat to virtue,
a situation—and most often a person—to cast its very survival into question, obscure its identity, and elicit the process of its fight for recognition. Remarkably
prevalent is the setting . . . the space of innocence . . . into this space, a villain, the
troubler of innocence, will come to insinuate himself, either under the mask of
friendship . . . or simply as intruder.[19]

In *December 7th* America, supposedly "safe and secure behind its military
rampart," is deceived by the Japanese overtures. This presentation differs
little from the feature films, especially *Bombardier*, as the military are
shown celebrating their state of innocence and virtue at a field mass at the
Kaneothe naval station where the priest suggests the type of gifts the men
might send home to relatives and other loved ones. The narrator points out
that into this tranquil situation comes the "Axis brand of war: a stab in
the back on Sunday morning."

The indignation expressed by the narrator in *December 7th* is "authen-
ticated" by the inclusion of excerpts from Roosevelt's December 8 address
to Congress. They reinforce the emotions expressed within the film, and
the positioning of the address at pivotal moments in the sequence of events
gives Roosevelt both a formal and an ideological function. In several films
his response to the Japanese action provides not only overall motivation

but the motivation for character change. The war demands "team players," as Captain Quincannon (John Ridgeley) explains to the rebellious Joe Winocki (John Garfield) in *Air Force*: "We need you just like we need the whole gang. It takes all of us to make this ship function. . . . You've played football, Winocki. You know how one man can gum up the whole works. You've got to play ball with us and play the game or I'll have to get rid of you." Winocki rejects this plea until the bomber approaches Hickam Field during the Japanese attack and Quincannon urges his crew to take a "good look at Pearl Harbor, maybe it's something you'll want to remember." This is reinforced by a selection from Roosevelt's December 8 address to Congress, and a close-up of Winocki occurs as the president is heard saying, "I regret to tell you that very many American lives have been lost." The edited version of Roosevelt's response concludes with his promise "always will our whole Nation remember the character of the onslaught against us." The scene concludes with Roosevelt's pledge that "with the unbounding determination of our people we will gain the inevitable triumph. So help us God." The climactic line is accompanied by the image of Quincannon looking at a small toy given to him by this young son prior to their departure at San Francisco, an image perfectly consistent with the over-determination characteristic of the melodramatic imagination as Roosevelt's promise is visually associated with the "innocence" of a child's toy.

In effect, the melodramatic pattern inherent in Roosevelt's complete address is not only simplified but, in the film, takes the form of a parable which provides an ethical context for the audience to understand the real basis of America's role in World War II. *Air Force*, like all of the combat and war-related films produced during this period, cannot fulfill the complete closure of melodrama; but as the B-17s take off on another mission at the end of the film, Roosevelt's voice is heard once again on the soundtrack promising retaliation against the enemy: "We shall hit him and hit him again wherever and whenever we can reach him, for we intend to bring this battle to him on his own home ground." Roosevelt's words in the film thus serve to remind the audience that the concerns of the text extend beyond the film itself, and that these concerns should not be denoted as merely "fictional." The plenitude usually offered at the closure of melodrama is projected into the future, as the written epilogue also promises: "This story has a conclusion but not an end . . . for its real end will be the victory for which Americans . . . on land, on sea and in the air . . . have fought, are fighting now, and will continue to fight until peace has been won."

Selections from Roosevelt's December 8 address are used in a similar manner in *Flying Tigers*. This film, as director David Miller pointed out, was completed before December 7, 1941, and additional scenes were shot to include the president's speech.[20] The address not only intensifies the anti-Japanese nature of the film but also "explains" the shift in the characterization as Woody Jason dies after saving Jim Gordon's life. The turning point begins with him listening to Roosevelt.

The first American film to refer to the Japanese attack on Pearl Harbor, *Yank on the Burma Road* (released January 19, 1942), began production on October 22, 1941, and was completed before the Japanese attack, when MGM made a number of changes, including a prologue which spells out the theme that was to dominate many films for the next two years: "On December 7th, 1941, Japan attacked the United States of America and engaged it in War. This is the story of one American who tackled Japan a little before the rest of us—and what he started the rest of the Yanks will finish!" The film's climax was also rewritten so that now the hero yells "that's for Pearl Harbor" after killing a Japanese soldier. It concludes with his final exhortation that "we're heading for Tokyo, Yokohama, and points East," which, while less subtle than Rick's speech to Ilsa at the end of *Casablanca*, provides the same basic message.

A number of combat films released in 1942 and 1943 contained narrative episodes which reinforced the "resurrection of innocence" developed in Roosevelt's Fireside Chats. Just as Roosevelt's speeches were placed at crucial points in *Air Force* and *Flying Tigers* to provide the motivation for a crucial change in characterization, other films included episodes that provided the audience with a summary of the overall narrative structure while foregrounding the reasons for fighting the Axis. A common device to present these parables were sentimental funeral orations of the kind delivered by Captain Cassidy (Cary Grant) in *Destination Tokyo* (December 21, 1943). When an American sailor attempts to rescue a Japanese pilot in the sea he is stabbed in the back. Cassidy then explains to his crew the difference in moral values between the Americans and the Japanese:

I remember Mike's pride when he bought the first pair of roller skates for his little five-year old boy. . . . Well, that Jap got a present too when he was five, only it was a dagger so that he'd know what he was supposed to be in life. The Japs have a ceremony that goes with it. At seven a Jap kid is taking marches under an army instructor, at thirteen he can put a machine gun together blindfolded. So, as I see it, that Jap was started on the road twenty years ago to putting a knife in Mike's back. There are lots of Mike's dying right now and a lot more Mike's will die until we wipe out a system that puts daggers in the hands of five-year-old children. You know, if Mike was here to put it into words right now, that's just about what he died for. More roller skates in this world, including some for the next generation of Japanese kids, because that's the kind of man Mike was.

Mike stabbed in the back was an overt metaphor for the unprovoked attack on innocence. Similarly, in *Gung Ho* (December 21, 1943), a recreation of the Carlson raid on the Japanese-held Makin Island in the early months of the war, an American chaplain accepts a white flag offered by a small group of Japanese soldiers. The Japanese then kill the chaplain as he walks toward them, and he dies reciting the Lord's Prayer. The Americans then avenge his death.

Earlier in the film the Raiders, enroute to Makin Island, inspect the damage at Pearl Harbor, and footage shot by the navy photographers is intercut with the reaction shots of the actors portraying members of the Second Raider Battalion. The sense of indignation is reinforced by an anonymous narrator:

Pearl Harbor! [heavy chord on the soundtrack] Five months following the day of infamy! Silence settles over the ship as we ease past the wreckage. There they are [wide shots of the *Arizona* and the *Okalahoma*], the *Arizona*, with her mast and torn bridge thrusting out of the water, the rusty hull of the *Oklahoma*, their guns are cold and unmanned. Mere testimony to the power of Japan. There are men in the Second Raider Battalion who lost brothers on those ships. Can we even the score? We dare not fail!

"Take a good look, Raiders!" one of the officers urges the men. "That's what the colonel meant when he told us about them Japs!" After the chaplain is killed on Makin, the marines shoot, stab, and bomb the Japanese.

Melodrama, Robert Heilman argues, is aways a kind of war, and it is the logical mode of expression whenever "reality" is reduced to the polarized state of "us" and "them."[21] The presentation of the events surrounding America's entry into the Second World War in President Roosevelt's December 8 address to Congress, his Fireside Chats, and the films released during this period were overt examples of making "reality" yield to the dictates of the melodramatic imagination. It is not the only example of this process in American history, as Korea, Vietnam, and the Gulf War demonstrated. Never again, though, did it have such striking success. The historical conditions lacked the moral intensity generated by the Japanese attack in December 1941.

The primal scene adopted, reiterated, and amplified by the movies was a crucial reason for the acceptance of Roosevelt's account of December 7, "the date which will live in infamy." When innocence was violated, a divided nation united under the sign "Pearl Harbor" where "American strength would be concentrated into an arrow point of resolution."[22] Energies had to be directed outward, toward the Japanese, and an intensive bout of self-examination and internal guilt would have effectively destroyed the moral sign of violation, indignation, and just retribution.

NOTES

1. Peter Brooks, *The Melodramatic Imagination. Balzac, Henry James, Melodrama, and the Mode of Excess* (New Haven: Yale University Press, 1976). See

also Jacky Bratton, Jim Cook, Christine Gledhill (eds.), *Melodrama Stage Picture Screen* (London: British Film Institute, 1994), particularly Simon Shepherd, "Pauses of Mutual Agitation."

2. Brooks, *The Melodramatic Imagination*, p. 21.

3. Peter Brooks, "The Melodramatic Imagination: The Example of Balzac and James," in David Thorburn and Geoffrey Hartman (eds.), *Romanticism. Vistas, Instances, Continuities* (Ithaca, N.Y.: Cornell University Press, 1973), p.199.

4. For perceptions of 'melodrama' other than Brooks, see Thomas Elsaesser, "Tales of Sound and Fury. Observations on the Family Melodrama," in *Monogram* 4, 1972; Geoffrey Nowell-Smith, "Minnelli and Melodrama," in *Screen* 18, no. 2; Frank Krutnik, "The Shanghai Gesture. The Exotic and the Melodrama," *Wide Angle* 4, no. 3; and the essays in Christine Gledhill (ed.), *Home Is Where the Heart Is. Studies in Melodrama and the Woman's Film* (London: British Film Institute, 1987).

5. See "The Dream and the Primal Scene" in J. Strachey, *The Complete Psychological Works of Sigmund Freud*, Volume XV11 (London: Hogarth Press, 1978), pp. 1917–1919.

6. The Wolfman's dream consisted of white wolves sitting on a big walnut tree. "In great terror, evidently of being eaten up by the wolves, I screamed and woke up." See Strachey, *The Complete Psychological Works of Sigmund Freud*, p. 29.

7. Brooks, *The Melodramatic Imagination*, p. 34.

8. Gordon Prange, *At Dawn We Slept. The Untold Story of Pearl Harbor* (London: Michael Joseph, 1981), p. 580.

9. Ibid.

10. Ibid., p. 582.

11. Ibid.

12. S. I. Rosenman, *The Public Papers and Addresses of Franklin D. Roosevelt. Volume 10, The Call to Battle Stations* (New York: Russell and Russell, 1969), p. 54.

13. Ibid., p. 54.

14. Ibid., *Volume 10*, p. 529.

15. Ibid., *Volume 10*, p. 548.

16. S. I. Rosenman, *The Public Papers and Addresses of Franklin D. Roosevelt. Volume 11. Humanity on the Defensive* (New York: Russell and Russell, 1969), p. 42.

17. See D. Ford, *The Unquiet Man. The Life of John Ford* (London: William Kimber, 1982), p. 167. See also W. T. Murphy, "John Ford and the Wartime Documentary," in *Film and History*, Vol. vi, no. 1.

18. One of Ford's cameramen, Brick Marquard, who saw the "full documentary before it was suppressed" described it as "political dynamite." See Andrew Sinclair, "John Ford's War," in *Sight and Sound* (Spring 1979): 101.

19. Brooks, *The Melodramatic Imagination*, p. 29.

20. See Lawrence Suid, *Air Force* (Madison: University of Wisconsin Press, 1983), p. 13.

21. Robert Heilman, *The Iceman, The Arsonist, and the Troubled Agent* (Seattle: University of Washington Press, 1973), p.147.

22. Prange, *At Dawn We Slept*, p. 738.

6

Losing the Peace: Some British Films of Postwar Adjustment

Brian McFarlane

When Trevor Howard, icon of British decency in so many British war films as well as the gentlemanly lover in *Brief Encounter*, turns up as an un-shaven non-hero fleeing from the law in Cavalcanti's *They Made Me a Fugitive* (1947), one knows that something has gone terribly wrong with life in postwar Britain. And he is not alone. The returning war hero who can find no satisfying role in the postwar world is a recurring figure in British cinema of the late 1940s and the 1950s. Sometimes—rarely—his difficulty in adjusting is played for comedy or for romantic drama; more often it is a matter of a man with a distinguished war record who finds himself, *faute de mieux*, caught up in dangerous and/or criminal activities. ("Man" is not used in a sexist way here: the protagonist of these films is virtually never a woman.) I want to argue that this motif of the man at a loss in the peacetime world occurs frequently enough in postwar British cinema to constitute a kind of sub-genre worth considering as such; that these films, viewed forty years on, or more, offer an instructive commentary on the social reality of the times in which they were made; and, more speculatively, that they offer an analogy between their characteristic nar-rative paradigm and the changing fortunes of the British film industry of the period. In the most general terms, one might simply claim that whatever is *common* in a given period is *ipso facto* significant for one's grasp of that period.

The title of this volume is *Screening the Past*. The films with which this chapter is concerned were of course dealing with what was at the time of their production a contemporary phenomenon. The significant past for their protagonists was no more remote than ten years or so; it was specifically "the War" which dominates *this* past and which casts a shadow over the lives represented in films from the late 40s on. Seeing them several decades later, as a group they make between them a telling comment on the loss of excitement, the sheer dullness, that—it is very easy to believe— was the lot of those returned safely from wartime dangers. There is a curious kind of "innocence" about the films I shall draw attention to. They were obviously conceived for the most part as "entertainments"; they are not presented as social history or as any other kind of history. However, they inevitably and perhaps sub- or un-consciously, in the decisions taken about narrative structures and outcomes, and in their representations of aspects of the contemporary scene, tell us a great deal about the thinking and behavior of their time of production. They become, in effect, historical documents of a very revealing kind, no less so since that was not what they set out to be. The novels of Jane Austen, recently seized on by filmmakers, were not written as social history, but to read them now is to be aware of insights into middle-class life of unusual vividness and precision. A film which may have seemed a bland entertainment at the time may now be seen to hold sociocultural information in its texture like a fly in amber.

Strictly speaking these films do not belong to any constituted genre in the usual sense of the word. That is, the films are not necessarily instantly recognizable tonally or in terms of iconography, or of formal structures. The fifteen or so films which interest me are essentially linked by a thematic concern: in one way or other, they foreground the problems of adjusting to the peace after a long and difficult war. Milton may insist that "peace hath her victories/ No less renowned than war"[1]—but they tend to involve less obvious heroics and to be less showily triumphant.[2] My aim is to group these films as a sort of synthetic genre, the study of which may yield a useful sense of how postwar British cinema went about coming to terms with the changed conditions of postwar British life. These films cut across a number of established genres including adventure, romantic comedy, realist drama, romantic melodrama, gangster thriller, and heist thriller. I believe it is just as useful to consider them on the basis of what they have in common as to place them in other genre categories constituted on different lines.

The films are grouped together because they help to answer the question of what postwar British cinema was like in its relation to the social reality, without, however, there being any suggestion of a mirror reflection. In the immediate postwar years, British cinema was dominated by stylish literary adaptations and social realist dramas, and in terms of prestige the British film industry reached a level of achievement it had not previously enjoyed. By the early 1950s, these two strands were no longer so dominant, and much of the euphoria had gone out of British film-making. In British society, a growing affluence[3] and a diversification of leisure interests had been accompanied by a sort of stagnation in the film industry—it remained prolific but lost much of its wartime and postwar verve. The films I want to discuss seem to me part of the cinema's reaction to the gradual loss of Britain's prestige that may be attributed to (1) the dismantling of the concept and reality of Empire, and (2) the sense that Britain may have won the war but seemed to be losing the peace.

What are the films like? The quintessential narrative paradigm involves a returning serviceman with a good war record, coming back to civilian life. His return raises issues of relationships, personal and/or professional, as he attempts to come to terms with a world which seems shabby, tired, and lacking in the excitement of the war years. Resolution of the problems confronting the ex-serviceman did not always take the form of a traditional "happy ending," but tended to foreground the protagonist's efforts at adjustment to the changing demands of peacetime life. Before looking at the important films of this genre, it may be useful to point to some films made during the war itself that suggest motifs that will be fully developed in the postwar cinema.

A key precursor film is Lance Comfort's *Great Day* (1945) in which a former World War I captain is reduced to pub boasting and stealing a ten-shilling note, having found nothing in the 25 years between wars to stimulate him. Captain Ellis (Eric Portman) is trapped in his memories, his rudderless peacetime life contrasted with the busy usefulness of his wife (Flora Robson), who works tirelessly during World War II for the village Women's Institute. His sense of uselessness is marked by his clinging to his army rank ("Maybe that's all he's got," remarks a sympathetic observer in the bar). He explains to his wife, after he has been caught stealing, "I was never frightened in the war. But I *was* frightened in peace," by the demands placed on him as father, husband, and provider. This will prove to be a prophetic remark in view of the later films in which meeting the challenges of post-World War II will be at issue. *Great Day*, a not very well-known film, nevertheless anticipates problems that will be endemic a few years later. It refuses to idealize British village life of which, beneath a surface of consensual activity, it offers an often abrasive critique. At this point, one might also add Val Guest's *Give Us the Moon* (1944), Basil Dearden's *They Came to a City* (1944), and Alexander Korda's *Perfect Strangers* (1945), as three others which, in their different ways, anticipate postwar problems. Piffling as much of it is, *Give Us the Moon* renders in comic vein the spectacle of war heroes losing their way in peace, opting for a life of idleness and luxury, opting out of serious work. *They Came to a City*, Ealing's version of Priestley's allegorical conversation piece, is informed by a need to ensure a "new" postwar world, in which women need not be confined to the home and in which class and wealth need no longer rule. As one character says, "I'd rather die. Going back there would be a kind of slow death." It is, as Charles Barr says, a film "ruthless with those who won't compromise their wealth and position and commit themselves to the socialist dispensation."[4] At the end of *Perfect Strangers*, the dowdy husband and wife (Robert Donat and Deborah Kerr), who have been transformed physically and emotionally by their wartime experiences, are brought to the point of mentioning divorce but conclude, "We're young," young enough to rebuild, as war-ravaged London will have to do. The idea of peace and the kinds of demands it will make on those who have been engaged in the long struggle of war is thus prefigured in different keys and tones before the actuality presented itself as a subject for film in post-1945 Britain.

"I joined the Force because it seemed the only legitimate way to get action in peace-time," says the well-bred policeman Archibald Berkeley-Willoughby in a long-forgotten comedy thriller of 1949, Godfrey Grayson's *The Adventures of PC 49: The Case of the Guardian Angel*. Even in so minor an enterprise as this, the preoccupation with the lack of challenge in postwar British life makes itself felt, though Archie's reaction to it is different from all the others I want to discuss. They tend to find "action" in *il*legitimate ways. In the neat "B" thriller, John Gilling's *The Quiet Woman* (1951), war hero Duncan (Derek Bond) has taken to smuggling, in a light-hearted way that earns him the rebuke of pub-owning heroine Jane (Jane Hylton): "You do it out of bravado. . . . You're worse than the real crook." In John Paddy Carstairs's thriller, *Dancing with Crime* (1947), Dave Robinson (Bill Owen), bored with peacetime life, gets involved with a crooked nightclub owner who has him killed when he demands his share of the "pile" to be made from postwar crime. His death is followed by this exchange at Scotland Yard:

> "Civvy Street seems strange to some of the boys."
>
> "Yes, and when they come out they don't know what to do."
>
> "It isn't only that. The job you did before the war seems small after six years."
>
> "And it costs more to live."

The first three comments of this exchange sum up a good deal of the motif examined in this chapter; the last points to one of the other incitements to postwar crime. The kinds of crime are very often connected with the obtaining of luxury goods, such as whisky, cigarettes, nylons, and furs, all at a premium in the queue-forming austerity of postwar Britain, where the rewards for having won the war seem not to be felt in everyday life. Postwar "spivs,"[5] in films at least, notoriously had access to these goods and lured disillusioned ex-servicemen into their network with the promise of much larger returns and much more excitement than their civilian jobs could offer. PC 49 may have found the action he needed in the "Force," but many more were finding it on the other side of the legal fence.

Alfred Roome's underrated chase drama *My Brother's Keeper* (1948) concerns the pursuit of two escaped prisoners handcuffed together. The war as such has no bearing on the plot, but one of the escapees, Martin (Jack Warner), an old lag, wants "to get right away from this country—to somewhere like South Africa or Australia where it's new and young." That remark could never have been heard in a prewar or wartime British film; it resonates with postwar disappointment in a Britain where nothing seems to have changed, a Britain from which, in fact, large numbers of people did migrate to Australia in the late 1940s and early 1950s.[6] The film ends with Martin killed after pursuit on—significantly—a minefield reflecting the dangerous aftermath of war. There are other films, too, which do not foreground the war's influence but which imply it in various ways. Charles de Lautour's *Impulse* (1955), for instance, never mentions the war, but the stasis in which the life of the hero Alan Curtis (Arthur Kennedy) seems to have become stuck and the insistence on how slow and safe everything is in the country town where he has lived and worked for eight years echoes Martin's remark in *My Brother's Keeper*. He is an American, married to an English woman, who takes their placid lives for granted; the film doesn't explain how he comes to be there, and one can only assume that he has stayed on after the war. The hero of Basil Dearden's *The Ship That Died of Shame* (1955) says in voice-over: "The beginning, like everything else about me, went back to the war." This appears to be the case with so many of the protagonists of postwar British cinema that it seems to be implied even when it is not overtly stated. The vaguely upper-class, caddish "Captain" (Dermot Walsh) in Terence Fisher's *To the Public Danger* (1947) uses his wartime (and class) resonances to entice a dissatisfied country girl (Susan Shaw) away from her dull boyfriend. There is a general air of postwar irresponsibility (epitomized in drunk driving), of freedom from restrictions and yet of boredom as well, now that the heightened tensions of wartime have passed. Some don't want challenges; they prefer to be seduced by flashy excitements.

There is very often a cautionary tone in these films, usually directed against the notion of succumbing to spurious and sometimes criminal temptations, but sometimes also in the way of a critique of the times for not offering more stimulating opportunities to those returning from the war. Losing the peace, that is, is seen as the fault of those who have not learned enough from the experience of the war. The old class barriers are seen still to be in place, the old conservatism now looks like stick-in-the-mud prej-

udice, the materialists are seeking to profit from the urge to postwar progress, the wartime recruitment of women to the workforce is in danger of
being superseded by the cliché of "woman's place is in the home."

Two of the rare comedies that belong to the adjusting-to-the-peace genre
touch on all these matters. These are Derek Twist's *All Over the Town*
(1949) and Jeffrey Dell's *It's Hard to Be Good* (1949). *All Over the Town*'s
protagonist, Nat (Norman Wooland), is the local hero of a seaside town,
who returns to his prewar job on the town's newspaper amid speculation
about whether this will be exciting enough for him. He feels a sense of
confinement, as he settles to dealing with local factions, but he doesn't want
to "chuck it and get out." He comes up against issues such as that of
women who did men's jobs during the war and now don't want to be
reclaimed into dull domesticity,[7] and the conflict between old gentry and
vulgar progress ("Progress with taste" is the slick motto of the developer
played by James Hayter). He talks of the folly of "fighting a war for freedom of speech and then putting a muzzle on yourself in your own town."
In this matter, there is the subplot of the ex-WAF, Beryl (Eleanor Sum-
merfield), who is charged with drunkenness and is depicted as another postwar problem. The magistrate hopes that her punishment will be an example
to others who have returned "coarsened" by their life in the services. Nat
gets into trouble for refusing to report Beryl's case, his boss claiming that
"The war's been made an excuse for every sort of licence and debauchery,"
showing no sympathy for her difficulties of adjusting to the routine of
peacetime life. Whatever serious notions are floated, albeit in the spirit of
comedy, the film settles for a romantic embrace between Nat and Sally
(Sarah Churchill), the woman who has replaced him during the war, and
a public meeting which is a victory for the need for care in postwar planning.

It's Hard to Be Good, on many counts an inept and tiresomely didactic
comedy, is only worth noting for its explicit address of the problems of
peace. Its VC-winning hero, Captain Gladstone Wedge (Jimmy Hanley),
returns from the war full of talk of "good will" and of "helping people,"
meeting suspicion and opposition from everyone, and confronted by doom-
laden Sunday papers and evidence of conformity and unneighborliness.
Since he has nothing to propose except abstractions, it is not surprising
that he is so unsuccessful. The film is lamentably short on any sense of the
actualities of daily life, nor does it have the dialectic vigor of *They Came
to a City*; but the very notion that the postwar world should be an improvement on what went before and that this might be achieved by a consensuality of effort is one that deserved to be worked out in livelier, more
convincing detail. Only Wedge's opportunist sergeant, Todd (Geoffrey
Keen), who can't break the habit of calling Wedge "Sir,"[8] strikes a sharper
note as one who is "on to something good" if only he can get the capital.

In this way he prefigures the key narrative protagonist of the films of this sub-genre that will be considered in more detail.

Two "B" film romances that have affiliations with my synthetic genre both echo more famous films. *A Song for Tomorrow* (1948), an early film by Terence Fisher, for the Rank Highbury operation, recalls the American film *Random Harvest* in its use of amnesia as a plot device for complicating the postwar life of its hero Derek (Shaun Noble). His difficulties in adapting to peacetime life are compounded by his falling in love with the singer, Helen (Evelyn McCabe), whose voice is his last link with the past. The film winds up its romantic action in somewhat arbitrary fashion with Derek returning to the prewar fiancée whom we never see, the issue of being at a loss in the postwar world raised but allowed to sink beneath the weight of novelettish conventions. William C. Hammond's *The Fool and the Princess* (1948) suggests *Brief Encounter* in reverse. "We'd hardly settled down before the war came and changed everything and pulled us apart," says a woman's voice on the soundtrack at the outset as the camera pans along a suburban street. In postwar Wimbledon, housewife Kate (Lesley Brook) sews prosaically while husband Harry (Bruce Lester) sits listening to Beethoven's "Appassionata" (cf. Celia Johnson and Rachmaninoff) and recalling Moura (Adina Mandlova), the (self-styled) princess with whom he fell in love in a displacement camp in Europe during the war. He has been unable to adjust to peace—"I'm just not going back to the old routine"—and feels he must return to Europe to see Moura again. With that arbitrariness in reaching a dénouement, which is perhaps a "B" movie failing, the film cuts from their meeting to Kate's receiving a letter from Harry saying, "This time darling, I'm coming home because I want to." Like Celia Johnson's Laura, he turns down romance and settles for a dull spouse, and there is no time for the film to wonder about how he will adapt to the "old routine." Another film which touches on this theme of painful postwar adjustment in a married relationship is Henry Cass's *The Glass Mountain* (1949). In this, the composer husband Ricky (Michael Denison) has difficulty in resuming his marriage to Anne (Dulcie Gray) after the war, as a result of a wartime affair with an Italian girl, Alida (Valentina Cortesa). This is a more consciously romantic film than was common in British cinema at the time, but the outcome is conventionally in line with middle-class proprieties; it is, however, touching nevertheless as a dramatization of a common postwar problem. Its resolution is, of course, in line with British film at large in the way suggested above in the reference to *Brief Encounter*: that is, the claims of duty inevitably win over those of passion. That such endings were endemic perhaps also tells us something important about the dominant ideology of the times. If this suggests a timorousness in the face of disruption, then that is also revealing about the times: a wanting to return to remembered prewar values, rather than striking out

for the new and challenging. These romantic melodramas all opt for the
status quo, though not without hinting at ways in which things might have
been different or without suggesting the adjustments that needed to be
made.

Failure to settle down to the old routine is at the heart of the four most
striking films I want to discuss in relation to the theme of this chapter.
They are Cavalcanti's *They Made Me a Fugitive* (1947), Guy Hamilton's
The Intruder (1953), and Basil Dearden's *The Ship That Died of Shame*
(1955), and *The League of Gentlemen* (1960). All four of these exemplify
the narrative paradigm that is central to this study. That is, each is concerned with the return to civilian life of men distinguished in war service
and unable in peace to find legitimate outlet for their skills and energies.
A historian or a sociologist—I am neither—might well be able to adduce
statistical evidence for the connection these films posit between wartime
distinction and peacetime boredom leading to crime. My concern is to draw
attention to a body of films, hitherto neglected both individually and as a
sort of genre, as offering grounds for supposing the phenomenon constitutes a significant response by the cinema to Britain's decline in postwar
stature. (There are other cinematic responses, too; these will be referred to
later.)

Clem Morgan (Trevor Howard), a former RAF ace, who is "bored . . .
bored" with peacetime life, and whose boredom provides the narrative
starting point for *They Made Me a Fugitive*, is probably the first fully-
fledged version of these ill-adjusted protagonists in postwar British cinema.
"He's got class," says one of the gang to which he is introduced, and his
class is signified not only in the background of wartime distinction but in
his general bearing and above all in his upper-class accent. Accent is, of
course, a major signifier in British cinema, but here it works to put Clem
at a further remove from the gang. The leader of the gang, Narcy (Griffith
Jones) recognizes Clem's aimlessness: "What you need is an outlet for your
energy," to which Clem's "popsy" Ellen (Eve Ashley) replies, "What he
needs is another war." This exchange may well be the first explicit statement in a postwar film of the particular postwar problem with the representation of which this chapter is concerned. The film is equally explicit
about Narcy, described later as "just cheap rotten after-the-war trash," not
"a respectable crook."[9] The choice of the two actors was no doubt important: both, formerly associated with a notably gentlemanly persona, are
now seen in roles that take them far from their usual purlieus into areas
of crime and danger. Such casting in itself can suggest a world in which
things have gone seriously astray, and the ambience in which these actors
now find themselves is created with a new concern in the thriller genre for
a tough, dirty, violent urban *mise-en-scène*. (Several years later, Trevor
Howard would again play a wartime hero looking for a niche in peace time

in Ralph Thomas's lively thriller *The Clouded Yellow* [1950]. A former major, he thinks that what he wants is "something quiet in the country." What he finds is, of course, anything but quiet; however, unlike Clem, the major does find some use for his wartime skills which had involved helping refugees to escape. It is a less resonant film than *They Made Me a Fugitive*; it is simply a well-told chase story at heart. But its texture is enriched by the knowledge that its roots lie in postwar alienation. The hero is not merely given a narrative action to perform; he is, as well, given an affectless, drifting way of life to pull himself out of.)

Clem is aware of what he has let himself into and plans to pull out after the warehouse robbery. However, he is caught as a result of Narcy's treachery. His sojourn in prison is created in a very controlled montage sequence (long shots of men working in fields, close-ups of breaking stones); and there is a later bleak montage of dogs, woods, and police cars to render Clem's escape and pursuit. The plot is resolved skillfully enough in thriller terms, but what now is particularly interesting is the film's insistence on sheeting home the blame to postwar neglect of those who have served the country well during the war. Inspector Rockliffe (Ballard Berkeley) asks Clem, "How did you come to get mixed up with scum like Narcy? You had a fine record." Elsewhere, Clem provides an answer to this: "I went on doing what the country put me in a uniform to do after they'd taken it back." As a thriller, *They Made Me a Fugitive* (a neglected film ripe for reappraisal) is unusually tough-minded, witty, and downbeat. There is a hard awareness of the facts of criminal life that is scarcely conceivable in prewar British cinema. However, its real interest as a document of its times is its twofold attack on the climate of postwar Britain: first, it has allowed "scum like Narcy" to prosper;[10] and, second, it has somehow failed those on whom it had relied for safety and survival.

The Intruder, another neglected film, also works as an escape thriller, but like the previous film it gains in resonance from its setting of a Britain that has let down its servicemen. Whereas the war has provided the opportunity for men to be their brothers' keepers, in the complacent postwar world the old class differences have kept them apart from each other, each immersed in his own concerns to the point of losing contact with former comrades. The key line in *The Intruder* is: "I'd also like to know what turns a good soldier into a thief." It initiates the two kinds of search that account for the film's plot and its structure. In terms of plot, Colonel Wolf Merton (Jack Hawkins) surprises, in his London flat, a burglar who proves to be Ginger Edwards (Michael Medwin), one of his best troopers in the war. Wrongly believing Merton has betrayed him to the police, Ginger escapes into the night, and Merton, who has not kept in touch with his men, now feels the officer's responsibility "to try and find him before he gets into serious trouble." Thus, the rest of the film—in narrative terms—is motivated by this double search: for the fleeing Ginger and for the answer to his question about what has happened to cause Ginger's descent into crime. Structurally, one might say that the film's hermeneutic is established at the outset: the rest of the film shows its articulation through an alternation of peacetime episodes and wartime flashbacks as Merton pursues Ginger literally across England, in order to persuade him to give himself up, and, in doing so, looking for the answer to the problem that puzzles and disturbs him.

Through patient searching, Merton finds some of the ways in which Ginger's peacetime experiences have let him down (e.g., his girlfriend's infidelity with a spiv who missed out on war service because of his flat feet) and how this has led eventually to the prison sentence from which he now runs. The film's double action is concerned to find Ginger and bring him to some kind of justice, however much it is disposed toward a sympathetic understanding of his situation, *and* it also needs to account for the anomaly of a good soldier's being reduced to a thief. The wartime flashbacks fill us in on Ginger's military career, and make us aware that this is a man whose situation warrants our interest and concern.[11] Hamilton has known how much wartime material he has needed to enable us to value Ginger and to contrast it with the meagerness of the opportunities open to him in peacetime. As to closure, the film opts for low-key realism, with Ginger quietly giving himself up to finish his sentence, and Merton agreeing to help his rehabilitation. The mutedness of the ending acts as warranty of the seriousness of the issues which have underlain the thriller format.

Guy Hamilton has recalled how "Lindsay Anderson came up to me not long after the film was released, and said, 'You've let the side down.' He meant that the burglar rejoined the Establishment when he really should have turned on the Colonel."[12] However, as Raymond Durgnat has noted, "Paternalist as . . . this may seem, it has to be looked at from another angle: a renunciation of pre-war *laissez-faire*."[13] (Eight years later, Tom Courtenay in Tony Richardson's *The Loneliness of the Long-Distance Runner* would spurn the inter-class rapprochement that marks the end of *The Intruder*.) What is revealing in Hamilton's film is that class, and the whole idea of hierarchy, is seen as operating in both war and peace. Though war may create a new sense of purpose and cause a cross-class bonding in the interests of getting the military job done, this doesn't mean that class as an issue goes away—not even in the wartime situation. War may seem to imply that the nation is working as a family, but the scene in the officer's mess makes clear that it is still a family with poor relations. Newly promoted from the ranks, George Summers (George Cole) behaves so gauchely on his initiation to dining with the officers that he longs to be off drinking with his old mate Ginger. Because this is an intelligent film, the upper classes—the officers—are not uniformly presented as swine. Perry (Dennis Price) is the most overtly snobbish;[14] he is also a coward and, unlike the humane Merton, he persists in using his captain's title in civilian life. But the officers played by Hawkins and George Baker provide balance. Class, the film seems to suggest, is deeply ingrained in British life. War may shift the barriers about a bit, but it will in fact create its own hierarchy. It may, as Carol Reed's *The Way Ahead* (1944) suggests, create a wartime family, sinking differences in the common cause, but *The Intruder*, ten years later, sees the family as having let down some of its less well-placed members.

The two films directed by Basil Dearden are very different in tone. *The Ship That Died of Shame* is a melancholy lament for the loss of wartime purpose and camaraderie, whereas *The League of Gentlemen* is a comedy thriller, albeit drawing on the same sense of loss. The former (based on Nicholas Monsarrat's novel) is in the Ealing tradition of male-centerd low-key excitement, stiffened by the melodramatic flair that characterizes the films produced by the Dearden-Michael Relph team. For gunboat commander Bill Randall (George Baker), "the beginning, like everything about me," in the voice-over near the start of the film, "went back to the war." His brief wartime marriage to Helen (Virginia McKenna) gave him a sense of "a purpose in things—even in this damned war." After the war, grief at her death and the loss of the urgency of naval action leads Randall into an aimless existence and makes him agree to take up the offer of a smuggling operation put to him by wartime comrade Hoskins (Richard Attenborough). They recruit their third gunboat mate Birdie (Bill Owen) and for a while Randall responds to the excitement of fetching and carrying "just a few things to light up the postwar darkness a bit," as Hoskins says. "Not much time to sleep but we revelled in it," says Randall's voice-over;[15] that is, he is responding to a revival of something like the old wartime challenges. But Hoskins's opportunist approach to postwar life (shipping those luxury goods in short supply) darkens when he agrees to transport a child-killer on the run. The thriller content and the metaphorical element indicated in the film's title now converge, instead of merely worrying at each other. Randall and Birdie become distanced from Hoskins as his cargo grows more dangerous, and the gunboat becomes increasingly "resistant": the ship stops suddenly with inexplicable engine trouble; its wheel throws Randall during a storm and Hoskins is hurled overboard. Finally Randall runs it aground on the rocks. "And so she died. She gave up and died. In anger and shame." At the time of the film's release, *The Ship That Died of Shame* may have seemed to reviewers like a conventional thriller with metaphorical pretensions. Producer Michael Relph recalls that the film was intended as a critique of postwar British society: "the ship represented what people had done with the country that they had inherited after the war. It was a sort of allegory."[16] In the hindsight of forty years, if one accepts the anthropomorphizing of the ship, the film offers a fascinating account of how the war and the decade following it were viewed and may be read now. It resonates with the sense of a nation settling into a complacent peace in which standards of conduct and morality are no longer reinforced by the sense of a common purpose. As one recent critic has said of it: "[It] is an exemplary film of its time, not only activating memories but, through its narrative structure, constructing and expressing a striking critique of such nostalgia and the drives which fuel it."[17]

The League of Gentlemen offers a satire on Britain's finest hour. It was, as Alexander Walker has noted, "a more wry, disenchanted kind of comedy than Ealing would have made," though it shared Ealing's "unflagging belief that the amateurs could outwit the experts."[18] It is, in fact, a film that looks forward to the cheekier 1960s in its sexual references and in its disrespectful, quite non-nostalgic attitude to the old days as well as to the present. Nevertheless, the caper that provides the film's climax is planned on military lines (and the montage of preparations is accompanied by martial music). Also, the ex-servicemen who have been recruited for the robbery by ex-officer Hyde (Jack Hawkins, in a role that parodies his 1950s star persona of square-jawed commander) have been chosen for their specific skills—as well for Hyde's knowledge of their secret vulnerabilities. These men are all sailing close to the legal wind when the story begins, and Hyde blackmails them all into acquiescing in his plans: "You're all crooks one way or another," he tells them when he first brings them all together. Hyde himself is merely embittered as a result of being declared redundant, but we are not invited to feel sympathy for him, rather to cheer the renewal of dignity he experiences as he directs the heist. A special, cynical pleasure for Hyde derives from the fact that the Army is providing the equipment (e.g., gas masks) for the operation, and one wants them to get away with it, because the film is quite sharp in its satire on an affluent, bureaucratic society. When Captain Peter Race (Nigel Patrick) is late for the first meeting, he blithely offers, "I took the wrong turning and not for the first time. Found myself in a room full of trade unionists cooking up the next wage claim. All Tories of course." That bit of dialogue sums up a good deal of the film's thematic and tonal irreverence. Crooks these men may be, but they can still rally to a call on the energies and expertise that war once demanded of them, albeit in a criminal cause! By 1960, after a decade of war films more or less unequivocally celebrating British heroism, it is interesting to find a film challenging the virtues that have entered the national mythology.

The foregoing by no means exhausts the titles that might be included in the generic category of "adjusting-to-the-peace" films. Indeed, one thinks at once of two further relevant Dearden-Relph works: *Frieda* (1947) in which the returning serviceman (David Farrar) wonders "whether [he] could pick up the reins" of his old job, his postwar life complicated by the German wife he has brought back to his conservative home town; and *Cage of Gold* (1950) in which ex-RAF officer Bill (Farrar again), who "never took anything seriously," can find no useful place in peace and disrupts the life of his former wife. And there is Lewis Gilbert's *The Good Die Young* (1954), which involves two American ex-servicemen down on their luck who join a decadent English playboy Rave (Laurence Harvey) in an ill-fated mail-van robbery. Their sense of postwar disillusionment makes the Americans an easy prey for the corrupt purposes of the upper-class Rave. Enough. I think that the batch of films adduced is sufficient to establish a significant strand in British cinema history, a strand which has been curiously neglected. If there is no obvious masterpiece among these films— nothing to compare with, say, the American classic, William Wyler's *The Best Years of Our Lives* (1947)—these are films of definite social interest. It is perhaps strange that this theme of coming to terms with peace did not attract the attention of the great stylists of the British cinema, Powell, Reed, Lean, and so on (though such concern does sometimes assert itself in films with other matters more importantly on their minds, as in *Great Expectations*). The films that do address this theme cover a wide range of conventional genres and have their place across several rungs of the British filmmaking hierarchy. As films they vary markedly in their aesthetic qualities. I have not examined them primarily, indeed scarcely at all, from this point of view, but have focused on their narrative paradigms and the social issues that they highlight. As historical documents, it seems to me that no one has yet begun to see their value as exemplifications of trends in postwar England. They do not set out to be documents or documentaries: as "evidence" they may be less suspect for the relative innocence of their intentions.

In terms of the British film industry, there may be an instructive parallel to be drawn with the narrative patterns of many of these films. British cinema, it is by now pretty generally accepted, broke free, during the war years, from the artificial traditions that constrained much 1930s British film production. The war gave a new urgency to British filmmaking, reflected in such ways as the documentary-influenced war films which represented a new cross-class consensuality at work in both the services and the civilian community. As well, there was the growth of a prestigious literary strain (*Henry V* is the prime example) and of a really popular indigenous cinema in the Gainsborough melodramas. The energy and talent that produced these strands of wartime British cinema were sustained in the immediate postwar years but began to peter out in a sea of financial troubles in the late 1940s. The 1950s may well be due for reappraisal, as I hope some of the films discussed above suggest, but there is an undeniable falling off in the creative energy at work in British cinema in what has been described as "a battleship grey decade. A good formulation because there were a lot of battleships about. I would certainly have thought the 1940s were a boom period in all ways—aesthetically, culturally and commercially. But I suppose the 1950s were a boom period numerically, because there was a domestic British cinema with some viability."[19] Analogically, one might venture that the life and quality was going out of British cinema at a time when the films discussed here were challenging postwar mores.

Along with the resurgence of war films celebrating wartime exploits (e.g., *Reach for the Sky, Above Us the Waves*) and outpost-of-empire films (e.g., *Storm Over the Nile, Nor the Moon by Night*), the films discussed here constitute another response to Britain's postwar decline, and a more honest one, refusing nostalgia of one kind or other. They suggest quite overtly a nation running out of steam: their narratives are typically imbued with an awareness of the loss of power, now clearly borne out by the facts of postwar British history; of the failure to value and rechannel the wartime effort. They are resonant with the debilitating exhaustion that follows a long hard war and the concomitant depletion of the nation's resources; an exhaustion that prevents the wartime progress in such matters as class and gender roles from being fruitfully extended. Anyone wanting to know what it was like to be a wartime victor and a peacetime loser might do well to look at them carefully.

NOTES

1. "To the Lord General Cromwell May 1652."
2. In this connection, it is interesting to note a reader's letter to the popular magazine *Picturegoer* 18, no. 728 (NS) (January 29, 1949): 18, echoing Milton in urging British filmmakers to maintain the "exceptional standard" they had reached during the war: "Peace is as thrilling as war if looked at in the right way. There is the battle for coal and for production, the miracle of the expanding health service— other achievements. Stories of absorbing interest could be filmed against the background of our struggle to beat the crisis."
3. Donald Horne writes of this matter in *God is an Englishman* (Harmondsworth: Penguin, 1969), p. 216: "The only trouble with both the increase in economic growth and the increase in exports was that, although they seemed all right in themselves, they were no good compared with the advances being made by other industrial nations." Seventeen years later, John Hill also challenges the basis of this "affluence" in his *Sex, Class and Realism* (London: BFI Publishing, 1986), p. 7, claiming that "although British economic growth had looked impressive in isolation, when compared with other industrial nations it looked decidedly poor (lagging well behind such European competitors as West Germany, France and Italy)."
4. Charles Barr, *Ealing Studios*, new revised edition (London: Studio Vista, 1993), p.187.
5. Postwar slang term, defined by the *Concise Oxford Dictionary* as "Shady character who avoids honest work & lives by his wits esp. in black-market traffic (orig. unkn.)."
6. "So many migrants were attracted that Australia's net gain through migration in the period 1947 to 1977 exceeded the net gain in all its previous history," writes Geoffrey Blainey in *The Tyranny of Distance*, revised edition (London: Macmillan, 1982), p. 332. Ronald Conway also notes, in *The Land of the Long Weekend* (South Melbourne: Sun Books, 1978), p. 15, that the "first segment" of the

post-1947 "wave of migration . . . comprised those arrivals from the British Isles with a sprinkling of Maltese and Cypriots."

7. Cate Haste, in *Rules of Desire: Sex in Britain—World War I to the Present* (London: Pimlico, 1994), summarizes the situation for women after the war: "Lauded though they may have been for their wartime participation in the economic life of the country, it was made fairly plain that women's continuation in work was no longer a priority, nor even a right. They were made redundant as the men return" (pp. 140–141). She quotes Mass Observation survey figures to show that many women wanted to stay in employment outside the home after the war.

8. Neither can Birdie (played by perennial "ranker type," Bill Owen) in *The Ship That Died of Shame* or Ginger (Michael Medwin) in *The Intruder*. It is not just wartime habit at issue here, but the postwar persistence of class lines.

9. Three years later, Basil Dearden's *The Blue Lamp* would echo this notion of "a new problem to the police" in the postwar world, deriving from "restless and maladjusted youngsters." One of these latter, Tom (Dirk Bogarde), reckons "a bit of a scare's good for your insides," claiming to like "a bit of excitement."

10. Cf. the prosperity of other spiv figures in postwar films such as those played by Nigel Patrick in Edmond Greville's *Noose* (1948) and Sidney Tafler in Robert Hamer's *It Always Rains on Sunday* (1948).

11. A review at the time claimed: "the flashbacks are as convincingly contrived as any I've seen on the screen." *Picturegoer* 26, no. 964 (October 24, 1953): 20.

12. "Guy Hamilton," in Brian McFarlane (ed.), *Sixty Voices: Celebrities Recall the Golden Age of British Cinema* (London: BFI Publishing, 1992), p. 114.

13. Raymond Durgnat, *A Mirror for England: British Movies from Austerity to Affluence* (London: Faber and Faber, 1970), p. 53.

14. Cf. the characters played by Eric Portman in *Great Day* and Dermot Walsh in *To the Public Danger*. Hanging on to one's wartime title is usually, in films, a matter for pity or contempt.

15. One recalls here the smuggler-artist hero (Derek Bond) of John Gilling's *The Quiet Woman*, who was smuggling luxury goods out of "bravado."

16. "Michael Relph," in McFarlane, *Sixty Voices*, p. 192.

17. Jim Cook, "The Ship That Died of Shame," in Charles Barr (ed.), *All Our Yesterdays: Ninety Years of British Cinema* (London: BFI Publishing, 1986), p. 362.

18. Alexander Walker, *Hollywood, England: The British Film Industry in the Sixties* (London: Harrap, 1986), p. 103.

19. Charles Barr, film critic and historian, in interview with the author, England, 1989.

7

The Scent of Distant Blood: Hammer Films and History

Sue Harper

Filmmakers have always put history to a wide range of uses. In British cinema, history was used for commercial ends, and was raided for political purposes by those from the left and the right of the cultural spectrum. It has operated as a weapon of reinforcement for those confident of their place in the order of things, and as an alibi for resisting change among those uneasy about their position in society. During the 1930s, British filmmakers recuperated key periods of history in order to allay the anxieties of specific social groups. In World War II, the Ministry of Information was enthusiastic about the efficacy of history for propaganda purposes, and it promulgated films that used Britain's heritage in an exhortatory manner. In the latter part of the war, yet another form of historical film emerged: the costume extravaganza, in which heroines wearing sumptuous frocks caused mayhem among the unsuspecting populace.[1]

The historical film, therefore, was a genre often deployed as a persuasive rhetorical tool by those with an axe to grind. The status of historical films altered according to the job they were required to do. Outright entertainment or titillation was usually accorded minimal status by the social or critical establishment; education or improvement automatically ensured a higher status. Of course, history can never be accurately represented by the cinema. Social reality was always tangential in historical film, which deployed whatever disguises or discourses its producers felt to be appropriate.

But the historical film and the costume drama are not identical. Although they do well at the box office, since both constitute a vital kind of social remembering, they have different provenances. Historical film deals with real people or events, which it deploys for a range of purposes. Costume film is a sub-genre within historical film and deals with mythic or symbolic aspects of the past, raided in an eclectic manner for the pleasures they can provide. Costume is a far more flexible form, but its very malleability makes it acutely unstable. It can change radically over short periods of time, and it tends to splinter into further sub-genres.

One of the key sub-genres of the costume film has been the historical horror film. In the 1930s, historical settings were occasionally used to give an extra frisson to cinematic explorations of the uncanny. In America in 1931, Universal's *Frankenstein* was set in an imaginary European past which both distanced audiences from its gory events and gave an up-market nod toward German expressionist practices. In Britain in 1936, George King (MGM) made *Sweeney Todd or the Demon Barber of Fleet Street*, in which the human pie saga was given extra picturesque qualities by its historical settings. But such films were rare. The combination of historical and horror/occult elements remained unusual in the British films of the following decade. British-National's 1945 *Latin Quarter*, Gainsborough's 1945 *A Place of One's Own*, and Two Cities' 1947 *Uncle Silas* were virtually the only examples, and they were all box office flops. The costume market was dominated by Gainsborough's flamboyant bodice-rippers, such as *The Wicked Lady* and *Caravan*, primarily aimed at female audiences. But it was also because horror or occult elements were not what audiences wanted during the 1940s. As Christopher Lee remarked, costume frighteners like Hammer's "had not been made during the war. There was enough horror then. People hadn't seen anything like these for a long, long time."[2]

All this changed in the late 1950s, when Hammer Films launched a cycle of horror films with historical settings. At that time, the company was run by James Carreras and Antony Hinds. Their horror cycle began with *The Curse of Frankenstein* (released 1957) and *Dracula* (1958). Prior to 1956, Hammer had specialized in the production of films that were already, in a sense, pre-sold; they made films based on popular radio programs, such as *The Man in Black* or *Life with the Lyons*. Most of their pre-1957 films had modern settings.

Hammer horror films developed the costume genre in a qualitatively new manner. The studio had begun to specialize with emotions *in extremis* with its *Quatermass Xperiment* (*sic*) (1955), which exploited the new X certificate and the more relaxed censorship conditions. With *The Curse of Frankenstein*, company policy changed radically. Over half the films produced between 1957 and 1974 had historical settings. These settings were a key part of the films' meaning and appeal. Although Hammer has been the subject of some excellent academic investigations, many paying attention to the production context and directorial authorship,[3] little so far has been written about Hammer's historical work. The historical context of their new horror films permitted them to allude to hidden or forgotten elements in British popular culture; but it also opened up a space in which notions of national identity could be examined in a new way, and in which anxieties about the body (especially the female body) could be explored and addressed.

Hammer's shift into historical horror coincided with a serious crisis in British film production. In the late 1950s cinema audiences were declining catastrophically. Teenagers, particularly male teenagers, were replacing family audiences.[4] The industry spent much energy campaigning against the effects of the swinging Entertainments Tax; there were sharp falls in investment, and a decline in overall confidence. The response of the Rank empire was to make fewer but more expensive films, and, by using international stars, to make money in American and worldwide markets.[5] Smaller independent producers, such as Ivan Foxwell, tried the same technique.[6] But the films produced by such policies were often anodyne and did little business abroad.

Hammer's approach to overseas investment was quite different from that of any other British studio, and it seems quite clear that the "costume" element in their horror films was a key factor in their search for international profits. It made little sense to duplicate contemporary American schlock/horror films such as *The Invasion of the Body Snatchers* (1956) and *The Blob* (1958), which were so carefully tailored for their own home audiences; Hammer's *Quatermass* films, which were comparable to these, were quickly dropped in favor of the costume horrors. In what looks like a classic two-hander, Hammer packaged European history so as to give American audiences a strong flavor of the exotic, and to give everyone else a version of the past that retained some familiar elements. The two-hander paid off. Only a third of Hammer's considerable profits came from Britain; another third came from America, and the rest from other overseas sources.[7] It was the overseas earnings that earned Hammer the Queen's Award for Industry in 1968.[8] The studio's modesty of scale also helped the profit figures. Paradoxically, it was the very "Englishness" of the films that made them marketable for international consumption.

Another challenge for the indigenous British film industry during the late 1950s was the incursion of Americans into the business. From 1956, American-financed production increased.[9] Until 1959 American/British films constituted a significant proportion of first-feature films produced in Britain. This led to shortage of studio space for "native" filmmakers, a general malaise, and competition for key technical personnel.

Hammer turned the tables on American producers. From the mid-1950s, it struck major deals with American distributors, and took the battle for profits into America's own backyard. James Carreras signed global distribution contracts with Columbia, Warner Bros., and United Artists, and was aggressive and innovative in handling them.[10] But Hammer's first contract was with Universal. It hinged on the question of copyright. Universal claimed ownership of the cinematic representations of the Frankenstein and Dracula stories and, after acrimonious exchanges, a deal was struck whereby Hammer's version of the tales should *look* as different as possible from Universal's. In return, Universal would give Hammer access to its worldwide distribution network. Hammer had evaded the problems that beset other British producers by modifying the historical appearance of its films.

How did Hammer produce these films, in which the past played such a crucial role? There were few senior executives, although further down the management ladder roles were flexibly interpreted. The executive producer, James Carreras, producer Antony Hinds, and associate producer Antony Nelson Keys exerted tight financial control. Hinds noted that "I was on the floor a great deal of the time (not very popular with my directors, as you can imagine!) and had a loudspeaker in my office linked to the microphone so that I could hear how every scene was playing."[11] Len Harris, the camera operator on the early costume horror films, recalled how his use of the loudspeaker and microphone permitted Hinds to solve any in-production problems with the shooting script.[12] Producers inaugurated additional forms of cooperation between key personnel once the cycle had begun: "When the horror films started and especially the Gothics, more inter-departmental discussion took place. It was especially important that the lighting cameraman co-operated with the make-up man and vice versa to get maximum effect."[13]

The historical element in the films required more rigorous forms of production control. Only one film was shot at a time, and back-to-back planning ensured maximum use of sets. *Curse of the Werewolf* was chosen because Carreras had found sets going cheap; the sets of *Countess Dracula* were snaffled and recycled from *Anne of a Thousand Days*, acquired from another company.[14] But although there was tight financial control by the executive, there was minimal interference with the visual side. Staff appeared to be highly motivated (they all got an extra £1 a week above union rates), and they all attended the rushes. Directors worked on a freelance basis and were hired for each film, but they were frequently re-employed, so there was team continuity. The production design and art department, led by Bernard Robinson, had a degree of autonomy.[15]

There were startling similarities with Gainsborough Studios which, between 1942 and 1947, produced a successful cycle of low-status costume melodramas.[16] However, there was one important difference. At Gainsborough, the producers held the scriptwriters on a loose rein. They were a privileged group at the studio, and were allowed their heads in matters of plot nuance and construction. A comparative analysis of Gainsborough costume films reveals that little care was taken to ensure that the script was the dominant language. The Gainsborough films are in effect a battleground in which different discourses (decor, costume, script, body language, music) struggle unsuccessfully for mastery. Not so in Hammer films. Producer control over the scripting process was so tight that, for many major—and mostly historical—projects Antony Hinds, the executive producer, also acted as scriptwriter, sometimes under the pseudonym John Elder. Jimmy Sangster, with whom both Hinds and James Carreras liaised very closely, wrote many other scripts. Michael Carreras, son of James, produced as well as scripted several films. So did Antony Nelson Keys, another executive producer.[17] The other scriptwriters tended to be fairly "jobbing" or junior figures who would not resist instruction from above.

This tight producer control over the scripts profoundly affected the manner in which history was deployed in the films, and the producers made more interventions with the historical than the non-historical scripts. In Hammer scripts from the 1950s to the 1970s, the plot structures are extremely symmetrical. *Devil-Ship Pirates* gains its coherence by the careful balance between the two fathers; one is weak and the other strong, and they are both killed in order to resolve class contradictions and allow the narrative to be resolved. In *The Evil of Frankenstein* there is a careful balance between the qualities of the ice in which the body is frozen, and the passionate fire which revives it; there is also a parallel between the dumbness of the mute heroine and that of the monster. In *The Gorgon*, there is a restitutive balance between the life-bringing virgin and the death-bringing crone—acutely at issue on the night of the full moon. *When Dinosaurs Ruled the Earth* rests on sharp oppositions between dark and fair, animal and human, male and female.

These oppositions and doublings extend to Hammer's view of history itself. In Sangster's script for *The Mummy* (1959), the experience of the past is purveyed to contemporary viewers through a double filter. First of all they are led into the early years of the twentieth century, which exhibits overweening certainties in its father/son relations, and an arrogant treatment of other cultures. The script then takes the viewer back into Ancient Egypt, via the maimed son John (Peter Cushing). The camera "pans down to the desk and the picture of the Princess Ananka. DISSOLVE to the interior of tent. Voice-over says 'in the year 2,000 BC . . . ' " As John reads aloud from the book, the audience penetrates the veil covering the ancient world. It is a world of breathtaking vividness and spectacle, and no effort is made to reduce its strangeness. The unfamiliar texture of the past is presented *flat*, as it were. The priest Karis (in his unwrapped state) intones, "Thou goest round heaven, Thou seest Ra," while rituals of bodily purification are presented in a matter-of-fact way. The unfolding of events per-

The funeral procession in *The Mummy* (1959) is a ritual that both cleanses and defiles. (Reprinted by permission of Hammer Film Productions, Ltd., United Kingdom.)

force follows the pace of John's voice; leisurely, insistent, interlocutory, it commands the sequence and interpretation of the historical events on the screen.

Immediately after this key sequence, the script debates the provenance of historical fact:

> *Uncle Joe*: The dictionary defines legend as historical fact.
>
> *John*: But don't forget half of it we know is fact. We know that Ananka died on a pilgrimage . . . if half the story is true, why not the other half?
>
> *Uncle Joe*: Because the other half is removed from fact, it's fantasy.
>
> *John*: Dad knew all about the legend. Perhaps having discovered that half of it was true, he let his imagination persuade him that the rest of it could have been.
>
> *Uncle Joe*: It's a fairy story, nothing more.[18]

Here, simply expressed, is a sophisticated debate about the constraints on the historical imagination. The script interprets history first as an intricate puzzle, second as a source of threat, and third as a lesson for the future. The pleasures that the narrative offers are thus twofold; of responding to the beauties of the past, and of escaping from its dangers. The script *separates* these two pleasures, so that the audience is spared a sense of guilt caused by their proximity.

Compare Sangster's script of *The Mummy* with that of Hinds's *Frankenstein and the Monster from Hell* (1974). Both films were directed by Terence Fisher. Both scripts are startlingly visceral and are preoccupied with the minutiae of the body on the slab. Both have an intense interest in sexual symbolism, and both deploy history as the site of hideous yet fascinating acts. The two scripts have a measured, even ponderous, pace. Indeed, Hinds agreed with director Freddie Francis that "you can always tell a Gothic horror film, it's twice as slow as the others."[19] This "slowness" in Hammer scripts is essential for the audience to experience the desired emotional conflicts.

Frankenstein and the Monster from Hell presents the past in a picturesquely Gothic way: "what little moonlight is able to penetrate the rising mist faintly illuminates the glistening gravestones." Here, as in *The Mummy*, the script suggests that the image should be as "busy" as possible, and there is a clear preference for a linear plot developed in labyrinthine settings. Hinds's script, like Sangster's, is preoccupied by transgressive individuals. The style of the film is constructed by the outrageously casual manner in which these transgressors respond to horrific events. As Frankenstein unconcernedly remarks of his bandaged but fast-unraveling monster, "he'll come apart any day now." In the script of *Frankenstein and the Monster from Hell*, history is a convenient disguise in which to express anxieties about the wholeness of the body, and a place in which to consider cannibalism, incest, and transvestism.[20]

If Hammer's scripts were the conduit through which the producers channeled their desires, what was the significance of other visual inputs into the films—those of the director and the production designer? Film historians confront the same difficulties as social historians; their interpretations are determined by the kind of evidence that has happened to survive. In the case of Hammer, this means that we have to grant a degree of prominence to the work of director Terence Fisher, because there is a range of interviews with him and papers by him that are not available from other directors.

Fisher had a sharp eye for detail, as shown by his corrections to Hinds's script.[21] His comments were practical and concerned pace and eye-line matches. He merely *nuanced* the script, excising the odd sentence. This was because there was a consonance between Fisher's own Manicheanism and that of the script. Fisher's notebooks display a preoccupation with history and myth. Costume films deployed the past because "putting them in period takes them out of present-day reality and gives them atmosphere and veracity." Fisher championed "the extension of the audience's current experience into its possibilities" by the use of history, and he favored films that depict it in a solid way.[22]

The emphasis on historical solidity is evident in a range of interviews. Fisher liked art direction that "tried to recreate period effects" and that would feed into "a fantastical materiality."[23] He preferred films set in the nineteenth century because of its combination of scientificity and the grotesque, which encouraged "a means of defamiliarisation. That is at the root of the costume genre."[24] He made an interesting distinction between those aspects of the film which should be realistic (acting style, set dressing) and those which should not (lighting, color, costumes); he preferred a mixed mode in which the only *overt* stylization was "in the period costumes but not in the actions or the feelings expressed."[25] Such an historicized mode should, he thought, be termed macabre rather than horror.[26]

Fisher was discussing the role of history in his own films; but what is significant is that his comments hold good for all Hammer's costume frighteners. In all of them, historical settings distance the audience from their own emotional habits; they lift the film of familiarity from the world of culture. Fisher resembles Holt, Gilling, Sharp, and the other directors far more than he differs from them. There is, of course, a consonance of visual style in all Hammer's historical horror films that should not be attributed to the directors but to the Production Designer for most of the films, Bernard Robinson.

Robinson enjoyed working within the financial constraints imposed by the producers; he claimed to be "the Marks and Spencer of his profession, giving value for the money."[27] Since the selection and sequence of projects was out of Robinson's control, he had to accommodate the dovetailing of sets. The only area in which he had artistic autonomy was in the arrange-ment of interior space and in the selection of objects that embellished the sets. Within these confines Robinson worked miracles of elegance and am-biguity. In the final scene of *Dracula*, the decor stimulates both the histor-ical imagination and a sense of anxiety. Pillars are habitually straight and are usually phallic signifiers: but in this scene they are curvaceous and fe-male. The staircase signals danger because it is precipitous and without banisters. The object which looks like a familiar globe turns out to be an astrolabe. The black-and-white marble floor is beautiful at first sight, but it has colored Greek inscriptions that would be indecipherable to most of the audience. So the state of mind inculcated by the decor is one of pro-found insecurity and overstimulus. Robinson's work for the banquet scene in *Curse of the Werewolf* merits detailed attention. The basic colors of the composition are neutral and restrained, and the clothes were all in shades of grey and beige. The central tapestry behind the cruel marquise is a blood red, which is picked out in the colors of the meat. The idea of blood is thus linked with fear and excess, and this is extended in a later scene in which the heroine is about to give birth. The room and the bed are white, but the bed-hangings and her wrap are in the same bloody shade. The werewolf child again evokes the themes of blood, aristocracy, and excess.

Great care was taken to ensure that the *mise-en-scène* (including cos-tumes and makeup) appeared authentic.[28] Nonetheless there was a flatness, or lack of inflection, in the way Hammer's sets delivered information about the past. Margaret Robinson suggested that her husband's sets were "very like you get in children's fairy story books . . . without the lighting these sets would have been like a children's puppet show set, very clear cut, very chunky, very clean, but once Jack Asher got at them with his lighting you forgot how toy-like they were."[29]

Jack Asher, Hammer's first lighting cameraman, who had worked on the Gainsborough costume melodramas, was removed by Hinds because he was too expensive.[30] He was replaced by Arthur Grant, who was faster. But even so, there is a broad similarity in all the lighting and camerawork in the costume horror cycle. Asher's placing of gelatin slides over some lenses, and his use of colored kick-lights, became standard Hammer prac-tice and an aspect of its visual style.

There was, therefore, a strong hierarchy in the textual languages in Ham-mer's costume films; because of the mode of production control, the script was the master discourse. In turn, the visual codes of decor, costume, and color depended on its guidelines. The result was a remarkable consonance in Hammer's interpretation of the past. Although different teams of script-writers and directors were employed to work on a historical period (on the Empire or Mummy cycles, say), the manner in which these periods were put to work were the same.

The historical periods evoked by Hammer were extensive. It pillaged prehistory, with films such as *One Million Years BC* (1966) and *When Dinosaurs Ruled the Earth* (1970), which dealt with ritualized contradictions between nature and culture. It reworked classic myths concerned with powerful females, in *The Gorgon* (1964) and *She* (1964). Ancient Egyptian culture was the point of reference for a range of films such as *The Mummy* (1959) and *Blood from the Mummy's Tomb* (1971), in which the past was a source of threat. Another cycle drew on aspects of late Victorian culture, typically *The Hound of the Baskervilles* (1959) and *Dr. Jekyll and Mister Hyde* (1971). The dubious ethics and negative effects of the British Empire were explored in a range of films including *The Stranglers of Bombay* (1959), *The Bridges of Kandahar* (1965), and *The Reptile* (1966). European culture was raided in *The Curse of the Werewolf* (1960), *Rasputin* (1965), and *Vampire Circus* (1972), in which the power of marginal figures such as gypsies and magi is assessed. In addition, both the Dracula and the Frankenstein cycles offered a specific interpretation of the past. In *Dracula* (1958) and *Countess Dracula* (1971), the Ruritanian idyll so beloved of 1930s British cinematic culture was dismantled, made darker, and converted into Transylvania. An imprecisely located mid-Europe was presented as the site of aristocratic excess in *The Curse of Frankenstein* (1957) and *Frankenstein Created Woman* (1967). What is significant about all the nineteenth-century films is that they emphasize the later and decadent aspects of the period, and the survival within it of energetic and residual groups.

Some periods were virtually ignored. The pre-medieval period was only used once (*The Viking Queen*, 1967). The medieval period was only represented by Robin Hood tales such as *Sword of Sherwood Forest* (1960), which deal with the period as the site of robust popular culture rather than courtly love. The seventeenth century was only deployed once, in *The Scarlet Blade* (1963). Significantly, this film reconstituted the cavalier ethic, and argued that the natural politics of England were those of the stylish Royalists, rather than the puritanical Roundheads, presented as subtle, devious, and unreliable. It is instructive to compare Hammer's *The Scarlet Blade* with the Associated-British *The Moonraker* (1958). In this film, with an almost identical story-line, the Puritan opposition is much more crudely conceived. But the main difference lies in the resolution of the narratives. In *The Moonraker*, the finale is predictable and neat. In *The Scarlet Blade*, the Cavaliers finally take refuge in a wood with a band of gypsies. With considerable flair, the film consigns both powerful but "forbidden" groups to the margins, combines them together and confers on them enormous symbolic weight.

Absences were remarkable, too. Hammer made no Roman films, probably because the Americans had captured the market with expensive epics such as *The Robe*. There was no Hammer treatment of the eighteenth century, doubtless because Augustan elegance and Enlightenment rationality were inimical to the tales of blood and ritual favored by the producers. There were no settings in the Regency period so beloved of earlier British film producers and popular novelists; this was probably because those forging Hammer's policy felt that the Regency was played out.

The class system in Hammer histories is dystopian; the films portray, in whatever period they deploy, an arrogant upper class and a sullen, oppressed underclass. This holds good for the Egyptian, Transylvanian, and Victorian settings. Social relations are rarely perceived from a capitalist/labor perspective. There is one exception to this, the extraordinary *Plague of the Zombies* (1965). Here, the Squire has learned the arts of Voodoo from abroad, but he uses his powers over the undead to create a compliant workforce in the tin mines, since the real workers cannot be persuaded to go there. Otherwise, Hammer histories evoke a world in which social contradictions are absent. Instead, archetypal contradictions are presented: male and female, human and animal, the quick and the dead.

What of marginal social groups and beliefs? In Gainsborough melodramas, those on the periphery of society generated energy because they were ambiguously poised between the sacred and the profane. But in Hammer histories, such groups are profoundly disruptive. Byronic aristocrats, gypsies and pirates are like loose cannon; fun to watch, but dangerous for those who get in the way. On the other hand, Catholicism, the religion peripheral to British state culture, plays a positive role in both Gainsborough and Hammer. In both, it operates as a source of exotic ritual; but in Hammer histories, it is more intensely present, because it is a form of religion which confers talismans. Its crucifixes and incense can be recycled into nostrums against pollution.

Hammer histories also enshrine forms of social explanation which are residual and outmoded. A recurrent metaphor which the studio evokes is that of mesmerism: that late-eighteenth and early-nineteenth phenomenon in which, through the action of eye or hand, one individual seems to cast another into submission and hypnotic trance. This motif is powerfully deployed in the Frankenstein, Dracula, and Mummy cycles, in *Rasputin, The Reptile* and many more. Mesmerism in Hammer histories is used as a way of *evading* explanations based on the power of social forces, and instead substitutes those based on personal magnetism and erotic charisma.

But Hammer's historical films do not celebrate sexual pleasure and power. The Dracula and Frankenstein cycles display a nervous preoccupation with the body: its orifices, its blood, its organs, its unfamiliar changes, its mutilation, and unratified penetration. The films provide a means of interrogating those anxieties, by broaching and breaking social taboos to do with the body. These taboos are usually dealt with in the context of a ritual; that is, by a pre-ordained and symbolic activity whose meanings are opaque. It is the business of the films to encourage the audience to distinguish between those rituals which pollute, and those which will ensure eventual freedom from defilement.[31]

It is the female body that arouses most intense anxiety in the Hammer histories. Some plots are structured around the oozings of female blood, which can be variously interpreted. Consider, for example, *Blood from the Mummy's Tomb*. This film was directed by Seth Holt, who died during production and who was replaced by Michael Carreras. The plot centers around the dead body of the Egyptian Queen Tera. On her death, her right hand is severed by the priests, who believe that they will thus inhibit her influence. Archaeologists subsequently attempt to control Tera's power, and each time one of them dies, the stump (seen in prolonged closeup) bleeds afresh. The blood symbolizes her occult and inhuman power. Female bleeding plays a similar role in *The Plague of the Zombies*. Here, both the heroines suffer deep cuts inflicted by the Squire. Each time he engages in Voodoo rituals, the wounds bleed copiously, and the bleeding (again seen in prolonged closeup) signifies the women's status as sacrificial victims. Or consider *Countess Dracula*, in which the menopausal heroine is rejuvenated by young virgins' blood. Its viscosity enables her to become, as it were, her own daughter, and to make love to her prospective son-in-law; this is a transgressive act, albeit an outrageously satisfying one, and the heroine is dispatched in consequence.

The oozing female blood in such films has a different function from the male blood which spurts in *Dracula Prince of Darkness* and elsewhere: it seems likely that menstruation is signified. This biological phenomenon, of course, habitually operates as a site of distaste and taboo in some cultures, and particularly in our own. Hammer histories evoke and intensify this distaste, and present female blood as polluting and "uncanny."

Many Hammer histories are concerned with manifestations of the monstrous-feminine: consider *The Reptile*, *Frankenstein Created Woman*, *The Vampire Lovers*, and *The Gorgon*. *She* is a prolonged meditation on the appropriate punishment to mete out to overreaching females. In the mythical country of Rider Haggard's original novel, "the women are what they please. We worship them, and give them their way because without them the world could not go on: they are the source of life."[32] But the Hammer film draws the line much more sternly between sacred and profane women. The protagonists enter the land of Ayesha (She-Who-Must-Be-Obeyed) through the legs of a giant statue of her. Entry into her dangerous historical country, where nothing has changed for thousands of years, is coterminous with entry into the mother of all, the consumer of all, and the lover of all, whose appetites will not be gainsaid.

The predatory Ayesha is strongly contrasted to the nurturing Ustane, who succors the hero. On Ayesha's orders she is thrown into a burning chasm, whose vaginal significance is rather overplayed. We see Ustane's

In *She* (1965), Ursula Andress exemplifies the Monstrous-Feminine who destroys what she nurtures. (Reprinted by permission of Hammer Film Productions Ltd., United Kingdom.)

remains: a dry dust, which is shocking but not disgusting. By contrast, Ayesha dies when she enters the immortalizing flame a second time, and this hubris results in her enforced return to the mortal condition. Her putrescence is wet and malodorous. The dry, nurturing dust of Ustane is preferable to the visceral slime to which Ayesha is reduced.

Clearly, then, Hammer used history and myth as a way of exploring male anxieties about the female body; its enveloping and accommodating nature, its seeming wounds, its connection with lunar cycles. One of the last Dracula films (*The Satanic Rites of Dracula*, 1973) contains a remarkable scene in which a young girl is ritually stabbed. There is a closeup of the bleeding wound, looking remarkably like a vagina. Through the good offices of the male celebrants of the ritual, her wound is healed; before our very eyes, the orifice is safely sealed and, raised from the dead, the girl turns and gives the camera a reassuring and complicitous smile. The magical ritual has worked. The manner of delivery here and elsewhere is one of *disavowal*. In most Hammer histories, the scripts encourage the audience to repudiate the importance of what they have seen or felt, and they achieve this through verbal or visual irony. Such disavowals neutralize the potential dangers of the spectacle.

In Freudian terms, of course, the process of disavowal is conceived as the habitual response of male fetishists to the absent object of their desire, which is the mother's phallus: "it is not true that, after the child has made his observation of the woman, he has preserved unaltered his belief that women have a phallus. He has retained that belief, but he has also given it up."[33] Freud's fetishists partake of the paradox of knowing something rationally, but then choosing to behave in what we can call a "nonetheless" manner. What is unique about the Hammer histories is that they invite viewers to replicate this psychic double-bind; and the ironies in the films co-opt the audience into a disavowal of sexual difference.

The representations of history at Hammer were precisely targeted at specific audiences. I suggested earlier that film audiences had changed radically since the 1940s, when they were predominantly female. Now they were predominantly male, and younger; and the canny producers at Hammer nuanced their product accordingly, making films which reoriented the costume genre in a radical way. The publicity campaigns are an important index of the studio's gender orientation. The posters and press books were unremittingly slanted toward a male audience. Many of the drawings showed the masculine protagonist in a version of the "missionary" position, or at least placed in a dominating role in the frame. The captions of the posters are significant, too. One urges the audience to see Dracula as "the Terrifying Lover Who Died—Yet Lived," clearly making subliminal reference to fears of *le petit mort*. Another advertises *Dracula Has Risen from the Grave* with the headline "You Can't Keep a Good Man Down," implicitly linking Dracula's revival with his tumescence (via blood, of course).[34] Some of Hammer's publicity techniques were more maladroit than this.[35]

There is little hard evidence on audience responses to Hammer films. However, there is one suggestive survey, which was carried out in 1963 on behalf of the Federation of British Film Makers. This established that those who preferred horror films did indeed tend to be male and younger. One young man's comment is illuminating:

"Sometimes I really want to go—like *Circus of Horrors*: you can shout out more at horrors. No, 'course I don't take them too seriously, they make me laugh better than comedies—sometimes they go too far, these horror pictures, (i.e., are taken too seriously): did you see that one where they had a minute break in case you wanted to die of fright—and after all it was only a head rolling down the stairs, dead funny."[36]

Circus of Horrors is a Hammer film, as is the second one referred to, *The Gorgon*. It is clear that for this viewer at least the scripts' disavowal techniques worked, insofar as the horrors were controlled. That was not the position taken by most film critics, who excoriated Hammer films so severely that the studio ceased giving trade showings.[37]

In conclusion, therefore, Hammer studios reoriented the costume genre in a radical way. They deployed history so as to make social and class contradictions invisible. This was a politically retrospective position in the 1950s and 1960s, a period in which class difference and class definition were in profound upheaval. In their sexual politics, too, Hammer histories were reactionary. In a period when many women were beginning to question patriarchal certainties, the studio presented the female body as the site of unspeakable danger and excess. In Hammer films, history was co-opted into the service of social and sexual disavowal.

NOTES

1. I have analyzed this process in detail for the period 1933–1950 in my book *Picturing the Past; the Rise and Fall of the British Costume Film* (London: British Film Institute, 1994).

2. Interview with Christopher Lee, in British Film Institute Special Collections, Hammer Film Productions, Item 17.

3. See, for example, material in P. Cook, *The Cinema Book* (London: British Film Institute, 1985): P. Hutchings, *Hammer and Beyond: The British Horror Film* (Manchester: Manchester University Press, 1993); R. Murphy, *Sixties British Cinema* (London: British Film Institute, 1992); D. Pirie, *A Heritage of Horror: The English Gothic Horror Cinema* (London: Gordon Fraser, 1973); D. Pirie, *Hammer: A Cinema Case Study* (London: British Film Institute Education, 1980); Vincent Porter, "The Context of Creativity: Ealing Studios and Hammer Films," in J. Curran and V. Porter (eds.), *British Cinema History* (London: Weidenfeld and Nicholson, 1983).

4. *The Hulton Readership Survey 1950–1955, Spending Habits of Cinemagoers* (London: Pearl and Dean, 1956), *The IPA National Readership Survey 1956–1957* and *ibid., 1959–1960*, and *The Cinema Audience: A National Survey* (London: The Screen Advertising Association, 1961).

5. *Films and Filming* (December 1958, January 1959).

6. Ibid., February 1958.

7. Hammer Film Productions in Special Collections, material on *Dracula Prince of Darkness*. See also "Lovers of *Frankenstein*: Are Horror Films Good Business?" in *The Economist* (December 6, 1958). There are plentiful references to profits; see, for example, material in Pirie, *Hammer*, and Murphy, *Sixties British Cinema*.

8. There is an amusing account of this in *Hammer Horror* (No. 6, August 1995).

9. These were technically British films and fulfilled quota requirements because an appropriate percentage of their production personnel were British. In 1955, the Americans only made six films in Britain; but in 1956 the figure was 17, in 1957 it was 27, and in 1958 it was 26.

10. See material in *Hammer Film Productions*, and in Pirie, *Hammer*. See also A. Aldgate, *Cinema and Society in the 1950s and 1960s* (Open University Unit OU420, 1992).

11. Letter from Antony Hinds to Vincent Montgomery, in Vincent Montgomery, *Hammer Film Production at Bray Studios*, unpublished M.A. Thesis (University of Westminster, 1987).

12. Interview with Len Harris, in Montgomery, *Hammer Film Production at Bray Studios*.

13. Letter from make-up man Phil Leakey to Vincent Montgomery, quoted in Montgomery, *Hammer Film Production at Bray Studios*.

14. See interviews with Ingrid Pitt and Antony Hinds in *Hammer Film Productions*. Part of the problem was shortage of floor space. From 1951 to 1968 Hammer was located at a country house called Bray, which was not extensive.

15. See interviews with Aida Young and Don Sharp in *Hammer Film Productions*. See also material from Antony Hinds in Montgomery, *Hammer Film Production at Bray Studios*. See also Porter, "The Context of Creativity."

16. See material in Harper, *Picturing the Past*, pp. 119–135.

17. Antony Nelson Keys produced and scripted *Frankenstein Must Be Destroyed* (1969). Michael Carreras produced and scripted *Slave Girls* (1966), *One Million Years BC* (1966), and *Creatures the World Forgot* (1971). Hinds scripted and produced *Phantom of the Opera* (1962), *Kiss of the Vampire* (1962), and *The Evil of Frankenstein* (1964). He also scripted *Captain Clegg* (1962), *The Reptile* (1965), *Frankenstein Created Woman* (1967), *Dracula has Risen From the Grave* (1968), and *Frankenstein and the Monster from Hell* (1974). Sangster scripted *The Curse of Frankenstein* (1957), *Dracula* (1958), *Revenge of Frankenstein* (1858), *The Mummy* (1959), *The Man Who Could Cheat Death* (1959), *The Brides of Dracula* (1960), *The Terror of the Tongs* (1961), *Pirates of Blood River* (1962), and *Devil-Ship Pirates* (1964). These lists only refer to historical scripts.

18. See shooting script of *The Mummy* in the British Film Institute Library. Of course, the freedoms of interpretation that were open to scriptwriters of historical vehicles were not open to those scripting contemporary dramas. See *Film and Filming* (September 1957).

19. Interview with Antony Hinds in *Hammer Film Productions*.

20. First Draft Screenplay, dated March 1972, in Terence Fisher Collection, British Film Institute Library. This is an interesting early version of the script because it shows Fisher's manuscript comments, cuts, and extra script pages.

21. See Fisher's copy of *Frankenstein and the Monster from Hell*, in Terence Fisher Collection Papers, British Film Institute Library. Here Fisher excises the judge's remark to the hero that "in a less enlightened age, you would have been sentenced to burn."

22. See large red notebook in Terence Fisher Collection. In the same place there

is an intriguing remark: "Melodrama—overstatement of the natural. Mine—understatement of the supernatural."

23. "Entretien Avec Terence Fisher," *Midi-Minuit Fantastique*, No. 7 (September 1963). Translation by the author. Fisher comments in this piece that costume is "a commercial stratagem."

24. *Midi-Minuit Fantastique*, No. 10/11 (Winter 1964/5). See also *Films and Filming*, July 1964, and an interview with Fisher in Item 35, Terence Fisher Collection.

25. *Mini-Minuit Fantastique*, no. 10/11 (Winter 1964/5).

26. *ABC Film Review* (November 1959).

27. Interview with Robinson's wife, Margaret Robinson, in *Little Shop of Horrors*, vol. 4: 70.

28. See letter from Roy Ashton to Vincent Montgomery in Montgomery, *Hammer Film Production at Bray Studios*. Here Leakey describes his historical research for makeup for *The Mummy*: "I endeavoured in historical drama to be quite correct."

29. Interview by Margaret Robinson with Vincent Montgomery, quoted in Montgomery, *Hammer Film Production at Bray Studios*. Interestingly enough, Hinds insisted that Robinson always got his way on matters of set design: see *Little Shop of Horrors*, vol. 4: 40.

30. *Little Shop of Horrors*, vol. 9: 96. See interview with Jack Asher in Montgomery, *Hammer Film Production at Bray Studios*. Asher had been trained by the great Arthur Crabtree.

31. I have found the analyses of Mary Douglas very useful as a way of conceptualizing aspects of ritual in popular culture: see M. Douglas, *Purity and Danger* (London: Routledge, 1966), *Natural Symbols* (London: Barrie and Rockcliff, 1970), and *Implicit Meanings* (London: Routledge, 1975).

32. Rider Haggard, *She* (London: Hodder and Stoughton, 1915), p. 120.

33. Sigmund Freud, "Fetishism," *Three Essays on the Theory of Sexuality*, Penguin Freud Library, Vol. 7 (Penguin: London, 1991), p. 353.

34. See an example in *Films and Filming* (July 1958), and *Hammer Horror*, No. 7 (September 1995). There is a range of posters and press books in the British Film Institute library.

35. Showings of *Dracula* were accompanied by posters encouraging patrons to become blood donors. Outrage ensued, and the posters were withdrawn, doubtless to the detriment of the Blood Transfusion Service: see *The Times* (July 7, 1958).

36. *Cinema Going in Greater London: A Study of Attitudes and Behaviour* (London: Marketing Trends Ltd., for Federation of British Film Makers, 1963), p. 65.

37. See the range of newspaper responses in the Hammer microfiches in the British Film Institute Library. An especially negative review is in *Tribune* (May 10, 1957). See also Derek Hill, "The Face of Horror," *Sight and Sound* (Winter 1958–1959). *Films and Filming* had a more measured position; see Peter John Dyer, "Some Nights of Horror," *Films and Filming* (July 1958), and Dr. Martin Grotjahn, "Horror—Yes, It Can Do You Good," in *Films and Filming* (November 1958).

8

Film Nazis: The Great Escape

Tony Barta

One of many marvelous Steven Spielberg moments in *Raiders III*: Indiana Jones and the treacherously beautiful Else (Harrison Ford and Alison Doody) have pantomimed their way as Scots tourists into the fairytale Bavarian castle where the former James Bond, Indy's father, is being held in a tower. The camera comes up to a ledge and spies down: "Nazis. I hate these guys." Being pantomime, where reversal is all, it is the moment of truth. "Nazis. We love them," say the creative and commercial geniuses of Lucasfilm, and they proceed in the next eighty minutes to show us why. A full-dress SS adversary in black uniform, heavy jaw, and piercing blue eyes, lots of machine-gunning field-grey goons bursting through doors and doing stunts on Wehrmacht-issue motor bikes, and swastikas everywhere. The crooked black cross of evil is cheerily emblazoned on Zeppelins and fighter planes, in airport foyers, and on automobile pennants. At a march past in the Reich capital, massed red banners fill the screen with a pageant of color the documentaries have only recently let us see—and now the big moment: Indy, in borrowed Nazi plumage, is face to face with his Führer. What does he do when confronted by the all-time greatest movie star? He gets his autograph.

How can we really hate those guys? The color, the action, the send-up keep us happy: anyone who wants to treat it too seriously should be sent back to the road sign that gives our heroes a choice of Venice or Berlin. And does it matter if they are mythic creatures rather than historical ones?

Film cowboys, tycoons, or femmes fatales aren't generally expected to re-semble the stockmen, corporate executives, or real women one might ac-tually have encountered in the past—why should it be any different for Nazis? Because, I'll argue, the mythic Nazi was from the very beginning the accompaniment of the nastier historical one and was designed—by the Nazis themselves—to create the cinematic representation of the future. Fairytale myths of the future are a free for all: under his black samurai helmet an archetypical Darth Vader (Dark Father? Death Invader?) can put the SS in space. In history there is a past, and there we need to keep check-ing that neither the imaginary Nazis nor the Nazi imaginary run off with the plot.

When Spielberg went to Auschwitz to film *Schindler's List* it was in his-torical earnest. The site of terrible actual events was meant to confer au-thenticity, the black and white cinematography would evoke the archive authority of documentary. The drama would use every trick of character and story development, of camera angles, lighting, editing, to create sus-pense and engagement over more than two hours. The test would be in separating drama from melodrama, history from fiction, conviction from suspension of disbelief. No one knows better than Spielberg the power of cinema to create its own world; everywhere critics recognized his success in making a film firmly removed from fantasy. At last rewarded with Best Picture and Best Director Oscars—and huge concurrent business for *Juras-sic Park*—he was long accustomed to critics who noted touches of senti-mentality, gratuitous spectacle, some lack of subtlety in character, story, and image. (Did the Shower Scene from *Schindler* really need those droplets against the light?) A larger problem goes beyond individual style. Spielberg knows that every movie refers to other movies; he is adept at paying hom-age to his predecessors. Yet here he seems only partly to have recognized—especially in his historically documented but classically configured SS vil-lain—how previous films power and disempower his own creation.[1]

The recognition that Nazis now belong to the repertoire of movie enter-tainment as much as to history is not new, and we know not to confuse cinematic representation with the practices of historians. However, I believe that the way images of Nazism first reached the screen and the process by which entertainment conventions helped the historical Nazis to escape, as it were, into the movies, pose problems for both historians and film theo-rists which are worth trying to pursue. We need both a comprehensive history and a sort of "Film Nazis: A User's Guide." What follows is cer-tainly written by an active user—which teacher of twentieth-century history is not?—but it is not compiled from the hours of late-night viewing and dedicated archive research that the true addict would get a kick from. I can't report on *Surf Nazis Must Die*, reputedly still doing solid business in American video stores, and I didn't persevere in my search for *The Goose Steps Out*, a British hit in 1942. So this will be a fearful disappointment to film buffs. My hope is that other users—purveyors and consumers of history on the screen—will take up some of the leads and begin to question much more intently how screen Nazis function historically.[2]

HITLER AS FILMMAKER

In a quite substantial, not at all metaphorical way, I see us as coping with a giant, sixty-year film epic in which the documentary record of the past and its reconstruction as fantasy have become inextricable in most people's understandings. For historical reasons in the development of screen media, the Nazis were able to create both the screen documentation and the images for subsequent fantasy as they developed their historical epic.[3] This is what prompted Hans-Jürgen Syberberg to undertake what is still the most radical reworking of the Nazi screen legacy. In his seven-hour *Hitler, a Film from Germany* he keeps reminding us that Hitler, the avid film consumer, was the author of a much more grandiose film production. He gives a key speech to Hitler's personal projectionist:

I am the man who knew Hitler's most secret wishes, his dreams, what he wanted beyond the real world. Every day two or three films: *Broadway Melody* with Fred Astaire, *Snow White* . . . Fritz Lang's *Nibelungen* . . . Yes, whoever controls films, controls the future, controls the world and there is only one future, the future of film and he knew it . . . I know that he really was the greatest, the greatest filmmaker of all time . . . Again and again, six to eight times in a row, he would watch films in order to burn into his memory every frame and every angle. And then I saw him bring the whole thing to a halt at the beginning of the war, no longer looking at feature films but only at newsreels alone with himself, . . . a war made on film exclusively for him.[4]

It was never, and this is the point of Syberberg's film, exclusively for him. It was first to exercise fascination over the German public and then over the rest of us. In the same year (1977) a very different, much more popular film also appeared in West Germany, Fest and Herrendoerfer's *Hitler, a Career*. The only thing the two films had in common was the starting point: Hitler as self-dramatizer and historical impresario. The way Fest and Herrendoerfer replay large slabs of Nazi-designed footage has probably done more to promote the Hitler mystique than to question it.[5] But it at least emphasizes how deliberately contrived the cinematic "live" staging was, and how carefully Hitler created his film persona for political effect—and for posterity.

We are so used to the combination of Hitler's image with oratory that we forget these performances were developed in the very first years of sound film. The instantly recognizable voice, the rehearsed pauses and gestures, the brilliantly barbered visual trademarks were crafted for the new medium.[6] To this day many people consider Hitler unlikely material for a star: don't listen to their movie tips. That he was the first and archetypal screen Nazi is of an importance hard to overestimate: his performance and its presentation on the screen was designed, literally, to upstage all others, to fix an image of the National Socialist movement and its dynamic Leader in the consciousness of a newly film-conscious world. His glamour role in *Triumph of the Will* was the most extravagantly produced of these promotions. His brief appearance in Riefenstahl's *Olympia* was perhaps almost as effective. Hitler liked to talk up the power of the spoken word in the set piece live encounter. He used two of the new media devices, aircraft and microphones, to inspired effect; and he used the reproductive technologies of radio and film to magnify the impact millions of times over. There is a telling clip near the beginning of *Hitler, a Career* which shows the Führer's Mercedes in a motorcade of camera cars. The cameramen filming from in front and behind are a major component of the whole show, and they are there to ensure it goes to a much larger audience than the crowd lining the route.

The audience—thanks to *Hitler, a Career* and other films recycling those same Nazi propaganda images—must by now number more hundreds of millions than Goebbels ever dreamed of, but he was a man of limited imagination. The global audience would certainly not have surprised Hitler, who knew that the epic he was creating for the film age would have no rival. It would give the world images of greatness, daring, and destruction that could function with equal force whether construed as good or evil. If the Thousand-Year Reich was a disaster blazing for only twelve years instead of a millenium, the historical box office, as it were, would certainly not suffer. The success of this epic, in part because it was an epic failure, is the first and last thing about film Nazis we need to understand. When history is made as cinema—and I do believe this was the first history consciously played out as film—we shouldn't be surprised that its imaginative hold increases as the reality recedes.

The idea that the "real" film was more important than any other was reiterated by Goebbels even as its end was in sight. Having drawn resources away from the front to complete *Kolberg*, the Nazi cinema's last, vast morale-boosting effort, he said (while the real town fell to the Russians):

Gentlemen, in a hundred years still another color film will portray the terrible days we are undergoing now. Do you want to play a role in that film which will let you live again in a hundred years? Every one of you has the opportunity today to choose the person he wishes to be in a hundred years. I can assure you that it will be a tremendous film, exciting and beautiful, and worth holding steady for. Don't give up![7]

What is it the Nazis had that will continue to make them irresistible to the movies? The Touch of Evil, of course, and its horrendous drive to destruction. The struggle of heroes and abused heroines to prevail against cruelty, the organized and disorganized killing, the disciplined power of the giant war machine. All this was built into the story from the start—though in the service of good, not evil. Violence, power, uncompromising victory were meant to be Coming Attractions when the movement was formed from the lost warriors of the 1914–1918 war. And because the movement would bring back purpose and discipline, visible in the willing obedience to the leader of the massed ranks of the led, much of the cinematic effect could be achieved in purely political action and pageantry. Hitler recognized that militarism, marching, and music were ready-made for a medium that loves a spectacle. His screen adaptation would have no competitor in action, content, and plot, and it would be the latest in modern fascist style. Before he had worked out the script of his epic he was designing the costumes and the sets. National Socialism as Dynamic Tableau was invented first as live presentation, experiential theater, and then refined for wider transmission and celebration by film.

There were willing helpers, unable to resist the symbiosis between fascist spectacle and film. Some were unsung newsreel cameramen, others made spectacular reputations. It will never matter how often Leni Riefenstahl repeats she was not a Nazi: she got the world hooked on Nazism, The Movie. Hitler couldn't have cared less whether her eyes shone with fanaticism or fascination: she knew how to make other people's eyes shine in places he would never see. *Triumph of the Will* matters not for the relatively small number of people who have seen all of it but for the millions over half a century who have seen some of it. It makes no difference if the original appears only in glimpses. The glimpses carry the grandeur and dynamism of the fascist propaganda spectacle. The title, chosen by Hitler himself, sums up the only historical message to be remembered. There was to be no banality, grubbiness, greed, or ordinary political ambition in the screen record of the Nazi movement, and no reminder of the institutionalized terror behind the spectacle.[8]

These images of the adored leader and the shining youth, the SS automatons later transformed into the Action Men of the newsreel war, are the film Nazis from the Third Reich that count, not any that were fictionalized in features. The first attempt at a heroic role model, *SA-Mann Brand (Stormtrooper Brand)* was a small-studio third-rater that couldn't be saved from "profound public indifference" by a grand premiere with thousands of storm troopers lining the streets.[9] The escapism which Goebbels knew was fundamental in the cinema could hardly attach to Nazis while they were politically in high earnest. More effort, and promotion, went into *Hans Westmar*, originally titled *Horst Wessel*, and into *Hitlerjunge Quex* (both late 1933). The ideological struggle between National Socialism and Communism is successfully made personal in both films, with more attention to artistic quality. History lived—many people took the staging of Horst Wessel's funeral to be a newsreel.[10]

The Nazis remained extremely cautious about letting movies interfere with reality while the original cast version was running. Neither Hitler nor Goebbels was enthusiastic about the early propaganda efforts; they both thought the public displayed discrimination in staying away. In the main, therefore, the political content of feature films produced in the Third Reich has to be sought elsewhere, in its absence from the main run of entertainment films (the most popular film of 1933 was the original *Viktor und Viktoria*, not less silly than the Blake Edwards remake) and in its displacement into the past. This was a potent ideological mix. While the political trauma was disguised by reassurance that it was business as usual in the everyday comedy of life and love, the lessons of Germany's weakness and greatness were played out on the grand canvases of the eighteenth century with Otto Gebühr showing that Frederick the Great also had to make tough decisions to save the nation in times of peril. The mixture of history, fantasy, and megalomania in the production of *Kolberg* was a fitting climax.

The positive images of epic heroism in defense of hearth and home and civilized values were much more important than the famous negative images that made one or two films notorious. Even during the war there were relatively few portrayals of Germany's enemies in crude propaganda terms. There were a couple of beastly commissars and bloated British plutocrats and, of course, *The Eternal Jew*. This was a singular, and risky, experiment. For most people, used to having their cinema programmed as newsreel and fiction feature, having it taken over by crudely propagandist documentary was not an acceptable wartime sacrifice. More palatable in fixing stereotypes into plausible form were again the servings of the past, where costumed fantasy could not be threatened by the contradictory perceptions of the present. The two powerful anti-Semitic features released—significantly— in 1940 followed this model. Neither *The Rothschilds* nor *Jew Süss* were to be promoted as anti-Semitic films, Goebbels instructed. Audiences should take them for histories in the form of stories, showing "Jewry as it really is."[11]

Showing Nazism "as it really is" never troubled the Nazi manipulation of the cinema. The escape from history into history was a cinema staple everywhere. In Germany it had the added attraction of leaving the present to be filled by real heroes. And if the Third Reich became history rather prematurely it at least supplied the Nazis' cinematic epic with a dramatically unsurpassable closure. Everything else about the Nazi cinema paled before this blaze, and it remained by far the most intractable problem for the future to deal with. It completed the imaginary of National Socialism which Hitler had taken such trouble to launch into the future. The role of cinema as entertainment was always kept separate from this grander enterprise. So innocuous did German fiction films seem to Allied censors after the war that of 1363 features produced in the Third Reich they found it necessary to ban only 208.[12]

By then, though, the action had shifted, to Hollywood.

HOLLYWOOD'S NAZIS

A few weeks before the outbreak of war in Europe, when Hitler had been in power for more than six years, there had still not been one Nazi in an American film. That might seem a little curious on a couple of counts. For one thing, many of Hollywood's most successful directors in that period were German and Austrian. Not all had come as refugees from Nazism, but many were exiles as a result of the Nazi ban on Jews working in the film industry. Furthermore, virtually the whole of American motion picture production was—just as the Nazis said—in the hands of Jews.[13] They were strong-minded men, and quite capable, as was later seen, of throwing their weight to a cause. What held them back?

First, their business interests. Germany was the second-biggest export market for American films; millions of dollars of income could disappear overnight. Second, in common with many Jews in Germany, they thought that provoking the Nazis would only make the position of their co-religionists worse. The Nazis were very good at keeping this idea in the forefront of people's considerations. Third, there was powerful isolationist—and Nazi—agitation in the United States reinforcing the prior reasons and bringing into focus the fourth. It is the one at the heart of Neal Gabler's book, *An Empire of Their Own: How the Jews Invented Hollywood*. What drove most of the movie moguls, Gabler argues, was their desire to break out of the world of immigrant furriers and scrap metal salesmen (Adolf Zukor and Louis B. Mayer, respectively) and to identify with all things truly American. They were thus peculiarly exposed to the anti-Semitism that tinged America Firsters, and determined not to move ahead of the consensus about America's interests. They were desperately anxious not to be tarred with Communism. When Maurice Rapf, son of an MGM executive, returned with positive impressions of the Soviet Union, Harry Warner raged, "I don't want to talk to no goddamn Communist. Don't forget you're a Jew. Jewish Communists are going to bring down the wrath of the world on the rest of the Jews."[14] His fear, in 1934, chimed in perfectly with the message Hitler sent out to the world while he filled the first concentration camps. Finally it dawned on the moguls that this paranoid strain could be turned onto the Hitlerite menace as well: the Nazis entered American films not as swastika'd storm troopers but as subversives and fifth-columnists—as a threat within. *Confessions of a Nazi Spy* (Warner Brothers 1939) is usually cited as America's first movie recognition of a Nazi threat; German settings, in *The Mortal Storm* and *I Married a Nazi* came only after war had broken out.

The way the Nazis made their entry into what Sklar has called "Movie Made America" was portentous. America may be unjustly famous for being preoccupied with itself, but internal threats, from Salem to the McCarthy hearings, have always been the most real. The formative wars in America were civil wars; questions of loyalty were central, and traitors could look just like you or me. The external enemies—Injuns, Germans, Japs, Russkies—all took on a kind of cardboard cut-out, comic book quality. While Nazis were also internal enemies their movies had a chance of character development, a hint of human complexity before the rigid ideologue was unmasked. As soon as the script writers and producers began to look abroad, to make movies about European conflicts, they were at hazard. Almost all those who did it with success were themselves European, re-creating something they knew at least in part. Hitchcock set *Foreign Correspondent* (1940) in London, Fritz Lang directed George Sanders in *Man Hunt* (1941), and it was Douglas Sirk (Detlev Sierck) who turned John Carradine into a repulsive Reinhard Heydrich in *Hitler's Madmen* (1942). Sometimes the bully-boy Nazis were real enough but the Americanization came through in the Good German hero. In *The Mortal Storm* (Metro 1940), Hollywood's first toe-in-the-water of Jewish persecution—much milder in the movie than was then going on—it's Jimmy Stewart who needs the largest pinch of salt.

If the German writers, directors, and actors helped Hollywood keep the stereotypes and disembodied Nazi iconography of later years at bay, they also help launch them on their career. The full-fledged jackbooted Beasts of Berlin in *Underground* still stand up well to any competition. The icy torturer of our blonde heroine has black SS livery, low regard for human life, and low camera angles to match. If he misses out on caricature it is because the melodrama is successfully pitched as close to the Nazis' own stereotype of ruthlessness as to the movie thrill of the chase.[15] Now, of course, we can see more than a hint of the future *Raiders* villains in *Underground*—and *Kiss of the Spiderwoman* already primping in the dressing room.

To send the whole thing up, to mock the grandiosity of the Third Reich, to make the hitherto invincible enemy bumblers and buffoons, was an alternative strategy from the outset. It had a serious political purpose, as Chaplin made explicit in the speech at the end of *The Great Dictator*, a huge and politically potent hit in 1940. But there were intimations of a future problem, too. Even as the real Nazis were fastening a ruthless occupation on conquered Europe, audiences in America and England coped effortlessly with screen Nazis you couldn't believe would hurt a fly. In *To Be or Not to Be* (also made in 1940 but not released until 1942), Jack Benny, having just impersonated "Concentration Camp Erhard," finds he has to deal with a genuine Nazi—if that's how we can even for a second regard Sig Ruhmann. Everyone is acting their hearts out, and we want to enjoy him doing it as well. The Lubitsch touch applied to morale-boosting comedy showed that the Nazis who took themselves so solemnly could be defeated in the theater of life even by this bunch of Polish Jewish hams. ("What you are I wouldn't eat," says one.) If only the Nazis had been less intent on carrying their fantasies into the theater of the world. As a screen spoof it's all in the timing, but the rigidity in the real Hitler's "Heil myself" was a threat to human existence.[16]

The Jack Benny forces get the better of their heel-clicking conquerors because they can think fast and they have a cause. The Hitler image is deflated, but at the same time let loose from its historical constraints. The entertainment Nazis act as political cartoons during the war years because they are caricaturing a political reality. Once the regime is dead they are set for their long and independent life.

British films, most classily Leslie Howard's *Pimpernel Smith* (1941), also liked to show the enemy as far from invincible, easily outwitted by democrats and liberals. Howard was such an effective propagandist, in his broadcasts to America as well as his films, that his death in April 1943 was suspected of being plotted by the Germans. To cover both sides of the Atlantic their plot would have had to deal with some other powerful screen presences. The Three Stooges were doing their bit with *You Nazty Spy, I'll Never Heil Again* and more in the same vein. Donald Duck chipped in with *Der Führer's Face*. A less successful export was George Formby, the most popular screen star in England. *Let George Do It* (1940) was tried out as *To Hell with Hitler* in New York.

It wasn't all fun. But even the *really* nasty Nazis were there to be outwitted by our chaps. The typical films were the spy and resistance thrillers (*Underground*, Fritz Lang's *Hangmen Also Die*, Fred Zinnemann's *The Seventh Cross*), combat films for Dana Andrews and John Wayne (though not for Ronald Reagan), and Awful Germany films, warning of the corruption of German youth. As Beast in Chief the movies were very lucky to have Erich von Stroheim (*Five Graves to Cairo, The North Star, Storm Over Lisbon*) left over from the First World War, where the German Officer stereotype was still allowed touches of chivalry. He helped the trend to separate the German military from Nazism—with an effectiveness that Wehrmacht officers busy saving themselves from association with the regime at its defeat could hardly have dared to hope for. In the biggest and most lasting hit, *Casablanca*, there is sentimentality, menace, and heroism, but no screen Nazis of either the fiendishly evil or ludicrously heel-clicking kind. This rendering harmless found support in the standard configuration of Stalag films which continued after the war. By the time we get to *Stalag 17* (Billy Wilder, 1953) the enemy are about to become allies, and even Otto Preminger as Kommandant seems a less than sinister opponent for William Holden and the boys. The game of escape and discovery produces deep feelings like: "I'll tell you one thing about those Nazis. They sure ain't kosher." The harmless Nazis of *Colditz* and the cuddly Nazis of *Hogan's Heroes* aren't far off.

At the end of the war the Nazis should have become more serious, less gentlemanly. The terrible atrocity of the death camps was uncovered, and Nazis were no longer enemies but criminals. In the movies it didn't happen, not for fifteen years. Instead—crucial in this story—a new threat, again internal as well as external, filled the space of current political concern. Collapsing defeated fascism into aggressive communism under the device of totalitarianism helped the new menace free the imaginary of Nazism from its historical referent. The *imagined* historical reality of Nazism became a historical reality in its own right, brewing potently in that cultural and psychological realm where imagination and ideology work their way on each other. Before 1945, fiction, documentary, and a sense of actuality had all been tied to current history; now there were only the Nazi-generated images and their Hollywood opposite numbers. They functioned best, ideologically, as generalized icons of evil in the almost hysterical Cold War atmosphere of threat. Everyone could more or less remember what they referred to, but the need to pursue Nazism into its history, to understand it in context, was overriden.

The urgent agenda now became to rehabilitate the German fighting man, again the front line defense against the Red Peril—just as Hitler had always told him he was. "Good Guys Wear Grey," as John Mariani put it, and have to fight and die as decently as they can even when their political leaders are bad.[17] James Mason's Rommel in *The Desert Fox* (1951) was more gallant than von Stroheim's (he was a bit meaner in *The Desert Rats* two years later). In *The Young Lions* (1958), Maximilian Schell, the new Screen Nazi *par excellence*, starts on his career in the Wehrmacht and takes the very pretty ice blond Marlon Brando along with him. He takes him to his death, and there is enough realism in the desert, in the hospital, in the meeting with the concentration camp commandant behind the collapsing front, to keep alive some misgivings about integrating the Nazi soldier with the Dean Martins and Montgomery Clifts reluctantly doing their duty for America.[18] The contrast with America was foregrounded in another carefully historical feature, *Judgement at Nuremberg* (1961). It used documentary footage, German actors (including Marlene Dietrich), and its premiere coincided with the sentencing of Eichmann in Jerusalem.

Sometimes in the 1960s we were reminded that the German way of death hadn't got them very far (to *Hitler, the Last Ten Days*) and that it might take all of us even further—with *Dr. Strangelove* (1961). Then, in the 1970s, possibilities for identification with the German Fighting Man went full bore. *The Eagle Has Landed, A Bridge Too Far, Cross of Iron* were all released in 1977.[19] This wasn't the Fascinating Fascism that Susan Sontag writes about; it was a detachment of Nazism from fascism, its installation in the combat pantheon where *Gallipoli* heroes also go when they've been stopped for eternity, frame-frozen in mid-charge toward the machine guns. James Coburn as Corporal Steiner is in the midst of the mayhem Pekinpah serves up in *Cross of Iron*, and his manhood matters more than any political messages. If those are the Russkies he's mowing down (in the real war they were our galant antifascist allies) it only seems natural:

they've been the enemy as long as most people at the movies can remember. Of course Steiner does, briefly, have to pause for an encounter with the softer sex, because his blood-soaked derring-do has earned him the obligatory rest sequence in hospital. None of that soppy *Farewell to Arms* stuff for our Wehrmacht hero, though: he belongs to death, to duty, to masculinity, and mateship. When he sees a truck with his unit heading back for the front on go his cap and his tunic. Love and happiness, or at least their temptation in female form, are left sitting on the bed.

Am I making too much of this? Or the subsequent voyeuristically set-up scene in which Steiner's patrol encounters a group of Russian women soldiers? There's an attempted rape, an emasculation, almost copybook from the sexual/military paradigm in Theweleit's *Male Fantasies*. Steiner remains throughout the contained, honorable, dead-inside Man of Iron. To see this as just substitute America, or pre-Rambo box office, is to catch part of the success, including the success it had in Germany. But the male fantasy it repackages for a new generation is also Hitler's fantasy, the flower of German manhood playing out their blood sacrifice for his newsreels. I see the cross-cultural appeal here in sexual-political terms because that's where all the signs point—any other appeal of fascism is splattered out.

For historical understanding it gets murkier yet. The alliance between the "normal" male sexuality of a Corporal Steiner and gory death was counterpointed from very early on by cinematic suggestions linking Nazism with sexual deviance. According to Ilan Avisar, the connection was first made by Rossellini in *Rome Open City* (1945) and again in *Germany Year Zero* (1946).[20] Visconti's *The Damned* (1969) made fascination with the imagery of Nazism more sexually fetishistic, and openly associated with sexual violence, than any previous film from a leading director, and it established a genre that other Italian filmmakers apparently could not resist. Neither could some of the stars. From *The Damned* to *The Night Porter* (Liliana Cavani 1974) and *Salon Kitty* wasn't a long journey, and Dirk Bogarde, Charlotte Rampling, and Helmut Berger were willing to risk going a good deal of the way. Mostly it's the women who have to be the attracted subjects and abused objects, but not invariably. If Helmut Berger rapes his mother in *The Damned*, Lina Wertmuller has an almost equally grisly fate in store for Giancarlo Giannini in *Seven Beauties* (1975). The homophobic Captain in *Cross of Iron* (Maximilian Schell again—and it's obvious he wants to be in it himself) puts his own unsavory slant on Nazi kitsch as erotic fantasy. For some admirers of Visconti as director here was a major attempt to comprehend the past through art. For others this tendency of representation was the worst perversion.

One emerges from *The Damned* [wrote Richard Schickel] with the strong impression that the yeast causing the rise of the Third Reich was exotic depravity—transvestism, child molestation, incest. No one denies that the pre-war German power

elite was, to put it mildly, an unhealthy organism. But to imply a cause-effect relationship between sexual perversion and political perversion is both historically
inaccurate and socially irresponsible. For it has an odd, insulating effect on us,
making us feel that totalitarianism is a rare bloom, one that can flower only in very
special soil.[21]

Michel Foucault and Saul Friedländer have taken up different aspects of
the association between eroticism, unerotic historical realities, and fantasies
that appear to work mainly on the level of kitsch. For some 1970s wearers
of SS insignia perhaps it was kitsch without fantasy, for others the full
blown "concentration camp." In either case it would appear sensible to
come back to the special nature of movies as medium—that environment
of brilliantly present light in past-free dark, where future consequences beyond the engulfing narrrative have no place. Historical associations are
absent or contingent precisely when the past is most vividly a present.[22]
The appearances may not carry the "substance of history" much beyond
the material substances denoted, and the connotations may be elemental in
ways as likely to be shallow as deep. The black SS regalia might conjure
up violent death, or might just look good. The appeal may be less to repressed fascism or fetishism than to repressed kinds of style. Either way we
need to recognize the combination of continuities that screen Nazis quarantine and stimulate. There was something both safe and dangerous in
loading all the ambivalences about rigid repression and violence as liberation into Hitler's lovingly crafted costumes. He expected the movies to be
unable to resist the apotheosis of masculinity's long love affair with the
uniform, and he keeps being proved right. In the actual past and in the
movie rerun, this is the only time men get to parade about in all that
marvelous gear. At least some contemporary references have got better:
where Riefenstahl and Cavani helped frame uniformed fascism with sim-
pering women, the men strutting their stuff in the eighties help frame the
fashion shots of Ms. Doody's self-possessed Nazi chic.

The *Raiders* films, even more than the Hitler wave of the 1970s, might
seem to mark the high point of the Great Escape: the escape of the Nazis
from history into the movies. In fact they are a lightheartedly ironic coda.
Virtually from the beginning, I have tried to show, Nazism inhabited a
kind of fantasy made for the cinema. It was where an epic larger than life,
sustained by a nostalgic saturation with death, belonged. The problem for
the later cinema was to reverse the Nazi heroics. Some directors—most
strikingly Fassbinder in *Lili Marleen*—knew how to invert and reinvert
vice, virtue, and movie vision round blazes of light and emblazoned uniforms. Less gifted practitioners expected the costumes of the drama to
speak for themselves. Since the Nazis could not be the heroes, their mythic
power was tapped as a metaphor for evil. Evil itself—this was meant to be
forbidden under the old Hollywood code—seemed to be the hero. Neither

the content nor the victims of the evil were ever clear; it was in fact Nazism without evil.

HOLOCAUST NAZIS: TELEVISION'S SUCCESS AND FAILURE

Holocaust (1978) was meant to put a stop to this fascination, to reconnect Hitler and his followers with the most terrible part of historical fascism. The epic family drama for the small screen was a serious and important attempt to show the generation born after the war what Nazism was and did. But there are big problems. The absorption of fascism as a whole into the genocide of the Jews is only one of them. More important is the losing battle against the imaginary of Nazism. If the new generation had no personal memory of the war, they did have some memory: movie memory. The war created on the screen was now joined by television narrative convention. Where *Holocaust* succceeded it succeeded with and in spite of these conventions. Where it failed it allowed the conventions to integrate the Nazi imaginary into the repertoire of soap. It did worse. It made genocide and the death camps part of that repertoire. Henceforth they would be the staples, the new powerhouse of the Nazi imaginary.

It might seem a most signal victory. The death camps were the one thing Hitler was determined to exclude from the film record. When the historical epic was complete there would be no memory of them. Filming was strictly prohibited at every murder site. Now film—and again Jews as filmmakers—had stepped in where both had been forbidden. Their version of the past would win the future. Photographic documentation of atrocity is incorporated into the fiction narrative record, and genocide as National Socialist policy is shown in its formation as well as its execution. Further, the character of Eric Dorf problematizes the standard presentation of the "armored" SS. We see the process by which a nice German boy is made into a desensitized administrator of killing. In one of its leading roles *Holocaust* gave the world a new Nazi: unheroic, weak, almost effeminate, a fragile masculinity held up by the black uniform. Whose male fantasy could identify with such a mummy's boy murderer? And fully human men, Dr. Weiss and the Warsaw Ghetto fighters, are offered as role models and heroes.[23]

I'm not convinced that either of these victories over the Nazi imaginary were real. The weakling Nazis of more recent films—Hoess in *Sophie's Choice*, Wilfried in *Heimat*, Höfgen in *Mephisto*, Goeth in *Schindler*—are a big improvement on the old ones where only the black armor was visible, but there's a way to go before that armor loses its attraction. In fact such made-for-television caricatures as David Warner's Heydrich and Ian Holm's Himmler leave only the uniforms with historical authority—and the deeds. An attempt to recapture the escaped Nazis and make them real perpetrators of a real crime needs more than juxtaposing a plainly actorish set of SS chiefs with the photographic record of atrocities they (and the audience of millions) have projected for them on the screen. Nor is recreating the atrocities of Gestapo torture and death camps in "gripping drama" the answer. This, I think, is the source of disquiet admirers and critics of the series share. The star of the show is the terrible, scarcely imaginable crime, and the enormity of genocide has given such a massive infusion of power to the perpetrators that they are likely to run with it forever.

War and Remembrance (1989) attempted a decade after *Holocaust* to throw every television and Hollywood resource (money, big stars, length, literature, publicity) at bringing to the small screen the largest historical perspective imaginable.[24] There would be statesmen at the top—Churchill, Roosevelt, and a grotesquely manic Führer—and the fates of ordinary people, some of them European Jews, at the bottom. In the middle would be a tired American hero (Robert Mitchum), his pert British girlfriend, and some awfully-played German functionaries and SS officers. Once again the immense documentary effort of the production, the incorporation of wartime archive footage, the location authenticity, "filmed on site at Auschwitz," is undermined by the hammy conventions. (The most striking case in point is the parody of Rudolf Hoess required of the actor who made him so plausible in *Sophie's Choice*.) Wouk's story tried hard to be a history, but that was in a book. Television "docu-drama," it seems, is only ever a site for television. When we finally arrived at the gas chamber, was anyone anywhere shaken to their depths?

ESCAPE AND REMEMBRANCE

While *War and Remembrance* was being made, Reagan, the first movie president, went with Chancellor Kohl to Bitburg. They were there to bury the Nazi imaginary in politics, to show they knew it was now sustained only by the movies.[25] They were both a little taken aback to find that the war did still have a real remembrance, and they hastily scheduled a visit to Belsen as well. Recent events in the Germany that was soon thereafter reunited have made people wonder whether the Nazi imagination has gone from European politics. In 1992 people were again being burned, but by kids for whom Hitler's policies had only the most elemental meaning. Certainly some were inspired by Hitler's epic, by the memory of German military sacrifice he swore would rekindle the flame. Their attraction to prejudice, exclusion, and self-assertion inevitably attaches to Nazi references in Germany, present in ways which do not depend on the movies. But glorification of unjustly rejected grandfathers and bits of Nazi memorabilia do not make a Nazi movement. As is the case in Germany's neighbors, the danger is more likely to come from politicians of the right careful not to be caught near a swastika.

In Germany the ongoing problems of dealing with the past would exist even if sixty years of screen representations had been suppressed. Yet the escape of the Nazis from history into the movies continues to have important historical effects. Screen melodrama provides a valuable foil for the actual nationalist right because it can easily distinguish itself from the jack-booted image. And Nazi apologists around the world can point to the lack of film documentation of gassings to suggest that Jews needed to make films to give authenticity to a fiction. The hope that graphic depiction drawn from genuine testimony—most recently in *Schindler's List*—will stop people from saying "it didn't happen" is a vain one. The very fact that memory has been converted first into the medium of fiction (Keneally's novel) and then into the fiction medium par excellence (Hollywood "realism") will exacerbate the rejection of testimony in those who would in any case reject it. There is no way out of this fallacy of authenticity for naturalistic television drama or for classical feature film.

The power of fiction film to constitute German history, especially outside Germany, is perhaps best illustrated by a film that keeps its distance from Holocaust images while playing on an inchoate amalgam of propaganda images in a vividly naturalist setting. Many people who cannot recall where they saw the adoring crowds rapturously reaching out to touch their Führer can straightaway cite the scene in *Cabaret* where the blond and shining boy stands up to sing "Tomorrow Belongs to Me." Very possibly he is the most powerful Screen Nazi since Hitler—and his song more widely known than any actually sung in Germany. The completely fictional sequence, evoking the Nazi's own Hitler Youth publicity, has by now become an independent historical actor of extraordinary influence. From a documentary-style observation of Nazi bullyboys and assorted Sunday afternoon drinkers in a Bavarian beer garden, we recall the clear solo voice as it impels all the "ordinary Germans" one by one to stand and join the swelling chorus. That both the song and the episode are pure inventions seems only to have boosted their power as historical testimony.[26]

Much as I admire *Cabaret*, I cannot think of any Germans who would see anything like their experienced reality in this scene, and neither Goebbels nor Riefenstahl would have had the gall to invent it. Perhaps it has escaped criticism because it occurs in a musical: very few people, even in America, have claimed their idea of Nazism was formed by *The Sound of Music*. In genre terms, *Cabaret* is not a musical—we don't recall its characters bursting into song to celebrate their feelings for each other—it is a cunningly made historical drama with brilliantly crafted musical propulsion. Its plot and subplot (poor Jewish boy wins rich Jewish girl) carry the gathering menace of Nazism in ways few could take exception to. There are good Germans, innocent Germans, and cynical Germans, and the Nazis are not grotesques. At the end they swim facelessly in the audience watching the grotesques on stage. Yet this reversal also does its bit for the Nazi imaginary. Leaving to one side the energies of Bob Fosse, Liza Minelli, and Joel Grey, Nigel Andrews suggests that like *The Damned* and *Salon Kitty*, "*Cabaret* derives most of its vitality not from the insipid love story at the centre but from the tangy, opulent corruption at the edges."[27]

The American rendition of their past that most influenced Germans also provoked the strongest German rebuttal. *Holocaust* moved Edgar Reitz to speak of German history being appropriated for American profits, and to make sixteen hours of *Heimat* (labeled "Made in Germany") in retaliation. A relatively small English-speaking audience has seen the televised version of *Heimat*, yet even among the discriminating and well-educated group who followed a subtitled German drama on a minority channel there was dismay at the absence of Nazis. Wilfried, the homegrown SS man, was not chilling enough, the massacre in Russia too matter of fact. And for some critics, the political context of National Socialism was not sufficiently visible. In the detailing of village life it appeared to have been actively suppressed.[28]

There are two problems here. One has to do with recapturing the German past and the other with recapturing the film Nazis who have escaped from it. This audience knew they would not be getting the repertoire of Nazis we genuinely love to hate, the sleazes who assault Meryl Streep in *Holocaust* and *Sophie's Choice* (she has the same ordeal, with the same expression on her face, in both movies) or Laurence Olivier in *Marathon Man*. Yet they wanted a version of the German past in which the real evil underlying these icons of evil fitted. The documentary past, perhaps: all the documentaries have been about evil. So it was bound to be discomforting— for some German critics, too—to have a past in which evil didn't dominate at all. Once a past is rendered in terms of memory rather than "history" its stories are likely to be very different from the Big Story history has always had an impulse, perhaps a duty, to tell.

Can real Nazis—attached both to experience and to historical knowledge—be presented in film stories? Can they help us understand the realities of German fascism as well as the contingencies of encounter, ignorance, and memory? Yes, they can. Probably the stories need to be made close to the European experience they depict, the Germans need to speak German, and the action needs to cut across the standard Nazi imaginary in some way. There are dozens of European films, made in all countries occupied by the Germans, that have experimented with naturalism, recollection, and distancing effects. Most of them work for audiences far from the experience, but the experience seems to have given them historical and artistic grounding. Nothing will take us closer to the murderous ideological core of Nazism than the unflinching realism of Klimov's *Come and See* (USSR, 1984). The less horrific ambience of Malle's *Lacombe, Lucien* (France, 1974) or *Au revoir, les enfants* (1987) has its own power. In Germany the banality of everyday evil, as Nazism came to dominate everyday life, was credibly delineated for a huge television audience in Egon Monk's two-part dramatization of *The Oppermanns* (West Germany, 1983). Comedy can of course be as effective as solemnity. Filmed from a stage play, *Der Bockerer* (*The Stubborn Mule*, Austria, 1985) brings to the screen aspects of Austrian character and experience Austrians can recognize and outsiders can understand. Schlöndorff's *The Tin Drum* (1979) makes fun of uniformed Nazis in a context of menace, ordinary life, and grotesque.

If American comedy—the *Raiders* epics, *The Producers*, or Mel Brooks' remake of *To Be or Not To Be* (1984)—goes for laughs rather than enlightenment, *The Pawnbroker* (1965), *Sophie's Choice* (1982), and *Reunion* (1990) demonstrate that not all American drama is ruled by the common denominators of television. In the larger company of European cinema *Schindler's List* (1993) is not the event that publicity and excellent timing in Spielberg's career made it, but it does show that an American director, by faithful research, careful casting, and skilled employment of classic cinema narrative, can create a convincing depiction of the Nazis at their worst. Whether Spielberg's (serious) addition to the pantheon of screen Nazis—Ralph Fiennes as Amon Goeth—will evoke the calculation, ideology, brutality, and panicky behavior of an SS commanding officer under pressure or rather a bundle of dangerously nutty characteristics already loaded into the screen by Brando, Schell, and hundreds of lesser lights has to be doubted. Whatever feeds the imaginary of Nazism can hardly be expected to create clarity in historical focus.

What kind of film can bring the imaginary of Nazism itself into focus is the final question. The narrative conventions of feature film and television make it almost impossible to reflect on movie messages of character, plot, and genre. Documentary, we need to remind ourselves, is not necessarily better off. Because of its dependence on Nazi-generated images (which include those "captured" by Allied film crews at Nazi atrocity sites), the images feed the imaginary in the way the Nazis intended. Claude Lanzmann tackled this problem by refusing to incorporate archive footage in *Shoah* (France, 1986). His success was striking but not complete.[29] Words, faces, encounters, sites, connect past policies and human suffering with the present and provide space for human response away from the noise and action emblems of the Nazis' own cover story. More radical German filmmakers have tried to devise strategies for opening the whole complex of film and history to scrutiny. Alexander Kluge, in *Die Patriotin* (1979) and other films, makes montages of past and present, individual enquiry and collective assumption, the daily realities of work contexted in a history of oppression, war and myth. A history teacher with a spade, he suggests, and a meditation on the knee of a soldier blown to bits, might get us closer to the realities of the past than the recycling of written and screened constructs usually passed off as meaningful.[30] Syberberg, determined to reduce the

Nazis below the scale of their own spectacle, made his *Hitler, a Film from Germany* (1978) in a studio with puppets, dummies, and cabaret actors. Certainly this is an extreme antidote to both kinds of film Nazis, dramatized and documentary, and one can understand what drove him to it. But recapturing the Nazi imaginary escaped into the movies is perhaps too tall an order for a film, even one that relies largely on pre-filmic theater, masque, and words.

Words, hours of words. For Syberberg "film is the most important art form the democratic twentieth century has produced," so his project is to attack the representation, the spectacle in which mass fantasies focused on Hitler's figure. He thought he would be able "to unmake the *image* of Hitler, to disclose the fundamental *void* of the Nazi projection of the masses: the absent body of Hitler."[31] His film does make its (non-mass) audience consider how the focus on the absent Hitler only refuels the fantasies. Replacing the Nuremberg rallies with an interminable discourse by Hitler's valet on the precise timing of the Führer's breakfast or his changes of underpants shows how the Allies' policy of blowing up his houses and palaces can't stop the virus of obsession multiplying in almost any site. Kitsch can stand in for grandeur or terror, and relieve the imagined reference of all connection to historical reality.

I'm convinced the condition Syberberg diagnosed in Germany, where people couldn't face up to where they stood with Hitler, is also endemic among us, his enemies. We are more like our enemies than we like to admit. The imperialism, the racism, the narcissism, the fragile masculinity armored in the role-playing of uniformed exhibitionism, the mad maleness of "justified" violence: there are deep historical and psychological affinities here. Germans are sick of hearing about "the inability to mourn," their blocking off of a past too dangerous to enter. We have never seriously been challenged to enter into that past as ours, or to deal with it as our historical responsibility as well. It has suited us to be cultural outsiders—which in key respects we undoubtedly are—and to be historical voyeurs. Most fictional film Nazis, and many documentary ones, reassure us that us that we, following them, have escaped the contamination of nasty historical realities.[32]

If the real historical Nazis hold their own against the movie remake we should be grateful. The early amateurish film records, the cinematic brilliance of Riefenstahl and the newsreel cameramen, the blurred fragments of atrocities, the full color of the pageantry and combat can be treated as historical materials even when they are constructed to resemble a feature. Film, as an art, contains within itself the means to reassemble, re-examine, provoke reflection. Employed as history, nothing previously screened is outside its processing and reprocessing potential.

Hitler is certainly not immune to the deconstructive and reconstructive possibilities of film and history. Starring in his own epic, he leads and misleads as he did from the beginning. He invites a contest between film and history. Trackers of Nazis, and the Nazi escape into the movies, could have a worse guide.

NOTES

This essay first appeared in *Metro*, No. 100, Melbourne, Summer 1994–1995: 3–13.

1. John Slavin, in *Metro* 98 and 99, provides a wide-ranging context for Spielberg's transformation of Commandant Goeth into "a classic Hollywood Nazi." Although the Jewish = Good, SS = Evil polarities of the film are certainly prominent, it is not only Schindler as Good Nazi who challenges preconceptions. I've been surprised at how little comment there has been on Spielberg's bold delineation of an unattractive Jewish character, with some of the early images verging on anti-Semitic stereotype. Among other robust responses to the film see David Thomson and Armond White in *Film Comment*, March-April 1994.

2. Curiously, given the millions of words written about Nazism and about film, there is relatively little writing about Nazis on the screen. In individual reviews, notably those by historians in the *American Historical Review*, there are useful comments on representations and historical understanding; other short articles (cited later) have appeared in magazines and film journals. Major books dealing with German cinema before and after the war discuss particular representations rather than the cumulative effect. There are valuable histories of combat films and wartime production—see, for instance, Clive Coultass, *Images for Battle: British Film and the Second World War, 1939–1945* (Newark: University of Delaware Press, 1988); *The Goose Steps Out* makes an appearance on p. 77. Although several books have surveyed films representing Nazi genocide, their focus on the portrayal of the Nazis responsible for the crimes is secondary. Annette Insdorf, *Indelible Shadows: Film and the Holocaust* (New York: Cambridge University Press, 1985); Judith E. Doneson, *The Holocaust in American Film*, (Philadelphia: Jewish Publication Society, 1987); and Ilan Avisar, *Screening the Holocaust: Cinema's Images of the Unimaginable* (Bloomington: Indiana University Press, 1988) are all cases in point, though Avisar gives more sustained attention to the representation of Nazism. The indispensable study by Anton Kaes, *From Hitler to Heimat: The Return of History as Film* (Cambridge, Mass.: Harvard University Press, 1989) shares some of the concerns of this chapter, though with a different focus. Interesting also are Thomas Elsaesser, *New German Cinema: A History* (New Brunswick, N.J.: Rutgers University Press, 1989) and Eric Santner, *Stranded Objects: Mourning Memory and Film in Postwar Germany* (Ithaca: Cornell University Press, 1990). For developments in fictional writing, parallel to those on the screen, see Alvin H. Rosenfeld, *Imagining Hitler* (Bloomington: Indiana University Press, 1985).

3. This has also been a neglected aspect in discussions of film in the "Third Reich." The standard histories, including Kracauer's pioneering *From Caligari to Hitler* (Princeton: Princeton University Press, 1947) relate documentary images to feature production in the past, but not to the future.

4. The full text of the film is translated in Hans-Jürgen Syberberg, *Hitler, a Film from Germany* (New York: Farrar, Straus, and Giroux, 1982) together with

a preface by Susan Sontag. This excerpt (a slightly different translation) is from Timothy Corrigan, *New German Film* (Austin: University of Texas Press, 1983), p. 158.

5. Wim Wenders reaction at the time is in his *Emotion Pictures: Reflections on the Cinema* (London: Faber, 1989), pp. 93–99.

6. For another solemn interview—with the Reich authority charged with care of the Führer's moustache—see Justus Reibesam, "Die Wotansbürste" (1944), in Klaus Strohmeyer, ed., *Zu Hitler fällt mir noch ein . . . Satire als Widerstand* (Hamburg: Rowohlt, 1989), pp. 65–70.

7. Printed by Saul Friedländer at the opening of his *Reflections on Nazism. An Essay on Kitsch and Death* (New York: Harper and Row, 1984). A different translation is quoted by David Stewart Hull, *Film in the Third Reich* (Berkeley: University of California Press, 1969), pp. 265–266. There are more extended discussions of *Kolberg* in David Welch, *Propaganda and the German Cinema 1933–1945* (Oxford: Oxford University Press, 1981), pp. 221–237, and Erwin Leiser, *Nazi Cinema* (London: Secker and Warburg, 1974), pp. 121–133.

8. On Riefenstahl see Susan Sontag, "Fascinating Fascism" in *Under the Sign of Saturn* (New York: Farrar, Straus, and Giroux, 1980).

9. Hull, pp. 25–26. The favorite escape was of course America: *I Am a Fugitive from a Chain Gang* did much better business. In the kind of interplay between realities and representations that I'm espousing, this is significant, too. Cruelty and punitive labor were more real in the American South than close to home, where the concentration camps had been in operation for three months.

10. Hull, pp. 29–34. See also Leiser, pp. 34–40.

11. Leiser, p. 76.

12. Hull, p. 8.

13. Jews were not allowed to work in the German film industry after July 1, 1933. According to a 1936 *Fortune* survey, 53 out of 85 production executives in the major American film companies were Jews. See Neal Gabler, *An Empire of Their Own: How the Jews Invented Hollywood* (New York: Crown Publishers, 1988), p. 2.

14. Gabler, p. 319.

15. For an exemplary essay on the way an Austrian-born director made one of the most powerful American films within this genre, see Jan-Christoph Horak, "The Other Germany in Zinnemann's *The Seventh Cross* (1944)" in Eric Rentschler, ed., *German Film and Literature: Adaptations and Transformations* (New York: Methuen, 1986), pp. 117–131. For an early critique of the failure of the film industry, particularly in Britain, to move beyond melodrama into serious representations of "real Nazism," and the real politics of Nazism's opponents, see Eric Jacobs, "Foreign Policy and Cinema," *Sight and Sound*, Vol.15, No. 59, Autumn 1946, pp.102–105.

16. Leland A. Poague, *The Cinema of Ernst Lubitsch* (South Brunswick, N.J.: A.S. Barnes, 1978), p. 92.

17. John Mariani, "Let's Not Be Beastly to the Nazis," *Film Comment*, January-February 1979, gives a snappy overview of film Nazis from the past forty years.

18. Television epics have not been so careful. When Byron's mates go down with their submarine in *War and Remembrance* they are replicating one of the most popular German films of the Nazi years, Pabst's *Morgenrot*; and when Pug's other

son plunges to his death in flames, Americans, too, show that they know how to die.

19. These three films are the occasion for Lenny Rubinstein's question, "Where Have All the Nazis Gone?" in *Cineaste*, Vol. 8, No. 2, Fall 1977, pp. 32–35.

20. Avisar, pp. 157–158.

21. Ibid., p. 157.

22. Interview with Michel Foucault, *Cahiers du cinéma*, July-August 1974, quoted by Friedländer, pp. 74–78.

23. An extended discussion of "Television and the Effects of *Holocaust*," without gender references, is in Doneson, Ch.4.

24. See Mike Harris, "Wouk at war," *The Bulletin*, April 18, 1989, p.136, and the Epilogue to Kaes, *From Hitler to Heimat*.

25. This was the occasion for some topical press reflection on connections between a movie president, movie Germans—and the force of image making in historical memory. See, for instance, Paul Attansio, "Why Nazis Make Good Bad Guys," *San Francisco Chronicle* (*Washington Post* syndicate), June 2, 1985.

26. Annette Insdorf on the whole approves of the effect created. "The most disturbing element in the scene is Fosse's eschewing of distancing devices: he leaves the the audience vulnerable to the emotion of the song, and it is only at the end that we pull back, horrified at the ease with which unified voices can become viscerally seductive. This scene affords an insight into the rise of Nazism, for it is the only number that gives the audience a chance to get into the act. These Germans [who have "insidiously wholesome faces"] feel important, part of a movement that offers a hopeful tomorrow." *Indelible Shadows*, p. 51. For the pervasive ways film fictions shade into historical understandings, and an interestingly parallel American example, see Robert A. Rosenstone, "JFK: Historical Fact/Historical Film," *American Historical Review*, April 1992, pp. 506–511.

27. Nigel Andrews, "Hitler as Entertainment," *American Film*, April 1978, quoted by Friedländer, p. 17.

28. See, for instance, Thomas Elsaesser, "Memory, Home, Hollywood," *Monthly Film Bulletin*; Leonie Naughton, "Backs to the Past," *Filmnews*, Santner, *Stranded Objects*, Ch. 3, and Kaes, Ch. 6. There is an excellent short review by Kenneth Barkin in *American Historical Review*, October 1991, pp.1124–1126. My own reflection, "Recognizing the Third Reich: *Heimat* and the Ideology of Innocence," is in B. Shoesmith and T. O'Regan, eds, *History on/and/in Film*, Perth 1985. For a related comment on some earlier German productions see Robert C. Reimer, "Nazi-Retro Films: Experiencing the Mistakes of the Ordinary Citizen," *Journal of Popular Film and Television*, Vol.12, No.3, Fall 1984, pp.112–117.

29. See, in particular, Ron Burnett, "Lumière's Revenge," *History on/and/in Film*.

30. See Kaes, Ch. 4, and Kluge, "On Film and the Public Sphere," *New German Critique* 24/25 (1981–1982).

31. Yann Lardeau quoted in Corrigan, p.157. See also Syberberg's script and introduction, and the commentaries by Sontag, Santner, Friedländer, and Kaes.

32. I am not of course arguing against the careful location of Nazism in its historically specific context. I do think we need to scrutinize what is at work in our voyeuristic historical fascination. Television histories such as *The Fatal Attraction*

of Adolf Hitler (Britain 1983) need to be analyzed in the light of Syberberg's critique and the consumer warning—intended as advertising—in the title. I have found it instructive to compare the gramophone imagery toward the end of Fassbinder's *Lili Marleen* with the Eva Braun pathos/bathos at the closure of *Fatal Attraction.*

9

Marcel Ophüls' *November Days*: The Forming and Performing of Documentary History

Stan Jones

What Marcel Ophüls tackles in his television documentary *November Days: Voices and Choices*[1] are by any account some of the most significant events in this century's history: the collapse of the East German regime in November 1989 and the unexpectedly rapid reunification of Germany up to July 1, 1990, when the West German Deutschmark replaced the currency of the defunct German Democratic Republic. To reflect those days he performed as interviewer, editor, and director so that he could produce a documentary as a complex retrospective montage, what he calls a "musical comedy" to stress its deliberate borrowing from a notably fictional form of film.[2] Why he made it was initially a matter of practical necessity. Ophüls emphasizes that he is a professional filmmaker who needed the work.[3] Secondly, there was the sheer pressure of events, what we like to think of as history, and which we expect to be reflected, constructed, and interpreted for us in the media. For Ophüls the immediate functions of *November Days* are an occasion to manipulate documentary form so that wider questions of freedom, the nature of democracy, the ethics and competence of government, civil courage, and racism are always present behind the individual performances.[4]

The film explores a further twist in the national history traditionally featured as the "German Question." It is a problem that has occupied Germans, and the rest of the world, with more or less alarm and intensity, for at least the last century. It connotes inquiry across a spectrum: What is it that defines the Germans and their nation? How should their state function? And, above all, what role should Germany play in the geopolitics of Europe? Since 1949 the "German Question" had focused on the ideological conflict and practical coexistence between two German states, with Janus always in the background whispering: "What if they got back together again?"

The Wall came to provide the supremely televisual symbol for the "German Question" in contemporary Europe. It sited the two Germanys in the power relationships of the Cold War, a function politicians and media commentators constantly cooperated to reinforce in popular consciousness. This was the place where the Western and the Soviet blocs confronted each other most directly. For the Germans it also signified something more ominous, namely the certain eradication of their countries and themselves in any serious conflict. With the extremely televisual breaching of the Wall came the breaching of its connotations for global politics. TV newsreels presented fundamental and historical change in a passage of what Dayan and Katz call "catastrophic time," when anyone could see the great symbol of thirty years of historical stasis suddenly begin to depict a process.[5]

As in the entire Soviet sphere, Mikhail Gorbachev and his reforms precipitated the restructuring of the German Democratic Republic (GDR). He issued his final counsel to the East German régime at his last meeting with it on October 7, 1989: "You have to acknowledge society's needs and do what is necessary. Life punishes those who come too late." His words in the German context have gone down in history as the essence of his reforms: acknowledge your economic obsolescence, the popular discontent, act to remedy it internally and, above all, do not involve yourself in the problems of your satellites. Big Brother was not going to send in the Red Army any more—which encouraged the dissidents in East Germany to go public with their demands. The head of the régime, Erich Honecker, had consistently refused to fall in with Gorbachev's reforms and was consequently toppled by his Central Committee on October 17. It was the first major move in a scramble to accommodate East German discontent and, above all, to dissuade people from making for the recently opened border to Hungary and thence to Austria. Less than a month later, on November 8, the entire Central Committee resigned and an interim administration began talks with its Western counterpart prior to holding elections. On March 18, 1990, the parties supporting unification with the Federal Republic got overwhelming support; the points, for Germany, were set.

Ophüls' treatment of Germany's immediate post-Wall history was first screened on November 9, 1990, as a BBC 2 "Inside Story," on the Luxembourg-based German station RTLplus and on the East German channel DFF2. It was the first anniversary of the breaching of the Wall and *November Days* revealed itself as a product marked by an inherent and multivalent irony. It participated in a broadcasting schedule that offered a further round of media mythmaking on the "German Question." At this point the myth aimed at establishing publicly and officially a new era in German history by celebrating the identity of the nation reunified as a fact now accomplished.[6] Yet the narrative of *November Days* reveals a period in the process when the myth might still be fluid, might still be evolving, with many personalities beginning to position themselves within it. The film does not attempt a complete account of events let alone an analysis of what they mean. In place of definitive conclusions it stresses the fact that the story is still under construction.

In a wider frame, Ophüls delivers all his East German subjects and imagery to an audience that is, at least initially, western and largely English-speaking. This goes with the identity of the filmmaker. Ophüls is a historically complex European personality. Uprooted by the advent of the Third Reich from his German birthplace, he grew up in America. By family background half-Jewish and working as a French citizen, he made the program for a British state corporation as a project partially financed by German private investment. The retrospective impulse of the film made it inevitably self-reflexive. It displays his authorship—presumably the reason why the BBC commissioned him in the first place[7]—in the ways it generates its irony: sometimes openly moralizing in cross-referencing its interviewees, with pointed references to the baleful afterglow Nazism still casts on the present.[8] Ophuls' "performative" technique reinforced this individual stamp, which James Saynor interpreted in the British *Listener* the week after the film first screened: "He manages to make remarkable links between the 'macro' level of public events and the 'micro' level of individual personal histories, and he's so obsessively interested in how the two interact, as though he's after a 'grand unified theory' of behaviour—a Stephen Hawking for the social realm."[9]

Both in the structure of his montage and more overtly in his screen persona as the interviewer playing his subjects, Ophüls places his own observing and involved self very much between his material and his viewers. He does not create the conventional interviewer, the fiction of a figure with the authority to ask the questions that we would like to ask, or, at least, think we would like to ask. He is rather the critical intellectual, a role which goes beyond Saynor's view and has to take account of Thomas Elsaesser's: "We now recognise that television has created a historically distinct public sphere, which can no longer be opposed to a private sphere."[10] *November Days* deals with a natural conjunction of the private and the public as individual East Germans formed into demonstrations to claim the identity of "das Volk," the people so assiduously celebrated in the Marxist-Leninist rhetoric of their repressive government. Once the reality of that government had gone, the slogan became "ein Volk" to envisage the new era of Germans as one people. The film personalizes the large scale public events by presenting them for the private sphere wherever TV is watched. Yet it simultaneously resists and investigates that very technique through its irony. The structure of *November Days* demands our assent to Ophüls' multiple roles in it and yet at the same time denies us both a neutral and objective attitude toward his documentary and any empathy with the personalities he displays. We do not get an analysis of its content but a network of associations, anecdotes and insights coordinated by the author as "performer." It invites evaluation and at the same time resists any cognitive synthesis because we have to adjust our position constantly in response to a very wide range of associated images. As much via an emotional response as through interpretative reason, we have to delay our first step toward understanding and then judging what he shows us.

Ophüls' actual subjects come in three broad types: there are the "ordinary" or "private" people, the anonymous faces in the newsreel film of the crowds meeting around the Wall and the checkpoints on November 9, 1989, and—identified as a subgroup—the minor state functionaries. We meet East German border police still on duty, several milk-truck drivers, a warder at the infamous Waldheim psychiatric clinic where dissidents were "reprogrammed," and the manager of what was the Communist Party's "retreat " outside Berlin, whose comments are counterpointed by the memories of the local populace on the bosses at leisure. There are the "intellectuals," semi-public personalities such as writers like Stefan Hermlin and the late Heiner Müller, Barbara Brecht-Schall, guardian of her father's literary estate, and dissidents such as the artist Bärbel Bohley, the conductor Kurt Masur, and the biologist Thomas Montag. There are the political *Prominenz*, public identities like Egon Krenz (who took over from Erich Honecker), Günter Schabowski (leading member of the Party's Central Committee), and Walter Momper, the mayor of the newly reunited city. Others are new celebrities: the former second-in-command of the secret police, Markus Wolf, and a figure eerie for his simultaneous significance and insignificance in German public life, the quondam leader of the Neo-Nazis, Michael Kühnen.

As counterpoint to these interviews, Ophüls inserts clips of BBC newsreaders and reporters who engaged with the unfolding events in creating documentary as ostensible record, the "news."[11] To these media images of recent history-in the-making he adds two further frames. One uses older examples of documentary images: clips from newsreels of postwar victory celebrations among the Western allies, a shot of Hitler at Berchtesgarden, and some stills of leaders and soldiers in the Third Reich. The other both parallels them and contrasts with them by quoting from films that are out-and-out fictions: John Wayne as "Ringo" in a sequence from *Stagecoach*; James Mason as Brutus or Marlon Brando as Marc Antony from Josef Mankiewicz's 1953 film of *Julius Caesar*, various forms of Nazis in Ernst Lubitsch's *To Be or Not To Be*; Marlene Dietrich as Lola, vamp-icon supreme, in von Sternberg's *Blue Angel*. Where he thinks it effective, Ophüls manipulates the soundtrack to his documentary images by quoting songs from musicals: "September Song" sung by Lotte Lenya, Gershwin's " 'S Wonderful," Bing Crosby singing "Song of Freedom," or "Money, Money" from the film *Cabaret*. Classical music figures with the Ode to Joy from a filmed performance of Beethoven's Ninth by the Leipzig Gewandhausorchester and a sound recording of Peter Schneider singing "Dies Bildnis ist bezaubernd schön" from *The Magic Flute*.

Ophüls' constantly shifting mosaic corresponds to a basic point made by Robert Rosenstone about how documentary film deals with history:

The documentary may seem closer to fact, but fiction almost always enters it in generous amounts—the most obvious example being the use of generic, illustrative images from the past that are not specifically of the scenes they purport to depict. Such elements only underscore the idea that film must be taken on its own terms as a portrait of the past that has less to do with fact than with intensity and insight, perception and feeling, with showing how events affect individual lives, past and present.[12]

November Days does not experiment with basic filmmaking techniques, like *mis-en-scène*, focus-shifting, or point-of-view, but it does disturb our perceptions by forcing us to cope with constant breaks in the film's narrative "flow," its "reality," caused by the contrast of texture, style, sound quality, and so on in film and still images from earlier times. We have not only to attend to the source and significance of the songs, to identify the "reality" of the historical images and of the famous fictions from the interpolated feature films, and to draw the parallel with the interview situation that the songs and the films accompany, but also to understand the dramatic scenes from television accounts of, for instance, the SED party rally in the Berlin Lustgarten on November 4, 1989, or shots of the dissident movement in Leipzig churches "before the Fall." These contrasting elements frame and qualify the "present" of the interviews Ophüls is conducting, the significance of their locations, the way he is included, either in the frame or via editing, and generate the film's overwhelming tone of irony.[13]

In the film's montage the dominant image is the Wall, but Ophüls shows surprisingly little of the "theatre of liberation" from November 9, when Berliners began climbing all over it and knocking bits off it. He shows instead people relating their memories of it: West Berliners, for instance, tell how it affected divided families, while Krenz and Schabowski interpose their versions as to how the East German border came to be opened. To generate a further dimension of memory, he has Heiner Müller relate how the sudden sealing of the border twenty years earlier had made people like himself, whom he defines as committed socialist intellectuals, feel a sense of relief and security at being able to develop socialism without interference from outside. Typically, Ophüls relativizes Müller's account with intercut stills of the construction of the Wall and of successful—and unsuccessful—attempts to break through it.

In the interview with the urbane Markus Wolf he raises the theme of the Stasi (the East German State Security Service), its effects on the East German state, and its continuing legacy in the newly unified one. Wolf's account of himself alternates with Müller's commentary on the "selective amnesia" of such personalities and, most pointedly of all, with scenes of farce from Lubitsch's *To Be or Not To Be* that ridicule the false ingenuousness of spymasters. Where "ordinary" people comment on the misery of the duplicitous informer culture and its crippling expense, their memories are validated by Thomas Montag, whose appearance as a vocal (and courageous) reformer before the rally on November 4 briefly elevated him from anonymity. Montag draws a historical parallel that still provokes debate. He compares his own experience of opposition with the treatment of the German resistance in the Third Reich to make the point that, although it could exact a terrible cost, civil courage in the Democratic Republic did not meet the same murderous response inflicted by the Nazis. Montag's remarks are also valuable for the subtle parallel he draws between the self-justification offered by people in positions of authority in East Germany and that of counterparts in the Reich: namely, that you had to cooperate with the state to protect your staff. Ophüls interpolates a photograph of a manager in civilian clothes (maybe even the legendary Oskar Schindler?) "negotiating" with a Gestapo officer, Himmler himself. The scientist is capable of elucidating the moral dilemma felt by dissidents and reformers such as himself in their response to the pressure from the authorities, namely the extent to which they could persuade themselves to compromise their principles to protect family, friends, and colleagues. It is one of the fundamental questions raised by the history of our century: what price must individuals be ready to pay in resisting dictatorship?

In representing those responsible for the East German regime, Ophüls indicates through his editorial cross-referencing the historical process that led to the Communist Party's losing its grip as events overtook it. There is no interview with Honecker, but the film's opening scene reaches back to the last days of the old regime to show his jovial arrogance in dismissing journalists' questions about what he planned to discuss in the fateful meeting with Gorbachev. This early Honecker image contrasts pointedly with the subsequent shots that comment on references to him. Ophüls shows a figure seen in longshot on supervised strolls, sometimes to the strains of "September Song," the fallen grandee who marks historical change in his own person. To suggest that his deposition marked the beginning of the end, Ophüls makes a moralistic comparison of both Krenz and Schabowski with figures from one of the most famous political fictions, the assassins of

Caesar in Mankiewicz's film. He even identifies Krenz by association as Brutus and then shows him denying the implication in the interview. Honecker's political bequest appears through an adept sequence of cross-cutting that begins by rapid shuttling between his two former lieutenants and the interpolation of television newsreel.

The dubious nature of their conflicting self-justifications is foregrounded at a further crucial juncture—enactment of the law permitting East Germans to cross into the West. By November the Party faced a crucial choice: suppress the popular demonstrations or officially sanction this final step. Its "crisis management" appears as a newsreel record of events from the cameras of an international press conference, scarcely the scenario to announce a repression of the populace. Instead a confused and harassed Schabowski reads an ad hoc formulation of the new law and confirms it under the pressure of the reporters' questioning. To apply the final ironic gloss to the "authentic" visual evidence of the effective end of the Party, Ophüls introduces the perspective of an East Berlin border guard who reveals he first heard he would have to police the scarcely credible new law from his wife. Then we have Schabowski and Krenz commenting on the anecdote. In the retrospective "present" of the interview it highlights their helplessness then and their evasiveness now before the record of the circumstances they created.[14]

Significantly, Schabowski's son observes his father's interview in the family's apartment. It is his generation that will have to inherit the consequences of the events with which *November Days* deals. In seeking insights into the "German Question" post-Wall, it works from the East German perspective characterized by Heiner Müller's comment on the impact of the open borders: "the GDR consisted in the first place of expectations and memories. There wasn't any present. And then suddenly there was only the present."[15]

The perspectives Ophüls recorded in the "present" of 1990 range from the straightforward expression of delight from "ordinary" people at their freedom of travel to the dismissive pessimism of Barbara Brecht-Schall's remark: "I've never been really crazy about the Germans." In the positive spectrum, a Herr Felgner Snr., comments on his times in the company of his family reunited from both sides of the city. He combines time with space in his travel plans as he intends, before considering the wider world, to go see the rest of Germany, a place he last visited as a member of Hitler's Wehrmacht. The Neo-Nazi Kühnen, younger but nevertheless one of the "Ewiggestrigen" (Forever Yesterday's People), sees the future already existing fully formed in the past; in what he deems a national reunification he sees tensions that will awaken a new appreciation of the order and security of the Third Reich. Inevitably, for Kühnen the new German state is just a stage toward reclaiming the lands to the East that Germany lost after 1945.[16]

The conjunction of past and future appears again where Ophüls gets Walter Momper to talk to him on the roof of the Esplanade Hotel within sight of the Reichstag. The mayor is upbeat on prospects for a part of Berlin with great symbolic significance: the wasteland that the Wall made out of the city center, the Potsdamer Platz.[17] Ophüls concentrates on the social aesthetic of the impending commercial development with his ironic speculations on whether managers can revive an environment in which "the pretty girls" would want to go strolling again. The editing cuts away to specify the involvement of Mercedes by showing its famous star on the skyline in the West and then linking that image with old newsreel footage of the prewar limousines that brought Hitler's guests to Berchtesgaden. The uncomfortable historical connotations of a leading icon for German industrial potency expand the historical frame placed on the Potsdamer Platz, but we have to pursue any further significance for ourselves.

What the future holds for the formerly prominent personalities, the film does not indicate, except in so far as it shows Markus Wolf reckoning with court proceedings.[18] Where Ophüls shows himself becoming involved beyond his screen persona as the interviewer—as distinct from the critical intellectual as editor who structured the ironic and critical montages accompanying his discussions with the former politicians—he draws the most remarkable responses on the future of the German Question. He asks Kurt Masur, as one of the prominent voices for reform in Leipzig, whether he feels let down by the populace that in the March elections so clearly chose unity with the Western model of consumer capitalism, the famous "banana vote," rather than socialist reform.[19] Masur abruptly suspends the roles in the film and refuses an answer on the grounds that Ophüls has no personal interest in that dilemma—his personal future is not bound up with it—and is merely looking for a journalist's sensation. At this the interviewer (what Bill Nichols calls the "initiator and arbiter of legitimacy")[20] shows himself abdicating that role and accepting the limits of the new position assigned him by his "victim." Ophüls indicates his awareness of himself as a historical subject: he may be a critical intellectual and a product of German history, but in his own person he is not now part of it.

By contrast, Heiner Müller does not challenge his inquisitor but instead both reveals and conceals fundamental traits in his relationship to his times. When Ophüls asks why he did not use his privilege of free access to the West to stay away, he says: "Staying away was never an option for me. That's certainly difficult to explain, but I probably needed this pressure, simply this dictatorship, because my reflexes come from the other dictatorship and I can deal with dictatorships, and democracy bores me." The subtle insight is constructed, half-smiling, by a German dialectician from his own personal history to present the motives behind his behavior. With it he parries the implication in Ophüls' question about his complicity with the East German state. He also sidesteps the question that Masur refused to answer, and hence any speculation on where the nation might go from here. Of all the subjects interviewed in the film, Müller is probably the only one who can "outperform" Ophüls in their debate. He can site his own personal history in that of his nation to trail the "bait" of "boring democracy" before his inquisitor. Ophüls' commentary on the interview appears in a *mis-en-scène* which is notably self-referential, by framing the two of them reflected simultaneously in mirrors, first in one and then in two, so that the camera team is also included. The complexity of these perspectives suggests strongly that we would need to shift our position as viewers only slightly to be included in the shot and then watch ourselves watching the people watching the interviewee. The exaggerated self-reflexivity creates a visual allegory for the irony of a documentary seeking from such a deliberately ambivalent personality as Müller answers to the "German Question" and its recent history.

November Days closes with an exchange where irony is tempered by the melancholy of a subject who, like Masur, reverses the roles. On July 1, 1990, Bärbel Bohley interprets the significance of the common currency as a further loss of freedom for the East Germans. They now have the Deutschmark—and are locked irrevocably into the Western system. They will have to work harder for even less of a share in the national wealth that they got in the socialist economy.[21] When she asks Ophüls how he sees the situation and the future, he shows himself (with his hand partially concealing his mouth) acknowledging the likely difficulties while affirming the general liberation of the East Germans. Then as editor he relativizes his own position again by the wittiest—and cruelest—sequence in the film. *November Days* becomes a "musical comedy" of parallel editing, with East Germans changing money as Liza Minelli and Joel Grey sing "Money Makes the World Go Around" in Bob Fosse's *Cabaret*. However, Ophüls is not content with just quoting. He creates a new frame of reference for the day's events by showing East Berliners "performing" the musical's refrain as they acquire their new Western marks and begin to distribute them. Coming at the end of the film's extensive montage, the willingness of some of the subjects, at such a crucial point in their changing times, to satirize themselves makes them appear somewhat over-cooperative dupes of Ophüls-the-director. His sequence leaves little question as to whether East Germans have "sold out" to a dominant economic system. Fosse's fictional treatment of a similiarly notorious period of German history creates a frame with distinctly ominous overtones.[22]

The counterbalance ensues as Ophüls closes on the comments of two East Berliners already featured coming through a checkpoint in a newsreel clip. Herbert and Karin Radunski reveal not only their pleasure at the new freedoms but their fears for their economic security and for that of pensioners, and reveal, with mildly ironic offhandedness, that they had been able to change 8000 marks "after 40 years" and that he has just lost his job. Ophüls uses their cheery newsreel image to wrap up his account, to the strains of Bing Crosby singing the "Song of Freedom": upbeat, certainly, but at the same time asking us if we accept the straightforward optimism of the closure.

The particular identity of *November Days* derives from its "micro" level, from the director's particular ability to get people to construct their personal histories, often anecdotally, before the camera.[23] The pronounced inclusion of his own life history is a further means of linking individual stories to the "macro" level of history writ large.[24] The sequences with Bohley show Ophüls agreeing to the role of the journalist asked to comment on the circumstances he examines with his subject—just as Masur refuses him the right to an opinion. With Kühnen, Ophüls takes a stance as a historical type when his subject identifies him as a stereotypical Jew and hence part of an abiding irritant to the German body politick, although he has nothing against Ophüls personally! "Nebbich!" (too bad) is the interviewer's immediate response to that proposition and, as editor, he reinforces his rejection of the Nazi by interpolating an item on a fiction, a musical comedy. He interviews Carl Jung, the star of a current production of *The White Horse Inn*, and points out to another member of Kühnen's generation of Germans the Jewish origins and identity of the play and, above all, of the leading role. Sitting on the stage, with the actor in costume, Ophüls deliberately eclipses his subject and the fictional role: he is a real Jew and really bald. He uses the wider cultural-historical dimension to challenge the fiction that has masked the real history of the musical since the Third Reich, and from the apparently innocuous entertainment shows how the central role of Jews in German cultural history is still denied.

When Markus Wolf reflects on the nature of his own Germanness, Ophüls raises the question of German Jewishness, but in completely the opposite manner to his rebuttal of Kühnen. He reaches back into the general historical context of their lives to remind the Stasi General that they are both Jews, the sons of families forced to emigrate in the 1930s.[25] Wolf's family went East to the Soviet Union while Max Ophüls, Marcel's father, established a name in Hollywood. To underline his speculation on what he might have become had he too gone East, Ophüls cuts to Brecht-Schall, with whom he shared American exile as a child. She tells how her father threw out his mother during one particularly intoxicated evening for being "zu deutsch" (too German). In such exchanges Ophüls is patently the "performer" constructing his own personality as one historical role in a range of possibilities. However, he is far from identifying with Brecht's daughter: he explodes her claim to have been distant from the regime with newsreel footage of her hobnobbing with Honecker.

The ironical montage is itself counterpointed where the TV journalist and his team generate a situation to which bystanders respond. Ophüls is filmed while trying to identify himself in German with his British BBC pass to the completely uncooperative police at the "Polenmarkt" (Polish Market) on the Potsdamer Platz. An observer intervenes very assertively before the camera to demand that he film the street-traders and is himself then rebuffed by an equally assertive woman, who defends Ophüls' right to film what he likes. Naturally, any "authenticity" we might perceive in such an exchange derives from the editing and is itself an irony on the overall function of the reporter/filmmaker whose very presence did, after all, generate the incident.

Since its initial broadcast *November Days* has been surrounded by controversy. It won recognition and exhibition, albeit in a projected video version, at the International Forum of the Berlinale in 1991 and additional broadcast on Austrian television. Some of the commentary did not run very deep. Ophüls reportedly felt the need to call his co-producer Renate Ziegler a "blöde Ziege" (stupid cow).[26] He wanted to augment the television documentary to produce a three-hour film version and claims he had interest from the German ARD network. His producers apparently refused permission on the simple commercial grounds that they had sold the international rights, and could not have afforded the concomitant licensing costs for the clips from feature films anyway.[27] So the nature of a fuller *November Days* remains a speculation in itself, an ironical prospect considering its theme of economic exigency pre- and post-Wall.[28]

The version we have is already a challenge to the term "documentary." Made for the popular media, it belongs to the group of television productions examined by Rainer Rother in his study "Jahrestag-Fernsehtag."[29] He stresses its free-ranging reference: "Ophüls does not respect any limits, and not those either that are ostensibly set for the documentary. He neither shies from making his partner the victim of his montage (and not making any secret of that), nor does he respect the division between documentation and fiction."[30] Rother defines the role of television coverage in the final days of the Democratic Republic to make the point that, while the collapse of the East German regime was due to economic pressures, the availability of Western German programs in the East exacerbated dissatisfactions. And once the public demonstrations began, they went out live to the world TV audience in broadcasts that then maintained—and even redirected—the inherent dynamic of events.[31] Within *November Days*, TV coverage intervenes most acutely in events where Ophüls shows Schabowski enacting the new travel regulations "on the run." The context of his film adds a particular irony and an unmistakably moralizing judgment on the event.

Ophüls is different from the other filmmakers in this particular group in one essential respect: they are Germans, whereas he is at once German and not-German. The journalist Christan Peitz put it pointedly: "As a re-immigrant he has it easier in Germany than elsewhere. Whether they know it or not, the Germans are thankful to the re-immigrants for the fact that at least they came back."[32]

The way he incorporates his own person in his film, his "performance" in it, raises wider questions for which German has the terms "Vergangen-heitsbewältigung" (coming to terms with the past) and "Lernfähigkeit" (capacity for learning lessons). They refer to the conscious treatment of history in the present and hence the influence of that history on the future. In getting Germans to talk about the recent past, at both micro and macro levels, to construct themselves as storytellers and commentators remembering before the camera, Ophüls demonstrates their willingness or otherwise to engage in a potentially traumatic confrontation.[33] Thomas Montag stands out, in contrast to, say, Heiner Müller, as the "honette homme" of the entire film, thanks to his clear enunciation of his own position. He also contrasts in another sense with two of his East German compatriots whom Ophüls traced from the newsreels, Steffi Rühmann and Klaus-Dieter Kubat. They say there that as campaigners for the rights of native American Indians they would support the GDR and its Wall before visitors. When they declare that they will be more critical of their state next time, Ophüls mocks their "Lernfähigkeit" by intercutting it with shots of John Wayne downing the redskins in *Stagecoach*. Representing them with a tragicomic pathos, the film is less severe than it is with figures such as Krenz or Brecht-Schall. It shows us its subjects in a performance of what Bill Nichols in his study of documentary drawn from American models identifies by the Freudian term "Nachträglichkeit":

The present approach to historical consciousness borrows from what Freud called *Nachträglichkeit* and Hayden White called "willing backward": "willing backward occurs when we rearrange accounts of events in the past that have been emplotted in a given way, in order to endow them with a different meaning or to draw from the emplotment reasons for acting differently in the future from the ways we have become accustomed to acting in our present."[34]

Ophüls shows us individuals involved in this process while we are constantly prompted by the montage structure to make judgments about them, in their relation to their sense of nation and history. His approach to the treatment of German history in film contrasts with the extreme fictionality of Syberberg's *Our Hitler*, as Rudy Koshar interprets it: "All the action, if that is what it can be called, occurs on a stage where actors perform monologues as they project themselves onto Hitler, 'the German Napoleon' of the twentieth century who is 'more of a nonperson,' as the circus master of ceremonies played by Heinz Schubert says early in part 1."[35] Syberberg is not interested in any sort of historical account, let alone analysis, of the phenomenon Hitler but instead displays various treatments of the myth-of-power that the figure has become in the contemporary collective memory as enshrined in visual fictions.

In 1983 Wolfram Schütte gave Ophüls and his work a different historical/philosophical context: "The work of this documentarist carries a sentence from Milan Kundera as its motto . . . 'The struggle of people against power is the struggle of the memory against forgetting.' "[36]

By now *November Days* is itself a messenger from its times, a form of remembering. Ophüls certainly makes no secret of his film being process depicting a process. He is the critical intellectual who constructs a "contrapuntal" montage, the irony of which constantly relativizes itself and leaves open a huge range of significance. Its multivalency demonstrates how remembering history in a German context is extremely difficult, and at its most extreme, the film's irony can even seem to mock our attempts to make any sense at all of the past. It seeks to exist in a form of permanent present, even though its subject matter may be receding.[37] It uses the basic nature of all visual media, which can only exist in the present, in the act of viewing, to refract its subject matter: East Germans reflecting on the "present" into which their part of the nation had suddenly been catapulted. At the same time it reminds us to remember what we, as viewers, are doing. So where the film invites us to seek allegorical significance, it aims also to inculcate a critical reflex toward the sort of media products *November Days* represents. As Pierre Sorlin puts it: "Their programs do not simply mirror the past, but contribute to its reactivation, even to its creation; an image of an event does not necessarily follow its occurence, it may be 'frozen' and resurface much later. The production of history, instead of being an objective assessment of past events, has become part of the media."[38]

At the start of the mythmaking about the reunification of Germany, *November Days* suggests that the individual historical actors—first among them the filmmaker—form and perform history as the film is made. They can entertain as they instruct us about the problematical and often contradictory workings of our dominant arena for constructing history as collective memory, the visual media. And that self-reflexive illumination, that "musical comedy," might just let the newest medium of history carry on being relevant beyond its times.

NOTES

1. Produced by BBC in association with Regina Ziegler and Arthur Cohn.
2. Quoted by K. Jackson,"Just Singin' 'Round the Wall," *The Independent* (November 9, 1990). Ophüls may also be alluding here to the way film musicals frequently reflect on themselves by depicting musical performance as part of their plot. See also Michel Sineux, "La défaite en chantant"(Going down singing; all translations by Stan Jones), *Positif* 370 (1991): 55–56, here p. 56. "Grâce aussi à une esthétique musicale, contrapuntique, qui confère au propos une aura fantomatique, irréelle, comme dans tous les bons cauchmars, oú les éclats de rire et les chansons d'amour sont les travestissements des plus redoutables menaces." (Thanks

also to a musical, contrapuntal aesthetic which confers on the subject a ghostly aura, unreal, like in the best nightmares where the outbursts of laughter and the songs of love are travesties of more redoubtable threats.)

3. He says of himself: "Ich bin Lohnarbeiter des Kinos in dem Sinne, daß ich mich in jener Tradition sehe, wo man sagt: gut, wir sind Autoren, aber der Beruf des Filmautors hat weniger mit Dichtern und Denkern zu tun als mit Zirkus." (I'm a wage earner in the cinema in the sense that I see myself in that tradition where they say, all right, we're authors, but the profession of film-author has less to do with poets and thinkers than with the circus.) "Einstellungsfanfare" in *CICIM. Revue Pour Le Cinéma Français* 29 (1990): 6–8. He is clearly well aware of the importance of entertainment as idea and subject matter in musicals—as well as its role in shaping television news.

4. Here the "rhetorical strategy" of allegory identified by Carol Plyley James in Ophüls' film *Le Chagrin and la Pitié (The Sorrow and the Pity)* from 1969 sheds a useful light on the techniques of *November Days*, as she says: "An allegorical text, then, is not merely self-reflective nor is it pointing to itself as an aesthetic object, but plays out in its own form the ethical conflict between proper and figural meaning." C. P. James, "Documentary and Allegory: History Moralised in *Le Chagrin et la Pitié*," *The French Review* 1(1985): 84–89, 85–86.

5. D. Dayan and E. Katz, *Media Events* (Cambridge, Mass.: Harvard University Press, 1992), p. 212. Normal broadcasting the authors define by contrast as "soap-opera time."

6. In 1974, Michel Foucault discussed the visual media and popular memory with reference to "Le Chagrin et la Pitié" and defined the process as follows: "So people are shown not what they were, but what they must remember having been." "Film and Popular Memory. An Interview with Michel Foucault," translated by M. Jordin, *Radical Philosophy* 11 (1975): 24–29.

7. Ophüls has been making films since 1957. He has only directed one feature film so far: *Peau de Banane* (Banana Skin) in 1963, and is best known for *The Sorrow and the Pity*, which caused considerable controversy with its investigation of French collaboration in the Second World War, and *Hotel Terminus. The Life and Times of Klaus Barbie*, 1985–1987, which investigates the Gestapo officer Klaus Barbie, tried in France for the torture of resistance fighters and the deportation of Jews. See also Rosenstone's definition of "filmmaker-historians," albeit postmodern ones, who "tell the past self-reflexively, in terms of what it means to the filmmaker-historian." R. Rosenstone, "The Crisis of History/The Promise of Film." *Media International Australia* 80 (1996): 5–11.

8. In its German context, the film's constant reference to living in the erstwhile GDR raises the dilemma expressed in Theodor Adorno's comment from 1944 on the Third Reich: "Es gibt kein richtiges Leben im falschen." (There is no right way to live in wrong circumstances.) T. Adorno, *Minima Moralia* (Frankfurt am Main,1989), p. 42.

9. J. Saynor, "A Grand Inquisitor," *The Listener* (November 15, 1990): 46–47.

10. T. Elsaesser, "New German Cinema's Historical Imaginary," in *Framing the Past*, ed. B. A. Murray and C. J. Whickam (Carbondale and Edwardsville, 1992), pp. 280–307, here p. 293.

11. Apparently, he located many of the "faces" they showed and from whom they sought initial reactions by simply placing advertisements in the Berlin papers.

12. R. Rosenstone, Introduction to *Revisioning History* (Princeton: Princeton University Press 1995), pp. 3–14, here p. 7.

13. On the subject of irony, Ophüls himself declares: "Ich bin bedenkenlos bereit zuzugeben, daß es, um den künstlerischen Einsatz von Ironie oder die stilistische Funktion von Anführungszeichen zu verstehen, vielleicht des Privilegs einer bürgerlichen Erziehung bedarf." (I am unreservedly prepared to admit that, in order to understand the artistic use of irony or the stylistic function of quotation marks, a bourgeois education is necessary) M.Ophüls, "Soll man Speer erschießen, anstatt ihn vor die Kamera zu holen?" (Should one shoot Speer instead of bringing him before the camera?), *CICIM* 29 (1990): 8–17, here p. 15.

14. Ophüls' particular hostility to both men—and his moralizing impulse—stands out in his cutaways to Schabowski's pet parrot, into whose beak he puts the words "Rat gegeben" (offered advice) and "Langue de Bois"(wooden–i.e., forked—tongue).

15. Quoted in S. Lebert, "Sprache ist stärker als Schmerz," (Language is stronger than pain), *Kulturchronik* 5 (95): 9–43, here p. 43.

16. Ophüls apparently had no scruples against paying Kühnen for his cooperation. See C. Peitz, "Ein Manuskript? Nie!" (A manuscript? Never!), *Die Tageszeitung* (October 9, 1991). Kühnen was to have no part in the future for Germany, as he died of AIDS not long after the film was finished.

17. In this place and in this role Ophüls role as an actual observer of the Berlin landscape gains a further dimension by contrasting him with the purely fictional phenomena from Wim Wenders's *Wings of Desire,* the eternally alienated recording angels.

18. Proceedings involving Krenz, Schabowski, and Wolf are still underway in 1996.

19. TV images showing East Berliners scrambling for bananas, which became suddenly plentiful after the collapse of the Wall, have provided one of the bitterest metaphors for what some see as the "buyout" of the East by the West.

20. Bill Nichols, *Representing Reality: Issues and Concepts in Documentary* (Bloomington: Indiana University Press, 1991), p. 52.

21. To judge from recent comments, Bohley's disillusion has apparently continued: "Den (Sozialismus) kannten die Menschen im Osten genau und wußten, daß er bis ins Mark hinein verrottet war, vor allem nachdem klar wurde, welche ökonomischen und ökologischen Probleme er neben den menschlichen hinterlassen hatte. Also wählten sie ein Modell, von dem sie vierzig Jahre ausgeschlossen waren, in dem Glauben, daß es wirklich liberal, demokratisch und sozial geworden war." (That [socialism] was what the people in the East knew all about and they knew that it was rotten to the core, above all after it became clear what economic and ecological problems it had left behind alongside the human ones. So they voted for a model from which they had been excluded for forty years, in the belief that it really had become liberal, democratic, and socialist.) However, she does maintain that: ". . . die Menschen sind nicht nur kurzblickend und selbstbezogen, sondern auch lernfähig." (. . . people are not only short-sighted and selfish but also capable of learning.) B. Bohley, "Wir brauchen eine Wende—überall." (We need the Turnaround—everywhere.) *Die Zeit* (September 1, 1995): 58.

22. See above all its final scene where the distorting mirror of the stage reappears and we are invited to look at ourselves reflected in it as an audience now marked with swastikas.

23. See the comment by Walter Benjamin: "The true picture of the past flits by. The past can be seized only as an image which flashes up at the instant when it is recognized and is never seen again. . . . For every image of the past that is not recognized by the present as one of its own concerns threatens to disappear irretrievably." Quoted in Bill Nichols, *Blurred Boundaries* (Bloomington: Indiana University Press, 1994), p. 7.

24. In the case of many of the "prominent" people, legal action has inevitably meant and still means that the "micro" and "macro" levels of their lives in their times are identical.

25. Ophüls, like Brecht, left Germany the day after the burning down of the Reichstag in February 1933.

26. See V. Leuken, "Destillat der Erfahrungen, was Deutschland heißt" (Essence of the experiences of what Germany means), *Frankfurter Allgemeine Zeitung* (March 28, 1992).

27. For what is ostensibly Ophüls' own account of the material not included in the extant version, see "Was nicht zu sehen ist" (What is not visible), *Die Tageszeitung* (November 14, 1991).

28. His latest product is "The Troubles We've Seen," an account of the reporting of the conflict in Sarajevo. See Ralph Eue, "Wir sehen Bilder, und es geschieht nichts" (We see pictures and nothing happens), *Der Tagesspiegel* (December 16, 1994).

29. R. Rother, "Jahrestag-Fernsehtag" (Anniverary Day, TV Day) in R. Bohn, K. Hickethier, and E. Müller (eds.), *Mauer-Show*, (Berlin, 1992), pp. 157–188, here p. 168.

30. Rother in *Mauer-Show*, p. 160. See also Ophüls' own remark: "Ein Dokumentarfilm ist nicht mehr und nicht weniger subjektiv als jedes andere Werk der Phantasie" (A documentary film is no more nor less subjective than every other work of the imagination), quoted in Wolfram Schütte, "Menschen erzählen. Zu einem Porträt des Dokumentaristen Marcel Ophüls" (People telling people. Toward a Portait of the documentary filmmaker Marcel Ophüls), *Frankfurter Rundschau* (January 29, 1983): 35.

31. See here especially the comment by Lindgens and Mahler: "Die am Geschehen beteiligten Akteure der Bürgerbewegung unterscheiden nicht zwischen der Darstellung der Revolution als 'Medienrealität' und der 'faktischen' Realität des Geschehens. In ihrer Sicht konnten die sozialen, politischen und ökonomischen Bedingungen als Ursachen des Umbruchs nicht einfach von Medien erfunden werden, und die Medien waren auch nicht selbst diejenigen, die eine Bewegung in Gang setzten. Ihre reale Funktion war es vielmehr, die von den Protestbewegungen ausgehenden Anstösse multipliziert zu haben. Die damit verstärkte Eigendynamik der Prozesse entsprach dann allerdings nicht mehr unbedingt den ursprünglichen Intentionen der Protestakteure." (Those agents of the citizens' initiative who were involved in the events do not distinguish between the revolution as "media-reality" and the "factual" reality of the events. In their eyes the social, political, and economic circumstances as reasons for the upheaval could not simply have been invented by the media and the media were also not even the ones who set a movement

going. Their real function was rather to have multiplied the impulses coming from the protest movement. The inherent dynamism of the process was thus amplified but it did not actually conform inevitably to the original intentions of the agents of protest.) M. Lindgens and S. Mahler, "Von Medienboom zur Medienbarriere" (From Media-boom to Media-barrier), *Mauer-Show:* 95–112, here p. 96.

32. Peitz, *Die Tageszeitung*.

33. The observations of Daniele Dell'Agli, another "outsider," of the Germans and their relationship to their history underlines the difficulty of this undertaking and of Ophüls' project with his film. In 1994 she interprets the mood of the crowds on the Berlin boulevard Unter den Linden on the anniversary of reunification: "Paradoxerweise schreckt gerade die opake Realität der symbolischen Stätten jeden intimen Bezug zu ihnen ab: die Leute trödeln unschlüssig, achselzuckend, bestenfalls unbekümmert umher; je näher sie hinschauen, desto weiter entfernt sich jede Bedeutsamkeit aus den Steinen; was die Monumente bezeugen, ihr historisches Gedächtnis, wird in der Konfrontation mit ihrer aufdringlichen Materialität gelöscht. Geschichte überlebt offensichtlich, wenn überhaupt, nur mehr im Fernsehformat, eine audiovisuelle Depotenzierung, für welche die Deutschen mit ihrem gebrochenem Verhältnis zu öffentlichen Kundgebungen besonders empfänglich zu sein scheinen." (Paradoxically it is precisely the opaque reality of the symbolic places that deters you from any intimate relationship to them: the people wander around indecisively, shrugging their shoulders, at best unconcerned; the closer they look the farther any meaning recedes from the stones; what the monuments commemorate, their historical memory, is extinguished by the confrontation with their intrusive materiality. History clearly survives, when at all, only in TV format, an audiovisual emasculation to which the Germans, with their disturbed relationship to public ceremonials, seem particularly susceptible.) D. Dell'Agli, "Transgermanien. Der Tag davor—Deutschvergessenheit Unter den Linden" (Transgermany. The Day before—German Amnesia Unter den Linden), *Lettre International*, 7 (1994): 25–27, here p. 26.

34. Nichols, *Blurred Boundaries*, p. 118.

35. R. Koshar, "Hitler: A Film from Germany. Cinema, History and Structures of Feeling," in Rostenstone, *Revisioning History*, pp. 155–173, here p. 160.

36. W. Schütte, "Menschen erzählen" (People Telling People), *Frankfurter Rundschau* (January 29, 1983).

37. See Rosenstone's comment that "filmmaker-historians" are successful when they "never forget that the present is the site of past representation and knowing," "Crisis/Promise," p. 7.

38. P. Sorlin, *Mass Media* (New York: Routledge, 1994), p. 8.

10

Braveheart and the Scottish Aesthetic Dementia

Colin McArthur

Edward Carson (James Mason): Did you consider this article in any way immoral?

Oscar Wilde (Peter Finch): It was worse. It was very badly written.
—*The Trials of Oscar Wilde* (1960)

Braveheart needs to be discussed in two quite separate ways: as a classical narrative film engaging with the border country between history and myth, and as an "event" in Scottish culture. In the last analysis the two are connected.

First, the question of historiography and popular narrative film. Let us put together a composite figure: a historian, preferably of Scotland; better still, a medievalist. He is in the best position to point out the widely-derided historical inaccuracies of *Braveheart*: the unlikelihood that Wallace and his army would have worn kilts and sported tartan of any kind since they were lowlanders and not highlanders, or woad, a feature of the Picts who had inhabited Scotland about a millennium before the period in which the film is set; that Isabelle (the French princess married to the future Edward II) might have been bedded and impregnated by Wallace since there is no evidence that they ever met, besides which the princess was only twelve years old when her marriage took place and delivered her first child several years after Wallace's death; and that English and Scots nobles would have been accoutred differently (in the film the former in metal and fine cloth, the latter in leather and rough homespun) since they were both of Anglo-Norman origin, had attained broadly the same level of material development, inhabited the same European code of chivalry and, very often, held lands in both England and Scotland. All of these inaccuracies are verifiable by reference to historical works on late medieval Scotland.

A more difficult problem concerning the historical veracity of *Braveheart* relates to its omissions of verified historical facts that might detract from its ideological construction of Wallace as implacable opponent, to the point of death, of any overtures to Edward I seeking less severe treatment after his defeat at Falkirk. Ranald Nicholson suggests that Wallace may have made such overtures early in 1304, but J. G. Bellamy is more definite, speaking of Wallace as being willing to "submit to his (i.e., Edward's) honest peace without surrendering into his hands body or head."[1] Such a fact is quite literally "unspeakable" within the ideological universe constructed in *Braveheart*. The film's populist nationalism has something in common with Trotskyist conceptions of the working class as ever ready spontaneously to rise and secure the communist revolution. What is equally "unspeakable" in *Braveheart*'s ideological scheme of things, with the commonality of Scotland flocking to Wallace's banner, is the well-documented fact of Wallace's having resorted to conscription and his willingness to hang those who refused to serve.[2] This repression of facts uncongenial to the work's ideological project is a feature of much historical fiction, most notably the work that arguably inaugurated the genre in general and historical fiction about Scotland in particular—Sir Walter Scott's *Waverley*.[3]

To return to our medievalist: having made these point about historical inaccuracy and omission, he is quite likely to adopt a position far at variance from that which he would take faced with a written document containing the same errors. None of this matters, he is liable to say, because *Braveheart* is "a ripping yarn," "a thundering good tale," implying that the film ought to be outside the protocols of historiography. Our historian's stance, curious on the face of it, is, of course, explicable by reference to deep-seated ideologies regarding popular forms such as cinema. Seeing cinema as irretrievably tarnished by one strand of its origins—that of mass entertainment—and therefore fundamentally other than the serious and elite business of academic historiography, he would simply be expressing the High Art position in the High Art/Mass Art debate which has riven European culture (and its colonial affiliates) certainly since the onset of industrialization and the development of mass markets, and arguably before that.[4] Such a position might be understandable, if not entirely excusable, in a medievalist who, after all, is not obliged by his calling to take a professional interest in debates about the origins and development of mass cultural forms. It is wholly inexcusable to find the same attitude in the writings of those journalists professionally concerned with cinema. The attitude to *Braveheart* of "Sure, it is historically inaccurate, but what the hell . . ." is to be found in a very high proportion of reviews, but it has seldom been expressed with such haughty disdain as by Alan Taylor in a piece in *The Scotsman* outlining why he was not going to bother even to see *Braveheart*:

> What I find most wearisome, however, is the bellyaching of those who are upset over the film's lack of historical accuracy, the actors' accents, the liberties it takes with Wallace's life and the Irish scenery. What do they expect? This is Hollywood, not a BBC documentary, and it's best to remember that everything is a sacrificial lamb to the demands of studio moguls and box office returns.[5]

Taylor is here expressing a knee-jerk anti-Hollywood prejudice (a position he contradicts elsewhere in his piece) rather than exploring a very real problem. The question of *Braveheart*'s historical inaccuracies and omissions is far from unimportant, but to note them and then celebrate the film or, the other side of the coin, note them and traduce it on that account, is to close off discussion of the crucial question of the interface between cinema and historiography, of what it means for cinematic institutions of our own time to represent cultures distant in time and space. With regard to *Braveheart*, the issue needs to be reformulated to enquire what determinants existed in the film's production process that required it to countenance historical inaccuracies and omissions. This must involve engaging with the Hollywood (or, more accurately, post-Hollywood) milieu, but in a much more cautious and nuanced way than Taylor's blanket condemnation. Exploration of the question requires reference to economics, aesthetics, and ideology, and to the interrelationship of all these. Still holding *Braveheart* within a framework relevant to historiography, the question might be posed, if it constitutes historical evidence, what is it evidence of? The widely acknowledged historical lapses suggest that the last thing it might be evidence of is the actuality of late medieval Scotland.[6] However, it does constitute evidence of two things: of a certain (post-Hollywood) classical narrative, genre filmmaking, and of the curious melding of two modern discourses. One relates to the construction, or narrativizing, of the medieval world, and the other to the constructing, or narrativizing, of Scotland.

To describe *Braveheart* as post-Hollywood is not to make a point crucial to its status as a historical film, it is simply to observe that it was set up as a commercial project through the route characteristic of the period following the demise of the major Hollywood studios as production mechanisms—roughly speaking, the early 1960s. That said, the winding down of the considerable resources the studios devoted to historical research in their heyday may contribute to the historical lapses of some post-studio productions. *Braveheart*, then, was put together as an independent packaging exercise built primarily round a "bankable" star (one whose name calls forth investment), Mel Gibson, and a workable script, all the elements being developed and financed by independent companies (Gibson's own company, Icon productions, and the Ladd Company), with the finished film being released by one of the majors, Twentieth Century Fox, in its modern role of distributor rather than producer. However, to describe *Braveheart* as a classical (post-) Hollywood *narrative* film is to begin to engage more directly with the reasons for its historical inaccuracies and omissions. Although at two hours, fifty-seven minutes, *Braveheart* is half as long again as the characteristic narrative fiction film, it displays all the necessary components of that form: a situation of dramatic stasis (medieval Scotland, prone to dynastic squabbling and threats from England); an inciting incident (the murder of Wallace's wife); a central *individual* protagonist (Wallace) and antagonist (Edward I); protagonist's motivations that are both internal/psychological (revenge for his wife's death) and external/social (the emancipation of his country); a series of struggles, gains, and reversals; and a return to a new dramatic stasis after the protagonist's triumph, literal or symbolic—symbolic in Wallace's case in his being constructed as the sacrificial John the Baptist who paves the way for Robert the Bruce's Christ.[7] Such a narrative schema implies a progressivist conception of history.

As well as being a classical narrative film, *Braveheart* is also a *genre* film, although it is not altogether certain to which genre it belongs, another factor which might help explain its tenuous relationship with historical accuracy. On the one hand it might be seen as an epic involving a quasi-mythical figure. The various versions of the Robin Hood story fall into this category, as does *El Cid* (1961). All such films set their shadowy heroes alongside actually existing historical personages. On the other hand, *Braveheart* might be seen as an historical bio/pic, a genre which has been present since early in the cinema's development but which fanned out and solidified into an important Hollywood genre in the late 1930s, particularly with Warner Brothers' series of biographies of important historical figures such as Benito Juarez (President of Mexico), Paul Ehrlich (the discoverer of salvarsan), and Paul Julius von Reuter (founder of the news agency of that name).[8] Whether *Braveheart* is epic or bio/pic, it delivers the three things required of both genres if they are composited: spectacle, heterosexual love (often, though not necessarily, involving the central protagonist),[9] and an ideological framework congenial to the film's primary consumers, the mass cinema audience throughout the world. Clearly, these three requirements overlap with the requirements of any (post-)Hollywood classical narrative feature film. Spectacle is, of course, primarily delivered in the battle scenes (a feature that many reviewers, including some not well disposed to the film as a whole, commented favorably on), but the generic necessity to deliver spectacle connects with one dimension of the film's historical inaccuracy, its tendency to undermine the geographically and historically key distinction between the Scottish highlands and lowlands and between highlanders and lowlanders, although the dominant post-1770 discourses within which Scotland has been constructed give powerful impetus to the erroneous view that Scotland is primarily a rural, highland society (of which more presently). Clearly, the generic requirement of delivering heterosexual love (along with the more formal requirement of minimizing the number of important characters) explains the historical inaccuracies relating to Princess Isabelle.

In celebrating heterosexual love (and in the case of *Braveheart* traducing homosexual love[10]), the epic and the historical bio/pic (and, indeed, all the Hollywood genres) are advancing an ideological framework congenial to the great bulk of the popular audience. But they advance a congenial ideological framework in a more general, political sense. *Juarez* (1939), for example, accomplished its ideological project of valorizing Benito Juarez by consistently identifying him with Abraham Lincoln, having actor Paul Muni dress in the same funereal clothes as the American president, instead of Mexican garb, and by having photographs of Lincoln on the walls of Juarez's rooms.[11] One of the mechanisms whereby an epic or historical bio/pic is rendered ideologically congenial to a popular audience is by linking the central protagonist to one single, oft-reiterated word that evokes a favorable response from the audience. In *Rob Roy* (1995), another excursion into Scottish history, the word is "honor" (a singularly inappropriate choice given what historians know about the actual activities of Rob Roy[12]), and in *Braveheart* the word is "freedom." This connects with another sense in which *Braveheart* is historically adrift. It constructs Wallace as a kind of modern, nationalist guerrilla leader in a period half a millenium before the appearance of nationalism on the historical stage as a concept under which disparate classes and interests might be mobilized within a nation state. As Nairn and others have argued, nationalism is the consequence of the uneven economic development produced by the English agricultural and industrial revolutions of the eighteenth century, the banner under which the bourgeoisies of France, Germany, Italy, and elsewhere mobilized the forces within their own geographical areas to catch up with Britain.[13] The reverse of the coin of *Braveheart* being marked by modern nationalism is that it feels no need to engage with the ideological structures of the late medieval period, most notably feudalism, the church, and the code of chivalry. Of course it is prepared to press into service limited aspects of feudalism that can be made to function within the film's modern ideological framework. This is true particularly of the *jus primae noctis*, the feudal right of the lord to one night of sexual access, before her husband, to a newly married tenant.

Braveheart assumes, and expects its audience to assume, that the *jus primae noctis* was unambiguously an act of sexual tyranny.[14] In this respect it contrasts interestingly with *The War Lord* (1965) which, although a classic narrative movie in the same tradition as *Braveheart*, was constructed round the *refusal* of a medieval lord to return the bride to her spouse after his exercise of the *jus primae noctis*. Clearly, the *War Lord* expected its audience to see the refusal of the lord, and the bride's connivance in the refusal, as the triumph of "modern" love over feudal convention. Nevertheless, with a subtlety altogether absent from *Braveheart*, it attempted to get inside the medieval *mentalité* by presenting the sense of outrage of the lord's tenants, not at his having deflowered the bride, but at his refusal to comply with the alleged feudal tradition and return her to her husband. The motivation of Liam Neeson's Rob Roy is also constructed partly in relation to the sexual abuse of his wife, as though modern filmmakers had difficulty in conceiving motivations that did not involve sexuality (but see above regarding the requirement of classical Hollywood narrative movies to deliver heterosexual love). A rare example of a film which, while dealing with sexuality, attempts to represent the otherness of the medieval world is Walerian Borowczyk's *Blanche* (1971). It does this partly by using distancing devices such as medieval music played on medieval instruments and incorporated diegetically into the film with medieval modes of musical presentation (unlike *Braveheart*, which has a lush, non-diegetic, romantic score based on vaguely Celtic motifs which, as it happens, sound more Irish than Scottish, perhaps appropriately so since the production was lured to Ireland from Scotland by promises of tax incentives and Irish Army reservists as extras) and a visual style based on the flat, non-perspectival look and range of colors of medieval painting. Significantly, *Blanche* is usually categorized and presented as an "art house" rather than a mass entertainment movie.[15] As well as offering evidence of the current determinants on (post-) Hollywood, classical narrative filmmaking, *Braveheart* offers evidence of a perhaps unique coming together of two modern discourses: the dominant narratives whereby the medieval world is constructed, and the dominant narratives within which Scotland is constructed.

Certainty about how to represent the past recedes the further back you go. The convention is that late Victorians are stiff and hypocritical at home and languidly supercilious in their imperial setting; Regency figures (and possibly early Victorians) are jolly and Dickensian; and eighteenth century figures are sexually rumbustious. Prior to that, however, things begin to mist over and certain "Dark Ages" tropes predominate: darkness; religiosity and/or mysticism; grinding poverty and filth; physical deformity and disfiguring disease; and, above all, unrestrained and unspeakable cruelty. These are the dominant tropes of *Braveheart*. This cinematic Dark Ageism, if such the discourse might be so called, can be tracked through Alexander Korda's *The Private Life of Henry VIII* (1933), in which Charles Laughton's messy eating and wife-beheadings are key tropes; Carl Dreyer's *Day of Wrath* (1943); Ingmar Bergman's *The Seventh Seal* (1957) and *The Virgin Spring* (1960); and Richard Fleischer's *The Vikings* (1958) to the cinematic adaptation of Umberto Eco's *The Name of the Rose* (1986). *Day*

(1991) explores brilliantly how *Monty Python and the Holy Grail* (1975) simultaneously presents and deconstructs this discourse, implicitly posing the question how can we, in the modern world, adequately represent the Middle Ages? Chris Peachment traverses some of the same terrain in a witty and accessible way shorn of Day's postmodern theoretical superstructure.[16] Cinematic Dark Ageism suffuses *Braveheart*, particularly the battle scenes, which are all gore, pierced eyes and genitals, cloven skulls, severed limbs, and awful screams.[17] It is present, too, in the morbid explicitness of Wallace's execution and the malignant leprosy of the Bruce's father. However, dominant as Dark Ageism is in the construction of *Braveheart* it is alloyed from time to time with another powerful discourse within which Scotland is constructed—Tartanry. This discourse has many facets, not all of which are mobilized in *Braveheart*. It emerged in the neoclassical period in the wake of James Macpherson's alleged translations (in fact inventions) of fragments of Gaelic poetry about ancient heroes such as Ossian and Fingal, and received periodic boosts through phenomena such as Sir Walter Scott's writings and Queen Victoria's imprimatur being conferred on the highlands, not least through her residence at Balmoral. The cumulative effect of the Tartanry discourse was to construct Scotland, in the eyes of pre-Romantic and Romantic Europe, as a magical landscape of hills and mists peopled by fierce warriors and wan maidens living close to nature, a realm with the power to transform strangers and teach them to dream. This discourse is, as Chapman and others have pointed out, an act of "symbolic appropriation" by pre-Romantic and Romantic ideologues who constructed Scotland in terms of the dreams, fears, fantasies, and repressions of their own societies just as they were to do with the South Seas, the Orient, and Africa.[18] The discourse of Tartanry was subsequently to dominate every form of signification relating to Scotland: novels, plays, poems, music, operas, ballets, easel painting, photography, advertising, right down to film and television in the present day.[19] So hegemonic did Tartanry become in the representation of Scotland that anyone seeking to speak about the country was drawn to Tartanry Circe-like, its pernicious tropes silently guiding the hands of artists and intellectuals of all kinds including, most grievously, Scots themselves. It is this subconscious dominance of Tartanry, therefore, that requires *Braveheart*'s Scottish personnel to wear tartan, although the historical evidence is that they did not, and to be seen in mountainous terrain although theirs was a lowland struggle. *Braveheart*'s overall aesthetic might be described as debased Romanticism, recalling that Romanticism has been called the cultural mode of nationalism.

This is not to say that a Romantic aesthetic cannot deliver serious and analytic screen history. Luchino Visconti's *The Leopard* (1964) triumphantly demonstrates this. Its lush musical score, based on the late Romantic music of Bruckner, Mahler, and Verdi, and the visual style of the film, based on Romantic painting, are entirely appropriate to the theme of the film, an analysis of the situation of an aristocratic Sicilian family at a moment of historical change in Risorgimento Italy. *Braveheart*'s debased Romanticism is unstiffened by the kind of precise historical analysis of *The Leopard*, which is a Realist work in the Lukacsian[20] sense of the term, its characters incarnating the social and political contradictions of their time. *Braveheart*'s Romanticism is closer to the popular meaning of the term, suggesting something very far removed from reality, dealing with heightened emotions, and displaying a certain vulgar pictorialism. The latter is evident throughout the film but is most gross in the scenes involving Wallace and the two women in his life, his wife Murron, and his lover, Princess Isabelle. Some sense of the vulgarity of *Braveheart* is conveyed in Figure 10.1, but its full realization in the film depends upon the orchestration of every dimension of the *mise-en-scène* at key moments: acting, lighting, music, the use of slow motion, and the like. The obverse of this sentimentality is the savagery of the battle scenes and the way Wallace's execution is mounted.

Any argument about the aesthetic insensitivity of *Braveheart* cannot be conducted in generalities, and must get down to the specific *mise-en-scène* of particular moments, but the argument will often be about the extent to which the film unerringly opts for aesthetic strategies that are "off the shelf," so to speak, clichéd, pre-existing, emerging from the filmmaker's working on automatic pilot rather than thinking carefully about the scene in question. One of the writers cited in the second half of this chapter refers to a particular scene in which the child Wallace, standing by his father's grave, is handed a thistle flower by the child Murron. The argument this chapter offers about the aesthetic crassness of *Braveheart* would raise questions about the casting of the child players, particularly the boy playing Wallace, who looks like a tearful, fetching urchin from a Joan Eardley painting; about the performances the director has asked the children to deliver; about the color and focusing of the shot; and, above all, about the music track accompanying it. The argument would be about how the *mise-en-scène* seeks to bludgeon the audience's emotional response. The same kind of analysis can be applied to the scene of Wallace's execution. To show a close-up of a bench covered with sacking and then to draw back the sacking to reveal the ghastly array of implements to be used in Wallace's hanging, drawing, castration, beheading, and quartering is to indulge in the pornography of torture. It is one of the paradoxes of film reviewing that tabloid reviews, for the most part retellings of the plot and superficial expressions of the reviewer's taste, sometimes cut to the heart of shallow pretentiousness in film acting and direction in a way the ostensibly more serious reviews in the quality press may not. Such was the case with the *Daily Mirror* review of *Braveheart* when it described the above scene with the children as "[smacking] more of a Bird's Eye advert than serious drama."[21] Narratives about certain societies—the ante-bellum American

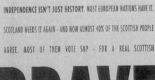
INDEPENDENCE ISN'T JUST HISTORY. MOST EUROPEAN NATIONS HAVE IT.

SCOTLAND NEEDS IT AGAIN - AND NOW ALMOST 40% OF THE SCOTTISH PEOPLE

AGREE. MOST OF THEM VOTE SNP - FOR A REAL SCOTTISH

BRAVE

HEART

PARLIAMENT WITH A DIRECT VOICE IN EUROPE, FOR SCOTTISH CONTROL OF

SCOTTISH OIL AND SCOTTISH RESOURCES, AND FOR INVESTMENT IN SCOTTISH

EDUCATION AND HEALTH. TODAY IT'S NOT JUST **BRAVEHEARTS** WHO CHOOSE

INDEPENDENCE - IT'S ALSO **WISE HEADS** - AND THEY USE THE BALLOT BOX!

INDEPENDENCE
We need it more than ever!

Battle stars: Mel Gibson has the leading role in the multi-million pound blockbuster

The Scottish National Party appropriates *Braveheart*. (Reprinted by permission of the Scottish National Party.)

South and Nazi Germany spring to mind—seem particularly prone to a
melange of savagery and sentimentality, and narratives about Scotland
show something of the same tendency. In *Braveheart* this noxious mix is
offset from time to time by other elements, most notably Mel Gibson's
playing of Wallace with some humor, a feature of his roles more generally.
The extent to which this is so may be judged by imagining how another
player associated with cinematic epics for a substantial part of his career,
Charlton Heston (an actor not given to self-mockery), might have played
the role. This, of course, cuts two ways. There are moments in *Braveheart*
when Gibson's repertoire of signs (particularly ironic movements of his
eyes) recalls the roles he played in the *Lethal Weapon* and *Mad Max* films,
posing the legitimate question of the repertoire's appropriateness for sig-
nifying a late medieval warrior within the film's own illusionist aesthetic—a
key element of which is that things look authentic.

No such ambiguities mitigate the thoroughly debased Romanticism of
Randall Wallace's novelization of his own screenplay for *Braveheart*.[22] To
adapt Oscar Wilde's remarks on Dickens's account of the death of Little
Nell, the man must have a heart of stone who could read Randall Wallace's
Braveheart without laughing. Usefully, however, this piece of sub-Barbara
Cartland pulp literature indicates the extent to which the devil's brew of
savagery and sentimentality is present in the writing as well as the direction
of the film. The quality of Wallace's writing may be gleaned from the following extracts, the first from the scene in which Wallace and Robert the
Bruce meet for the first time, the second from the scene of the first encounter between Wallace and Princess Isabelle:

Wallace stood with his feet planted as wide as his shoulders, and for a man with
shoulders so broad, the posture could have looked bullying. But his face contained
none of the surly arrogance of the brute. He was handsome, strikingly so; manly,
calm and self-contained—young Bruce could see why tough men like the Highlanders [*sic*] would follow this man into battle. It was a face women would like,
with softness in the pale green eyes and light playing in the blondish hair. His chin
was up, his mouth set, his eyes still. And young Robert the Bruce knew . . . that
before him stood a man who never had nor never would subjugate himself to any
other man.

And while the princess reminded William Wallace of everything he had loved and
lost, he haunted her with everything she wanted and had never found. Tall, powerful, commanding, his shoulders thick, his hair wild, his eyes soft, even pained. A
man facing the hatred of the world's most powerful king; a man who had won
great battles and commanded armies, yet who looked as if he could spur his horse
away right now and ride away from adoration and glory and never miss any of it.
She had never seen a man like this. She had never known such a one existed.[23]

What Randall Wallace's novelization offers that the film does not are a
prologue and epilogue outlining his own take on the story of Wallace. The

epilogue, in particular, is remarkable for its mélange of authorial hubris; mystical, quasi blood-and-soil ideology; and a sensibility of staggering vulgarity and sentimentality. In the following extract, Randall Wallace has returned to the area in London called Smithfield where Wallace met his end:

I wanted to visit that sanctuary [a church on the site] again to find a private place away from the crowded street, where people passed neither knowing or caring about the long-dead Scot remembered on the plaque or the American who stopped before it, gazing up at it with tears in his eyes.

The church was closed that day. So I stood in the arched shelter of its entryway, beside its graveyard. I had meant to pray inside the church, but where I now found myself seemed no less fine a place for prayer. So I thanked God for my family and friends and for my calling as a storyteller. And I thanked God for William Wallace. I wondered if William Wallace was just as glad I had come upon his story. And then something strange happened. I can't say that I saw him; it may be an overstatement to say that I felt his presence. But I felt . . . that I could talk to him there. I thanked him personally. I told him I had no idea if we were related by blood, but I had come to feel a kinship with him and felt that somehow I was meant to be there, seven hundred years after he was, to tell his story. I told him there were few promises I could make him as to what would become of this telling of his tale, but I could make him the same one I had made to God and to myself; I would do my best to convey the truth as I saw it to those around me . . . [24]

In Randall Wallace's universe, even a piece of ostensible reportage takes on the character of a Romantic trope—the swearing of an oath to a departed "ancestor." The key question is how the ludicrously debased Romanticism of Randall Wallace's writing and Mel Gibson's production should provoke such a powerful response within Scotland.

The indices of *Braveheart* as "event" in Scottish culture are diverse. A useful starting point is the decision of the producers to mount the European premiere of the film in Stirling, a medium-sized Scottish town somewhat to the north of and equidistant from Edinburgh and Glasgow, but deemed appropriate for the premiere since it was close to the site of Wallace's victory over the English in 1287 and also of the Wallace Monument, raised in the 1860s as part of the culture of nationalism's "invention of tradition," ably described in the book of essays of that title.[25] It is an open question as to the extent to which the producers' awareness of the nationalist/separatist ideology of the film was a factor in the siting of the premiere in Stirling, a factor about which they (particularly Mel Gibson) were to be somewhat coy when the Scottish National Party appropriated the film as a whole into its party rhetoric and images from the film into its party literature (of which more presently). Most societies are, to some extent, dazzled by the idea of Hollywood, particularly by the opportunity to see stars in the flesh. It is a mark of Scotland's provincialism that it has regularly feted (in the form of breathless national and local media coverage) those Hollywood stars who have come there and, what is worse, celebrated those films which have constructed Scotland within regressive discourses.[26] This dazzlement, with regard to *Braveheart*, was most evident in the local newspaper, the *Stirling Observer*, which announced delightedly on the front page of its edition of August 2, 1995, that the European premiere of the film would be in Stirling. The sense of local pride, in that account, vied with a quite hard-nosed appreciation of the likely tourist spin-off from the premiere and the film itself (the recently-released *Rob Roy* had been massively tied in with the Scottish Tourist Board). Subsequent issues reported the arrangements for the premiere and, a variation on a regular feature of the paper, ran a competition, the prizes for which were tickets to the premiere. The issue of September 1, contains the advertisement in Figure 10.2 and the culmination of the coverage came with the special *Braveheart* Souvenir Issue of September 6, which carried four pages of stories and pictures about the premiere, the stars and the great and the good attending it, and the ecstatic response of the local people who had waited for up to eight hours in pouring rain to catch a glimpse of the notables. Such was the local demand for the souvenir issue that the relevant four pages were reproduced in the issue of September 8. The tabloid end of the Scottish national press was no less ecstatic, the *Daily Record* of September 4, including in its report a quotation from a Stirling old-age pensioner: "I've lived here all my life and I've never seen anything like this. Stirling has become the centre of the world." It was left to an *English* quality broadsheet, *The Guardian*, to describe the premiere in altogether more sardonic terms.[27]

Another index of the extent to which *Braveheart* had become an event in Scottish culture was its intertextuality, its capacity to be referred to, quoted from, analogized on, in sites far removed from cinema. The film became a fruitful source for political and other cartoons in the press (see Figure 10.3); a newspaper talked of a mythical snooker player as "Braveheart of the green baize"; a travel feature on walking in Scotland was headed "For the Brave Hearted"; a staff recruitment advertisement by Scottish Enterprise was headed "William Wallaces wanted"; a football match report referred to East Fife manager Steve Archibald as "Brave Arch!" and, a sure sign of intertextual status, the television comedy program *French and Saunders* included an item which satirized both *Rob Roy* and *Braveheart*. It was spot-on in sending up the heavily macho ethos of both films and the aesthetic grossness of *Braveheart*. *Braveheart* is not unique with regard to intertextuality. Certain films, most notably *Casablanca*, are profusely intertextual.[28] The point being made here is the fecund intertextuality of *Braveheart* in the Scottish context—the first film since *Local Hero* (1983) to function in this way—pointing to its status as event in Scottish culture.

The third index of *Braveheart*'s status as event is its appropriation by

STIRLING

Town Centre

Open Sunday 3rd September, 1995
for
The European Premiere of the Movie

BRAVEHEART

Scotland's premiere town is hosting this great event and to celebrate it
our shops, restaurants and tourist venues will be open.

The Thistle Shopping Centre open 12.30-4.30 p.m.

+ *Mel Gibson & Loads of Hollywood Stars*
+ *Street entertainment (throughout the town)*
+ *pub parties*
+ *old town costume performances*
+ *medieval extravaganzas in the Castle (all day!)*
+ *be amazed at the profusion of banners*
+ *be dazzled by the special floodlighting*

Come early and make a day of it - shopping, leisure and fun

'The City Experience in the Countryside'

Braveheart becomes hegemonic in the local tourist industry.

the Scottish National Party (SNP). The Tory Secretary of State for Scotland,
Michael Forsyth (who is also the Member of Parliament for Stirling), and
his parliamentary shadow, Labor MP George Robertson, both attended the
premiere and made halfhearted attempts to square their own parties' un-
ionist politics with the clear independence message of the film, but everyone
knew that there was no way they could construct the Wallace of the film
as anything other than separatist.[29] The SNP's deployment of the film in

"Blairheart" by Steven Camley in *Scotland on Sunday*. (Reprinted by permission of the artist.)

party literature has already been mentioned (see Figure 10.1), but it also figured substantially in the address of the party's National Convenor, Alex Salmond, MP, at the SNP's annual conference soon after the film's premiere, the entire opening section of the address being structured round the film. It is worth quoting in some detail:

A funny thing happened to me on the way to the *Braveheart* Premier [*sic*]. There was the hero draped in tartan just waiting to be cheered by the thousands lining the streets as he entered the cinema. And what happened? Well first he got booed in. Three hours later he was booed out. For this wasn't the Hollywood hero but the local hero—not Mel but Michael—the Secretary of State Against Scotland—the man whom Lady Thatcher once described in her memoirs as a "Young Lochinvar." They (Forsyth and Robertson) were certainly having trouble explaining away the message. Michael said that Wallace was a fighter for Scottish "interests." George said he fought for Scottish "identity." Notice this difficulty with the "i" word.
    The one word they didn't want to mention was INDEPENDENCE which is what Wallace was actually fighting for . . .
    The *Braveheart* screenwriter Randall Wallace tells of how he talked to some local youngsters in the shadow of the Wallace monument. They knew it was called the Wallace monument but couldn't tell him anything about the man it commemorated. . . . The story of Wallace should and does inspire us, but the story of the youngsters who had never heard of Wallace should make us pause and ponder. . . .

We should be ashamed that it has taken Hollywood to give so many Scots back our history. . . .

And George and Michael should also be worried because now, as anyone who knows the story and has seen the film will know, the real villains are not the English but the establishment leadership of Scotland who bought and sold their country for personal advancement.[30]

Salmond then went on to deal with more substantial issues of policy, but the ideological capital of the film's bringing back to public attention the shadowy historical figure of Wallace was cashed once more in the final words of his address: ". . . we can say with Wallace—head and heart—the one word which encapsulates all our hopes—Freedom, Freedom, Freedom."[31]

This essay began by suggesting that, in the last analysis, there is a connection between *Braveheart* as aesthetic object and *Braveheart* as event in Scottish culture. To be more concrete, there is a connection between its debased Romanticism, its post-1789 populist nationalism and xenophobia, and the way it has been appropriated by individuals and institutions in Scotland. The eminently knowledgable and serious Scots journalist Neal Ascherson, who understands, better than most, the universality and virtual inevitability of nationalism in the modern world, and its appalling dangers, wrote about the seductive appeal of *Braveheart*'s populism in a piece about heroes, popular and official:

Seeking heroes, I went the other day to see *Braveheart*. As an account of the real William Wallace, or of late 13th-century Scotland, it is a joke. The list of cultural howlers and historical distortions rolls on for ever. As in the similar *Rob Roy*, the English feature as degenerate, upper-class sadists. . . . You go to scoff . . . and yet there are moments when this shilling schlocker takes you unawares. One strong-minded, progressive friend found herself in tears. Another Scottish colleague reacted with a furious attack on the film for reducing his country's struggles to crude anti-English racism. Both went to the film certain they were immune to its allure—but neither was. They saw a child give a flower to a boy standing at his murdered father's grave, and the flower was a thistle. They heard a man speak easily of his country's "freedom" without seeking a lesser word. Suddenly, they were undone. Wallace is a real hero, which means that he lives on in the shadows at the back of people's heads.[32]

Ascherson's point about the seductiveness of *Braveheart* is repeated, with a much diminished sense of its dangers or the affront to aesthetic sensibilities on which it is based. Thus, Brian Pendreigh writes that: "*Braveheart* provides one of Scotland's great heroes with a monument as impressive in its own way as the one outside Stirling. But, more than that, it provides the Scots with a powerful creation myth which will surely help to focus our national sense of identity."[33] And the actor James Cosmo, Wallace's righthand man in the film, is reported in the *Stirling Observer* as "bursting with pride." It is as if an aesthetic dementia had gripped the Scots, rendering them blind to the empty populism, the slavering xenophobia, the sheer stylistic vulgarity of *Braveheart*. This is dismaying enough in individuals, but it is decidedly sinister when a national political party aligns itself with such a truly appalling film. One of the *Stirling Observer*'s parting shots on the topic of the *Braveheart* premiere was a photograph of a kilted Mel Gibson in a prominent place on the front page of its issue of September 8 under the heading "It's Mel Mania!" At the bottom of the same page, under the heading " 'Anti-English' alert," was an item about the local police looking for information concerning leaflets and graffiti canvassing the sentiment "English Go Home." The *Stirling Observer* made no connection between the two items, although a film more calculated to encourage the sentiments expressed in the leaflets and graffiti could not be imagined. One would heartily wish that *Braveheart*, to quote Trotsky, "will be swept into the garbage heap of history." One's fear, however, is that, available on video, it will play to packed buses of Scottish soccer and rugby supporters en route to matches against England, whipping them into a frenzy of xenophobia.

AFTERWORD

This Afterword was written some months after the above essay. In the intervening period *Braveheart*'s delirious intertextuality has continued apace, culminating in the discursive "braveheartization" of the Scotland versus England soccer match during the Euro 96 competition in June 1996. Throughout the latter one could scarcely open a newspaper or listen to a sports broadcast without hearing the Scots team described as "bravehearts," and this was, indeed, the trope deployed on the cover of the Scottish edition of *Radio Times* concurrent with the competition (Figure 10.4).

However, the discursive visibility of *Braveheart* had a curious effect on the rhetorical construction of the England team, particularly in the English tabloid press. This could be described as the "medievalization" of England. It was as if the tabloids, aware of the heroization of the Scots in terms of the figure of William Wallace/Mel Gibson, sought to construct the English in analogous terms. This resulted in extensive referencing of the English team as "lionhearts" and—a central hero on the scale of Wallace being a requirement in this narrative—the accoutring of Paul Gascoigne in the masquerade of Henry V.

However, I am happy to report that—despite the waving of lifesize cutouts of Mel Gibson at the game—the dire foreboding about the effects of *Braveheart* on the Scots fans with which I ended the above essay proved unwarranted. No doubt there were complex reasons for this, including the excellent spirit within which the competition was played and better stadium facilities, stewarding, and police intelligence. However, I would like to

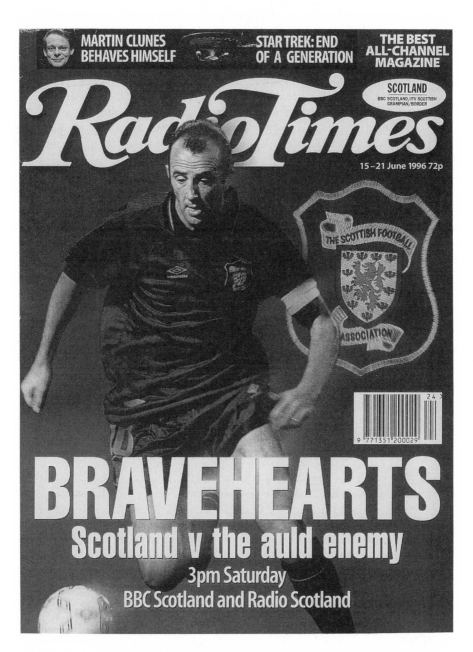

Braveheart makes the cover of the Scottish edition of *Radio Times*. (Reprinted by permission of *Radio Times*.)

think that Richard Giulianotti's intriguing theory had something to do with it. His argument, based on the evidence of the World Cup in Italy in 1990, is that the Scots fans, the "tartan army," now construct their identity dialogically in relation to the identity of the English fans. The latter had arrived in Italy in 1990 with a well-earned reputation for xenophobia, moroseness, and violence. Wishing not to be associated with this, Richard Giulianotti argues, the Scots constructed themselves as internationalist, convivial, and placid. The most important part of his argument is that the Scots fans projected this "new" identity (their own historical one had itself been rather alarming) through the same range of icons, tartan scarves and kilts, and saltire and lion rampant flags, as before. By suggesting that these icons are empty vessels waiting to be filled with either progressive or regressive identities, Giulianotti calls into question the position of those writers (the present one included) who see such icons as irretrievably tarnished by the uses to which they have been put and the range of attitudes associated with them.[34]

NOTES

The arguments in the above essay were first rehearsed at two events, one at the University of Aberdeen, the other at the University of Glasgow. With regard to the former, a panel of discussion, I would like to express my thanks to the chair of the discussion, Professor Alan I. Macinnes; to my co-panelists, Dr. Grant Simpson and Dr. Peter Murray; and to the committee of the Aberdeen University Historical Society, Dawn Bailey, Alison Cathcart, Rosie Fell, and Karen Jillings. With regard to the second event, thanks are due to Dr. Irene Maver and Dr. David Limond of the Department of Scottish History.

The essay is dedicated to the memory of Barbara Grigor who, with her husband Murray, did so much to contest regressive accounts of Scottish history and culture.

1. R. Nicholson, *Scotland: The Later Middle Ages* (Edinburgh: Oliver and Boyd, 1974); J. G. Bellamy, *The Law of Treason in England in the Late Middle Ages* (London: Cambridge University Press, 1970).

2. As will become clear, this chapter is not a crude attack on historical films, in particular those made within the Hollywood tradition. At the same time, historical films should not be let off the hook of historical veracity because they are dramatic reconstructions. After all, academic works of historiography are themselves acts of reconstruction, albeit using a different rhetoric from that of narrative fiction. The distinction False Invention/True Invention has been illuminatingly discussed in Robert A. Rosenstone, *Visions of the Past: The Challenge of Film to Our Idea of History* (Cambridge, Mass.: Harvard University Press, 1995), pp. 72, 76, his example of the former being *Mississippi Burning* (1988) and of the latter *Glory* (1989), the one because it is seriously at odds with verifiable facts, the other because it follows them closely.

3. In a novel devoted to the 1745 Jacobite Rising, it is astonishing that the key battle, that of Culloden (1746), should be, to all intents and purposes, repressed.

However, the repression does facilitate the pro-unionist closure of the novel. Claire Lamont, "*Waverley* and the Battle of Culloden," in Angus Easson (ed.), *History and the Novel* (Cambridge: D. S. Brewer, 1991): pp. 14, 26.

4. James Naremore and Patrick Brantlinger (eds.), *Modernity and Mass Culture* (Bloomington: Indiana University Press, 1991).

5. A. Taylor, "Tinsel town history," *The Scotsman* (September 4, 1995): 12.

6. Many historians and students of film, operating from diverse theoretical positions, would regard this as a foregone conclusion. Sorlin stresses the inevitability of historical films being about the time and place in which they were produced and not the time and place of the events they represent. Pierre Sorlin, *The Film in History: Restaging the Past* (Oxford: Basil Blackwell, 1980). Day talks about the impossibility of grasping "the Medieval Other," and Rosenstone, under the influence of postmodernist attempts to eclipse history, canvasses a form of historical film that is self-referential, palpably as much about its own take on the past as the past itself. D. D. Day, "Monty Python and the Medieval Order," K. J. Harty, *Cinema Arthuriana* (New York and London: Garland, 1991); Robert A. Rosenstone, *Visions of the Past: The Challenge of Film in Our Idea of History* (Cambridge, Mass.: Harvard University Press, 1995).

7. A more detailed account of the operation of classical Hollywood narrative and how it privileges *individual* and not collective solutions to problems is to be found in K. Bordwell and D. Thompson, *Film Art: An Introduction* (New York: Knopf, 1986).

8. George F. Custen, *Bio/Pics: How Hollywood Constructed Public History* (New Brunswick, N.J.: Rutgers University Press, 1992).

9. L. Grindon, *Shadows on the Past: Studies in the Historical Fiction Film* (Philadelphia: Temple University Press 1994), writes interestingly about Romance and Spectacle in historical films, in particular about Spectacle as bearer of the transindividual, historical elements of the film.

10. The American organization GLAAD (Gay and Lesbian Alliance Against Defamation) demonstrated and leafleted against *Braveheart* at its opening in nine U.S. cities on account of its construction of Edward I's son and his gay lover.

11. Grindon, *Shadows on the Past*, p. 12.

12. It is well established among historians that Rob Roy was, among other things, what would today be called a "supergrass (stool pigeon)," acting as an informant for the Hanoverian government against his erstwhile Jacobite comrades. J. Allardyce (ed.), *Historical Papers Relating to the Jacobite Period, 1699–1750* (Aberdeen: New Spalding Club, 1895); A. Mcinnes, *Clans, Commerce and the House of Stuart* (Edinburgh: Tuckwell Press, 1996).

13. T. Nairn, *The Break-up of Britain* (London: Verso, 1977).

14. It is widely assumed that *jus primae noctis* actually existed in medieval Europe, but a search of the historiographical work relating to the period reveals a curious absence of the concept. The idea is dealt with in the *Encyclopaedia Britannica* under the heading *droit de seigneur*: "The evidence of its existence in Europe is almost all indirect, involving records of redemption dues paid by the vassal to avoid enforcement. A considerable number of feudal rights related to the vassal's marriage, particularly the lord's right to select a bride for his vassal, but these were almost invariably redeemed by a money payment or 'avail'; and it seems likely that

the *droit du seigneur* amounted, in effect, only to another tax of this sort" (Chicago: *Encyclopaedia Britannica*, 15th ed., 1973, p. 670).

15. S. Neale, "Art Cinema as Institution," in *Screen*, no. 1, 1981: 11, 39.

16. C. Peachment, "All you need is mud . . . ," *The Independent*, September 7, 1995: 8.

17. The representation of violence in *Braveheart* seems to have set new standards. It is reported that the producers of *The Bruce*, yet another foray into Scottish history, ordered its battle scenes to be reshot since the first version did not reach the level of gore achieved in *Braveheart*. M. McBain, "Bruce has his bloody encore," *Scotland on Sunday*, January 14, 1995: 1.

18. M. Chapman, *The Gaelic Vision in Scottish Culture* (London: Croom Helm, 1978); F. Fanon, *Black Skin, White Masks* (New York: Grove Press, 1968).

19. C. McArthur, *Scotch Reels: Scotland in Cinema and Television* (London: British Film Institute, 1982).

20. Gyorgy Lukacs (1885–1971), philosopher, literary critic, and political activist, formulated in works such as *The Historical Novel* (1937) a sophisticated, antimodernist theory of literary realism. This was too hastily discounted by the modernist left in its elevation of Bertolt Brecht, with whom Lukacs had a stinging debate in the inter-war period (Ernst Bloch, Gyorgy Lukacs, Bertolt Brecht, Walter Benjamin, Theodor Adorno, *Aesthetics and Politics* (London: Verso, 1980).

21. Simon Rose, "Mel of a super hero," in the *Screen Mirror*, September 7, 1995: 3.

22. Randall Wallace, *Braveheart* (London: Signet/Penguin Books, 1995).

23. Wallace, pp. 146–47, 163.

24. Wallace, pp. 276–77.

25. Eric Hobsbawm and Terence Ranger (eds), *The Invention of Tradition* (Cambridge: Cambridge University Press, 1983).

26. *Brigadoon* (1954), *The Maggie* (1954), and *Local Hero* (1983) have in their time been rapturously welcomed in Scotland. It is a mark of the self-lacerative qualities of the Scots (nowhere more apparent than in their response to *Braveheart*) that they consistently mistake shit for manna (see Colin McArthur, "*The Maggie*," in *Cencrastus* 12, 1983). That said, *Brigadoon* in particular (arguably one of the more complex films on the question of the representation of Scotland) drives Scots intellectuals to distraction. It is repeatedly, indeed talismanically, cited as the very nadir of mawkish Tartanry.

27. Erlend Clouston, "Little Mel Walks Tall in Adulation of Scots Fans," *The Guardian*, September 4, 1995: 2.

28. Colin McArthur, *The Casablanca File* (London: Half Brick Images, 1992).

29. Arnold Kemp, "Battling Over Braveheart," *The Guardian*, September 11, 1995: 13.

30. SNP News Release 1995.

31. SNP News Release 1995.

32. Neal Ascherson, "Now is the time for official heroes to come to the aid of the party," *The Independent on Sunday* September 24, 1995: 20. Ascherson's call for a proper place to be accorded popular national heroes echoes that of Raphael Samuel (Raphael Samuel, "The people with stars in their eyes," *The Guardian* September 23, 1995: 27). Both their essays are considered responses from the left to the remarks of Dr. Nicholas Tate, Chief Executive of the School Curriculum and

Assessment Authority, who had argued for the resuscitation of British national heroes/heroines such as Alfred the Great, Horatio Nelson, David Livingstone, and Florence Nightingale so that children might once again become proud of their national past. Tate's remarks were an intervention from the right into the essentially political struggle over the content of the national curriculum. For the extent to which the struggle over the meaning of the past is not simply a British preoccupation, but characteristic of all advanced capitalist countries concerned about their "place in the world," see Frank Füredi, *Mythical Past, Elusive Future: History and Society in an Anxious Age* (London: Pluto Press, 1992).

33. Brian Pendreigh, "Gibson turns Wallace into Mad Mac," *The Scotsman* (September 4, 1995): 4.

34. Richard Giulianotti, "Scotland's Tartan Army in Italy: The Case for the Carnivalesque," *Sociological Review* (Vol. 39, no. 3, 1991): 503–527.

11

Borders and Boundaries: History and Television in a Postmodern World

Ina Bertrand

It is not clear whether Huyssens' "Great Divide"[1]—the border between modernism and mass culture—is a mountain range or a deep crevasse. But the dominant metaphor of the postmodernist turn away from modernism does seem to be spatial: "If this fracture lies in the very bedrock of modernism, then the language of topography—of mapping boundaries, schisms, borderlines—certainly seems adequate to the quagmire of postmodernism."[2] The problem is that these borders and boundaries are harder and harder to locate: for, if the project of modernism was to draw them, then that of post-modernism is to dissolve them.

One of the arenas in which this breakdown of boundaries is clearest is academia, particularly in the humanities, where the old disciplines are under siege. In "the current trend away from subject-specific academic work in favour of more general cultural considerations,"[3] there are now departments of Women's Studies, Australian Studies (and their equivalents in other post-colonial cultures), Afro-American Studies (and their equivalents among other minorities), Media Studies, Communication Studies, Cultural Studies, and so forth.[4]

The discipline of History has been shaken to its roots. Where it was once a master narrative with a clearly recognized place in the schoolroom and between the pages of serious books and journals, it is now everywhere—and nowhere. But if postmodern theory denies History, it allows the return of that repressed as "history," linking (historical) time with (present) space, in what has been called "schizophrenic temporality and spatial pastiche."[5] The postmodern view of history is summed up by Frederic Jameson: "The approach to the present by way of the art language of the simulacrum, or of the pastiche of the stereotypical past, endows present reality and the openness of present history with the spell and distance of a glossy mirage."[6] Giuliana Bruno further clarifies the spatial aspect: ". . . with pastiche there is an effacement of key boundaries and separations, a process of erosion of distinctions."[7]

But the blurring of boundaries extends to definitions of postmodernism itself: there is what Hayward and Kerr call a "slippage back and forth between postmodernism as a set of stylistic phenomena and postmodernism as a socio-economic phase." The same authors credit Jameson with being "the first critic writing in English to propose a homology between the cultural form of postmodernism, its stylistic superstructure, and its economic base."[8]

In a postmodern world, then, we may approach history through culture (images/simulacra), where matters of style and economy meet, expecting to find blurred boundaries or border skirmishes with modernism. We may even write history in film and television.

I am attracted to John Hartley's view of journalism as "the sense-making practice of modernity" and therefore "the most important textual system in the world."[9] The corollary might be that film and television are the sense-making practices of postmodernity, becoming more important textual systems as postmodernism seeks to overtake and displace modernism. Jameson himself has claimed two main features for postmodernism: "the transformation of reality into images, the fragmentation of time into a series of perpetual presents."[10] Both are central to the textual systems of film and television, fiction as much as non-fiction—whatever that distinction may mean in this context. To break down the distinction is to suggest that the cerebral (for the purpose of education) and the emotional (for the purpose of entertainment) may not, after all, be mutually exclusive.[11]

Within a postmodern world of blurred and shifting boundaries, intellectual fashions change rapidly. Currently, narrative—which is seen as a relic of the modernist preference for rationality—is out of fashion, and subject to what I consider to be unnecessarily harsh criticism. After all, popular culture cannot survive without narrative, and I would claim, with Dana Polan, that "Narrative logic and postmodern paralogic can even coexist in the same work."[12]

BORDERTOWN AND AUSTRALIAN HISTORY

In early 1995, the Australian Broadcasting Corporation began to advertise a historical television miniseries, *Bordertown*. It was set in a rural migrant hostel in the 1950s, one of those staging camps where post-war immigrants from Europe waited before being dispersed to work in rural or urban industries which desperately needed their labor in the post-war boom. There "wogs" and "balts" and "dagos" were transformed into "New Australians," learned to speak English and to abandon—or to disguise—the culture that alienated them from the society they had chosen as their new home.

For most present-day Australians this is an uncomfortable story. The attempt to produce an Australian nation by "assimilating" all the diverse peoples inhabiting the continent into an Australian variant of British culture became intensely unpopular. It was resented by both the immigrants to Australia and the indigenous Australians for whom it was initially devised, while the knowledge of its enforced application left a burden of guilt on those Australians with a largely British heritage. Immigrants subject to the assimilation process found they had to come to terms with memories, both painful and exhilarating. On the one hand was the physical and emotional deprivation in the camps, on the other the comradeship that helped to make the camp experience bearable.[13] The replacement of the policy of assimilation with that of "multiculturalism," attempting to encourage ethnic diversity within a national unity, has been broadly, though still not universally, applauded. The next logical step seems to be republicanism, the cutting of the final legal tie with Britain. Recent opinion polls suggest that it has widespread support within the Australian community in principle, though debate still rages about the details of how and when it will be put into practice.

Given the emotional weight of the issue of postwar immigration, both historically and within current debates, the assumption that a television program concerning it would be a consciousness-raising or conscience-pricking drama was understandable. People expected high culture from the national broadcaster, something along the lines of the classic serials made famous by the BBC.[14] They expected a serious discussion of the social problems of immigration, particularly as the same production team had earlier brought to the screen such worthy—as well as entertaining and high-rating—programs as *The Leaving of Liverpool* and *Brides of Christ*.[15]

When it turned out to be something very different the critics were dismayed,[16] and the public turned off.[17] For this was postmodern history, a discussion of a sociocultural issue (the perennial debate about the construction of Australian national identity) through a representation in which aesthetic/stylistic and generic/formal boundaries are permeable and fluid, so that the grotesque and the abject, in all their tastelessness, can also be represented.

There is an Australian city called Bordertown, on the border between the states of Victoria and South Australia, but the program was not located there. Rather, it was in a conceptual "bordertown," a neutral space between the old world and the new, a place which marked a Rubicon to be

The association of the administration of the camp with the national government is made explicit in this image of the second camp commandant (Henry Bates, played by Geoff Morel) saluting the Australian flag. (From *Bordertown*, produced by the Australian Broadcasting Corporation, 1995. Reprinted by permission of the Australian Broadcasting Corporation.)

Cora (Pat Bishop) is a socialist and a fierce nationalist: among the films she screens for the camp residents is *The Overlanders,* an ambivalently "local" production, made in Australia by British Ealing Studios. (From *Bordertown,* produced by the Australian Broadcasting Corporation, 1995. Reprinted by permission of the Australian Broadcasting Corporation.)

crossed, an ultimate boundary between the past and the future. So the camp was given an invented name—Baringa rather than Bonegilla—sufficiently anonymous to represent the experience of all.[18] Neither was it located in any specific district, or near any identifiable town or city.

Time was equally vague. Although costumes and sets and decor are all in period, the nearest reference to an actual date is Bev's slip of the tongue as she conducts the ceremony to open the new ablutions block in episode 3: the assembled crowd is invited to sing "God save the King—I mean Queen," placing the incident some time shortly after the death of King George VI on February 6, 1952.

The effect of this floating in a spatial and temporal vacuum is to produce a community apparently entirely enclosed and self-sufficient, but still unable to prevent intrusions from the past and the outside world. Within the surface narrative, new busloads of residents arrive (bringing key figures into the story, such as Nino, Diomira, Bianca), old residents leave (Pieter and Maeve die, Dante goes to his trial and execution, Bianca is deported back to Italy). "Old" Australians also enter and leave: Colonel Forsythe is replaced by Retired Colonel Henry Bates as camp commander, the gypsy boy

Dom encroaches and is sent away, the local Aboriginal community is invited in and then dismissed, the law descends on the camp and departs with its criminal/victim, Cora arrives and leaves with the traveling picture show. But there is also another layer that is non-narrative—flashbacks and flashforwards, moments of dream or nightmare, daydream or fantasy. These carry the basic story out of its time and place, setting up complex spatial and temporal resonances.

So this Camp Baringa, this bordertown, has at the same time clearly delineated borders (even marked by a high fence and an entrance capable of being patroled to keep the residents in and the outside world at bay[19]) and, in the permeability of these borders and the absence of realistic representation of that outside world in either time or place, no borders at all. Nevertheless, the nation at a critical point in its history is being represented here in microcosm. The concept of assimilation required that the nation be a "melting pot," in which difference was eliminated in the interest of the community as a whole, the past gave way to the future. In episode 1, Louisa describes this process in a reference to a chalk map of Europe on the ground, as: "Bit by bit the map wore away." But Baringa as nation demonstrates the undesirability, the impossibility, of the goal of assimilation.

Genre and Style

Despite such fundamental issues underlying the narrative, the program was not received as a serious discussion about the formation of national identity. In fact both critics and audiences were puzzled and confused by it.

First, it was difficult to locate in generic terms. Television genres were once clearly distinct, and one of the distinguishing marks was the difference between the past (presented as documentary compilation, fictional miniseries, or classic serial) and the present (presented as news, current affairs, and fiction in telemovies or soap operas). These generic boundaries have now been eroded, both in programming policies within the television institution,[20] and within production houses as they construct programs, acknowledging hybrids in new terms such as "infotainment." In Australia, television serials are now likely to have elements of both past and present,[21] or to be contemporary.[22] The storyline of *Bordertown*, however, is unequivocally in the past, and so it was received as a traditional historical television miniseries—a genre that is currently out of favor with those critics who are suspicious of nostalgia.[23] But any judgment of the program on generic grounds is undermined by its style.

Bordertown is not so much in an alternative style as moving in several stylistic directions at once, threatening all of them. The traditional Australian Broadcasting Corporation high-culture audience, which might have coped with its magic realism, found its tastelessness unacceptable.[24] They would not have appreciated its soap-opera-style narrative: a meandering story with multiple climaxes, a multitude of characters, and a very artificial (even ambivalent) happy ending. Each episode allowed certain of the characters to step forward to center stage and backgrounded the others: audiences, therefore, were required—as soap-opera audiences are accustomed to do—to shift identification both from one episode to another, and within a single episode as the point-of-view of the narrative shifted. But soap-opera fans, who would find this narrative structure familiar even with an untypical final closure, were not likely to take kindly to the program's magic realism and graphic violence. In fact, there was no readymade audience for this mix of styles and genres: any traditionally-defined audience would have been discomforted.

By avoiding realism, the narrative concentrates on our mental images of the world of the past, the "pop images." So, each of the characters starts as a stereotype—not surprisingly, in a narrative concerned with national identity, often a national or racial stereotype. Anal-retentive British schoolteacher Kenneth Pearson is unable to express his love for his only daughter. Joe della Virgine, the Latin lover, seduces and abandons all the pretty women in the camp. Maeve McAloon, the dour Scot, runs the store and post office like a martinet. Dutchman Pieter has rescued his Jewish wife Adrianna from the Nazis and has nightmares about it. Excitable Hungarian Mihaly Bassa spends all his spare time in his garden and protecting his beloved shovel. Dom—the dirty, cheeky and amoral gypsy boy—steals first from Mihaly's garden and then from a nearby farm. The local Aborigines live in a primitive camp by the river, where the women sit around drinking into the night.

But these stereotypes are then embroidered, again in two—not always compatible—directions at once. Realistic drama buries the stereotypical origins of its characters under overlays of individuality, and there is some of this in *Bordertown*: Kenneth Pearson harbors literary ambitions and fantasizes about his wife Peggy in terms that challenge any simplistic interpretation of him as merely the "stiff-upper-lip" Britisher, inarticulate and inhibited. Comedy, on the other hand, carries the stereotype to excess, till it tips over into either parody or a challenge to the notion of the stereotypical itself, as the "wogs" of *Wogs out of work* have done with the concept of ethnicity.[25] Both of these functions of excess apply in *Bordertown*, often producing comic effect within an otherwise dramatic context. So Joe's affair with Adrianna is presented as straight drama, but his attempts to seduce Bev eventually become parodical. Each of the stereotypes finally collapses under its own weight: in the case of Pearson, there is a very funny (but also touching) episode in which he overcomes his inhibitions enough to confess to his daughter Louisa that he loves her very much, without knowing (as the audience knows) that it is Nino, hiding under the bedclothes, who hears his confession—Nino the simpleton, who has failed to master English, but has succeeded in seducing Louisa. Published critiques of *Bordertown* noted only the fundamental stereotyping, without appreciating the complex superstructures of this or their function in critiquing Australian attitudes.

Subjectivity—Language and the Abject

Ihab Hassan has suggested that postmodernism is the ultimate tribal notion of all the world as one, a "postmodern United Nations."[26] *Bordertown*'s goal is the establishment of a national tribe, also creating unity out of diversity. By addressing the construction of national identity through the "pop images" of our culture, and specifically their ethnic roots, the issue of subjectivity is made central. And central to that, in turn, is language—heteroglossia in a polyglot culture, defined as: "the dialogically-interrelated speech practices operative in a given society at a given moment, wherein the idioms of different classes, races, genders, generations and locales compete for ascendancy."[27]

All texts are polyphonic, with a plurality of voices coinciding within any one text, and natural language is only one of the channels of the "voice" of a film: "Film dramaturgy . . . has its special tact, its ways of suggesting through camera placement, framing and acting, such phenomena as intimacy or distance, camaraderie or domination, in short all the social and personal dynamics operating between interlocutors."[28]

But within a national cinema, natural language may well be a determining element: in Australia's case, staging the polyphony of a heteroglot culture. Within Baringa, language is certainly one of the key organizing principles—after all, it is essential to the purpose of the place that all the residents learn English. But this is not a simple matter. In the cacophony of tongues that is heard in the camp, the varieties of English play an important role too: Maeve's Scottish burr, the Colonel's broad Aussie twang, Louisa's almost impenetrable Liverpudlian. The unsurprising result is that the accents of the residents for whom English is not their first language are also varied. Joe insists that Nino speak English even to him, but one of the signs of Nino's simplemindedness is that he fractures the language, producing a version of English that is not like even the Italian English that Joe himself speaks. Within the narrative, the government inspector is not impressed by the progress of Kenneth Pearson's students, and, within the critical discourse surrounding the program, viewers were not impressed with what they saw as "phoney fruit shop accents."[29] However, within a postmodern text, which does not claim to be realistic, the authenticity of accents may be irrelevant. A more important issue is the function of language as a boundary-marker, with the breakdown of boundaries signified by the breakdown of the specificity of language and dialect, accent and intonation.

So, language remains a signifier of difference, but that difference is just as likely to be among speakers of the same language (Bev and Kenneth Pearson, or Nino and Joe) as among those struggling to learn English as a common language. For that matter, there are also those for whom language itself is a struggle—the inarticulate, whether from intellectual disability like Nino or psychological inhibition like Henry Bates or Kenneth Pearson. One of the effects of this heteroglossia is a "schizophrenic" breakdown of the temporal order: ". . . as temporal continuity breaks down, the experience of the present becomes powerfully, overwhelmingly vivid and 'material.' The world comes before the schizophrenic with heightened intensity."[30] It is not surprising that such a world should be viewed through a magic realist vision, one in which the boundaries between reality and fantasy are no longer absolute, the grotesque periodically erupts, and the abject has become explicit.

In psychoanalytic terms, the abject is that which threatens subjectivity by exceeding or undermining the boundaries of the symbolic order (that associated with language and the law). These threats are represented physically, through the traumas of birth or death, but also through the substances expelled from the body—blood (particularly menstrual blood), waste matter (urine, feces, sweat, tears), pollutants (vomit, pus). Sexual activity, in which sexual fluids are exchanged, is part of this scenario. Our physical revulsion (abjection) from all these substances is an expression of our drive to establish the clean, whole body, and represents also our desire to sever the pre-oedipal connection with the Mother, to abandon what Kristeva calls the "semiotic." Kristeva argues that the abject is "rooted historically (in the history of religions) and subjectively (in the structuration of the subject's identity) in the cathexis of maternal function—mother, woman, reproduction."[31]

The result of both the breaching of physical/psychic boundaries and the impossibility of preventing the semiotic from permeating the symbolic, leads to insecurity and thence to fear and abhorrence of the abject, and its cultural repression/suppression as it is conventionally considered unrepresentable. Barbara Creed suggests that this is the reason we look away at certain times in the horror film—those moments when we cannot bear to watch the unrepresentable being represented.[32]

But the postmodern, which seeks to challenge all boundaries, should be able to accept the problematic nature of the boundaries of subjectivity. In that case, there is no longer any cause to fear the abject, which becomes entirely representable after all. This is what happens in *Bordertown*, where the abject is not only visible, but repeatedly and publicly celebrated. All of the physical manifestations of the abject listed above are present: from the sublime and/or terrifying (the Colonel tenderly and respectfully washing Pieter's dead body, or the glimpse of the tiny grey leg of Bianca's aborted baby as Louisa prepares to deposit the parcel in the camp incinerator), to the banal and mundane (Mihaly lancing Dom's boil, or Pieter emptying Adrianna's chamber pot).

Some key iconic signifiers are drawn from the abject, sometimes resonating with other signifiers of excess, such as those which suggest the grotesque or the carnivalesque. For instance, the interplay between the signifiers "blood" and "food" begins innocuously enough. In episode 1, tomatoes mature and ripen overnight in Mihaly's garden because they have been watered by the tears of the simpleton. The red of the ripe tomatoes becomes suggestive of both blood and wine as Nino treads the crop in the vat in preparation for making sauce. The sale of contraband food through Joe's secret store is one of the signifiers of his anti-authoritarian position within the camp, but his position is never secure, and it is always possible for others to manipulate him, which is how he is inveigled into butchering sheep for the commissariat.

This is the first of the truly unpleasant and confronting episodes: when Joe slits the throat of the first sheep, blood spurts dramatically, splattering all over himself and his companion Pieter, while Nino stands appalled. Joe returns to camp covered in the blood of the sheep, and with his own hand cut and bleeding. But when Bev's ministrations lead to a sexual encounter which has been brewing for the previous two episodes, Joe is disgusted to find that Bev is menstruating. Here the role of the abject in maintaining gender difference is first made explicit, then challenged as the audience is invited to empathize both with Joe's initial dismay and with Bev's sense of betrayal. The next day, Joe and Nino return to the slaughtering, reconciled to the task, and to each other, through a ritual of painting each other's faces with the blood of the sheep. This time, when they return to the camp, Joe is able to apologize to Bev, and, though she initially tells him "It's too bloody late," they are reconciled before the end of the episode (3) and the affair continues its bumpy progress. Much later, in episode 7, the theme of blood recurs, again linked with desire and sexual difference. Dante dyes Maeve's hair red, then slits her throat, destroying in one action both the women who have betrayed him—Maeve literally and his unfaithful redhaired wife Diomira symbolically. The graphic spurting of Maeve's blood recalls the slaughter of the sheep.

Further recurring evidence of the abject is in the images of pollution, decay, and putrefaction, which also have a key role in the narrative. We have been aware from the arrival of the first busload of residents of Pieter's obsession with the inadequacies of the toilet block, as he collects signatures on a petition of complaint. After the explicit representation of Cesare vomiting at the close of episode 2, the new ablutions block is officially opened. But even this cannot help Pieter, who suffers from chronic constipation, spending long periods sitting on the toilet, reading Shakespeare while a line of disgruntled residents waits. After Pieter dies in episode 4, his wife Adrianna insists that he be buried under a paperbark tree on the camp site.

Kenneth (Hugo Weaving) has every reason to be nervous of the scissors in the hands of Baringa's new barber Dante (Petru Gheorghiu): it is in this chair that Dante will later slit Maeve's throat. (From *Bordertown,* produced by the Australian Broadcasting Corporation, 1995. Reprinted by permission of the Australian Broadcasting Corporation.)

While Adrianna and the Colonel argue for days about this, Pieter's body lies in the infirmary, with the residents increasingly distressed by the effects of the heatwave on the corpse. Then the drains of the new ablutions block begin to flow backwards, covering the floor with shit. When Pieter's missing false teeth are discovered to have blocked the drains, the whole camp declares this the Dutchman's revenge. The Colonel gives in and conducts the funeral on the site. These events—including washing the body, the shit on the floor, the discovery of the teeth—are shown explicitly, with fewer of the concessions to audience sensibilities than we normally expect. In *Bordertown* we are not left to infer illness from a pale face lying languidly on a pillow: instead we see the victims repeatedly "throwing up." Such a vivid depiction of the abject, avoiding the closure that protects the symbolic by returning the abject to social control, is untypical of classical narrative.

Kristeva writes that it is ". . . not lack of cleanliness or health that causes abjection but what disturbs identity, system, order. What does not respect borders, positions, rules. The in-between, the ambiguous, the composite."[33]

In *Bordertown*, structures of difference are established, only to be challenged. The boundaries that mark the differences are constantly in flux, threatened by the narrative, by the eruption of fantasy into the real world, and of the abject into subjectivity. Bianca, the albino, is one character who stands squarely on such a boundary—in-between and ambiguous. Her excessive whiteness is a constant challenge to the concept of racial difference, and this is made still more explicit when she befriends the black women and persuades them to "blacken" her with soot from the campfire in a rebirthing ritual that echoes the women's business at the birth of a black child. Bianca's expulsion from the camp and repatriation to Italy is one of the few examples of the containment of the abject within this narrative.

Even the final resolution in a wedding ceremony is not simply the conventional establishment of the heterosexual couple. It is a double wedding with one bride grossly pregnant and the other expecting no more than six months of fidelity, its very excess exposing its ambiguity and its inadequacy as a social boundary marker.

Such representation of the unregenerate abject allows for the possibility of a subjectivity which is not forced to abandon the semiotic when it enters the symbolic. If we read this narrative as an allegory, we can conclude that the Australian nation does not have to choose between becoming a republic and maintaining the tie with the British motherland. As alternatives within a modernist paradigm, neither now carries finality or certitude, yet from a postmodern perspective both remain viable elements within a complex and evolving national consciousness.

CONCLUSION

Bordertown is postmodern history. It addresses the past through simulacra of stereotypes. But in doing so it does not entirely abandon narrative or mimesis. Rather it combines "narrative logic and postmodern paralogic.[34] The narrative is sequential, with all actions motivated and each subplot reaching some form of closure. By the end of the last episode the two central romances end in marriage, Dante is executed, and the camp is to be closed. However, within this narrative logic, realism is accompanied by symbolism, and mimesis by metaphor.

Symbolically, the nation has achieved subjectivity: the double wedding symbolizes the union of postwar British and European immigrants with each other and with earlier immigrants, the ambivalences within the unions suggesting an uncertain future. Death has been used to represent cleansing of the national spirit: Cora passes on the flag to Bev (though she also chooses, eventually, not to die in the process), Dante's death expunges guilt, Pieter's symbolizes the fitting end for weakness. Marginal groups (Aborigines and gypsies) have returned to the margins, marking potential sources of conflict but remaining for the moment outside national consciousness.

The expressions on the faces say it all. This double wedding is not the traditional "happy ending": (L to R) a very pregnant Louise (Christine Tremarco) is marrying simpleton Nino (Mitchell Butel), a rather disgruntled Bev (Linda Cropper) is marrying promiscuous Joe (Joe Petruzzi). (From *Bordertown*, produced by the Australian Broadcasting Corporation, 1995. Reprinted by permission of the Australian Broadcasting Corporation.)

Bianca—the most recalcitrant and destabilizing element of all, threatening national subjectivity through skin color and gender as well as national allegiance—has been expelled by deportation.

Through this logic, the impermanence and permeability of borders and boundaries is addressed, both in narrative (in the discussion of national identity) and in genre and style. There is a complex and rich paralogic that defies complete verbal exegesis, and also confronts the audience with a basic paradox. There is, after all, something rather perverse in an attempt to discuss the construction of national identity through a postmodern worldview in which boundaries of any kind are suspect.

Such paradoxical representation is, in fact, closer to our lived experience than is much traditional realistic narrative. We live in chaos, but also in time. We spend our lives attempting to reconcile these incompatible elements: we experience the chaos of existence sequentially, and we understand it as narrative. We may slip out of time occasionally—in sleep or in ecstatic moments—but we always return to time, take up where we left off, continue sequentially. So history (and particularly historical narrative) is fundamental to our self-concept (both individual and national) in the sense of memory constructing subjectivity and in the sense of narrative "making sense" of experience. We can choose to think of history differently—no longer as the grand narrative that explains everything—but we cannot abandon history (or narrative) entirely.

Neither can we avoid economics: if time is money, then history (time) is always already about economics. The history of immigration to Australia is about finding a workforce for Australian industry while also finding living space for people displaced by war. Film and television, as it happens, are also about money—finding the money to produce programs, finding the audience to pay for them. The audience may pay directly through the box office or indirectly by purchasing advertised products, or it may just be through their taxes at work in the national broadcaster. In the latter case, ratings flops are always read as a waste of taxpayers' money.

So, was *Bordertown* such a waste? Part of the role of the national broadcaster is to encourage talent and innovation by being willing to take risks. In doing this it treads a fine line between supplying what the public already knows it wants, and what it may be encouraged to try out. In the case of *Bordertown*, destabilizing the boundaries of subjectivity proved to be more than the audience in 1995 was prepared to accept, but that need not mean it was a waste.

Jameson could have been talking about *Bordertown* when he wrote:

Cultural production is . . . driven back inside a mental space which is no longer that of the monadic subject, but rather that of some degraded collective "objective spirit": it can no longer gaze directly on some putative real world, at some reconstruction of a past history which was once itself a present; rather, as in Plato's cave, it must trace our mental images of that past upon its confining walls. If there is any realism left here, therefore, it is a "realism" which is meant to derive from the shock of grasping that confinement, and of slowly becoming aware of a new and original historical situation in which we are condemned to seek History by way of our own pop images and simulacra of that history, which itself remains forever out of reach.[35]

In 1995, *Bordertown* was too much of a shock for television critics and viewers: perhaps by the time the ABC has the courage to re-screen it, the audience will have caught up. But by then there will be still newer ways of re-presenting the past, for, whether we are speaking about historical events or the styles of their representation, ". . . the only truly irremediable error would be to believe that this present will endure forever."[36]

NOTES

1. Andreas Huyssen, *After the Great Divide: Modernism, Mass Culture, Post-modernism* (Bloomington: Indiana University Press, 1986)

2. Anne Friedberg, "The Mercator of the Postmodern: Mapping the Great Divide," *Camera Obscura* 18 (September 1988): 68.

3. Philip Hayward and Paul Kerr, "Introduction," *Screen* 28, no.2 (Spring 1987): 4.

4. This is discussed by, among others, Will Straw, "Shifting Boundaries, Lines of Descent: Cultural Studies and Institutional Realignments," in Valda Blundell, John Shepherd, and Ian Taylor (eds.), *Relocating Cultural Studies: Developments in Theory and Research* (London: Routledge, 1993).

5. Giuliana Bruno, "Ramble City: Postmodernism and *Blade Runner*," *October* 41 (Summer 1987): 62.

6. Frederic Jameson, in Anthony Easthope and Kate McGowan (eds.), *A Critical and Cultural Theory Reader* (North Sydney: Allen and Unwin, 1992), p. 200.

7. Bruno, "Ramble City," p.62.

8. Hayward and Kerr, "Introduction," p. 5.

9. John Hartley, "Journalism and Modernity," *Australian Journal of Communication* 22, no. 2 (1995): 20.

10. Frederic Jameson, "Postmodernism and Consumer Society," in E. Ann Kaplan (ed.), *Postmodernism and Its Discontents: Theories, Practices* (London and New York: Verso, 1988), p. 28.

11. A longstanding criticism has been that, in contrast to the written word, images and sounds are incapable of speaking with any degree of specificity to the intellect, despite their undoubted power to speak directly to the emotions. This view of film and television as sense-making practices, however, begs the question of whether they have always had this capacity or whether it is something specific to what might be called "postmodern film/television."

12. Dana Polan, "Postmodernism and Cultural Analysis Today," in Kaplan, *Postmodernism*, p. 55.

13. Glenda Sluga describes this process as the creation of a "migrant dreaming," in Kate Darian-Smith and Paula Hamilton (eds.), *Memory and History in Twentieth-Century Australia* (Melbourne: Oxford University Press, 1994): Ch.10.

14. The term "classic serial" was coined for those series of programs located in the past, recreating either history or a respected literary work or both. It is particularly associated with the BBC's reconstructions of classic novels, from Dickens and Thackeray to *Brideshead Revisited*.

15. Promotion for the program described it thus: "From the makers of *Brides of Christ* and *The Leaving of Liverpool* comes a completely new television experience. *Bordertown*—a place of miracles" (*Good Weekend*, September 30, 1995). "One of the Australian film industry's top decision-makers" was quoted as saying: "In the case of *Bordertown* we have a very worthy and socially relevant story about an important era in our history. . . . Fine cast, expensive sets, attention to period detail—it's all there. But it's boring." (*Age Green Guide*, October 26, 1995).

16. Debi Enker (*View*, October 8–14, 1995: 19) was one of the few critics who wrote "In praise of *Bordertown*."

17. In Melbourne, where new Australian drama usually rated about 30 the first week, and often grew over the course of a serial, it rated 13 the first week and later fell as low as 6 (*Age Green Guide*, October 26, 1995: 10).

18. Bonegilla, eight miles outside Albury on the border of New South Wales, was the location for the major reception camp for immigrants in the postwar period.

19. In episode 10 the camp is quarantined, with army sentries at the gate.

20. What is now the difference between news and current affairs?

21. Fictional reconstructions of the recent past have begun to blend into the police procedural, like *Phoenix* or *Joh's Jury* or *Police Crop*.

22. *Corelli*, also broadcast on Australian Broadcasting Corporation in 1995, is an example.

23. To label a film or television program "AFC-genre" (Australian Film Commission–genre)—using the term coined by Susan Dermody and Elizabeth Jacka, *The Screening of Australia*, 2 vols. (Sydney: Currency Press, 1987, 1988)—is currently the ultimate derogatory evaluation of "seemly respectability" through pretty nostalgia.

24. This was evident from the letter pages of newspapers like *Age Green Guide* and the viewer responses read on the ABC's *Backchat* program.

25. I am grateful to Rose Dalgarno for this insight.

26. Ihab Hassan, public lecture, La Trobe University, Bundoora, August 24, 1994.

27. Robert Stam, "Mikhail Bakhtin and Left Cultural Critique," in Kaplan, *Postmodernism*, p. 121.

28. Stam in Kaplan, *Postmodernism*, p. 125.

29. *Age Green Guide*, October 26, 1995: 10. Jim Schembri agreed: "The one miracle that doesn't occur, however, is the one about convincing ethnic accents, especially Italian ones" ("Boredom Town," *Age*, September 28, 1995.

30. Frederic Jameson, quoted in Bruno, "Ramble City," p. 70.

31. Julia Kristeva, *Powers of Horror: An Essay on Abjection* (New York: Columbia University Press, 1982), p. 91.

32. Barbara Creed, *The Monstrous-Feminine: Film, Feminism, Psychoanalysis* (New York: Routledge, 1993), p. 154.

33. Kristeva, *Powers of Horror*, p. 2. I am grateful to Terrie Waddell for drawing this connection to my attention.

34. Polan in Kaplan, *Postmodernism*, p. 55.

35. Jameson in Easthope and Mcgowan, *Critical and Cultural Theory Reader*, p. 202.

36. Warren Montag, "What Is at Stake in the Debate on Postmodernism?", in Kaplan, *Postmodernism*, p. 102.

12

Television and Our Understanding of History: A Distant Conversation

Pierre Sorlin

PIERRE SORLIN   Why are there historians? Why do societies entrust scholars with teaching what happened in olden times, and why do they buy the books these scholars produce? Anxious to fully explore the intellectual and scientific aspects of their work, historians often miss its social function. But, one day, they find themselves in the situation where some in their society call into doubt the accepted version of the past while others want it reaffirmed. This conflicting demand becomes plain when there are moves to do away with a whole block of memory, when, for instance, doubts are cast upon the legitimacy of a war action—Hiroshima, Vietnam, the Falklands, the Gulf War. Historians are asked to verify, to certify, that what everybody believed had happened, had really happened. Others, of course, ask them to employ the maximum of critical sense to show things in a different light.

TONY BARTA   Don't people often expect historians to uncover a quite different version of events, to satisfy a popular belief that the story given out at the time was not the whole story?

PIERRE SORLIN   My point is rather about the construction of a common past. There are groups of human beings who do not want to maintain a memory of their common past, but most societies build up an image of their evolution and use it to organize and give meaning to their present life.

Historians are not independent researchers, they are the scribes of the memory people want to keep.

This memory is based upon a few recurring events that help people to define their position in their country. For instance, the Civil War and the Glorious Revolution are still a reference period for the British who never stop pondering its influence and aftermath. It is the task of historians not only to tell the story again and again but, more importantly, to tell it in a manner intelligible to those living at the same time. Gardiner's erudition was impeccable, but nobody reads him because the British no longer care about dynastic conflicts or religious polemics. Historians are under some pressure to adapt their accounts of the past to the ongoing concerns of their fellow citizens.

TONY BARTA   Yes, but isn't it just as true that they therefore continue to produce revised and questioning accounts, rather than a sort of updated consensus?

PIERRE SORLIN   Of course; perhaps both kinds. All I have said up to now is trite, but it was necessary to come to my point. Television has become the most important means of communication and education of our time. Do historians, who boast about the widening of their horizons and the opening of new fields of research, realize that it is television that has broadened our view of the world? We see perfectly well how Gardiner was influenced by the spread of dailies in his age. Why would we be more media-proof than him? What I would like to suggest is that, when teaching history, when writing books, we adopt a style profoundly affected by the techniques of television.

TONY BARTA   I doubt whether that's so among academics. I'd say it's very much open to question.

PIERRE SORLIN   A prior question, inviting less argument, is the role played by the media in the popular reach of history. Our great-grandfathers learned more from the novels by Walter Scott, Alexandre Dumas, or Charles Dickens serialized in papers than from school books. Then movies, which were attended by huge audiences, had a prominent part in the building of the common knowledge of history. Right from its first days, cinema has been in touch with history and has known how to use it. In Europe as well as in the United States about ten percent of the films made during the first half of our century dealt, be it indirectly, with a period which, because it was remote or because of its cinematic treatment, could be labeled "historical." It has often been noted that the tendency of Americans to see their history in terms of images derived from films creates a virtually impenetrable barrier to seeing the events on which they are based in verifiable historical terms. They are seen as "metahistory," that is to say as a contrived but very effective reconstruction of the past. Little Big Horn, which was not a big battle and in which the conflict between two Indian tribes was more important than the attack on the U.S. army, has become a national event, a long series of films has made Custer more famous than many American presidents.

TONY BARTA   I see metahistory rather differently: I'd say it has more to do with the "impenetrable barrier" you cite. Most people never see it as an ideological construction that affects all their readings of history, written or screened. Will television change that?

PIERRE SORLIN   Today, cinema is challenged and even threatened by television and, as historians, we have to wonder whether the new medium will merely develop and strengthen the tradition of history-telling created by the movies or whether it is likely to modify our understanding of the past. I am convinced that television is going to transform our comprehension, and that the historiography of tomorrow will be fairly different from the one we have been used to. Cinema changed our vision but did not influence our intelligence of the past. On the other hand, it is our very conception of history that will be modified by television. This may sound a bit odd or exaggerated. I'll have to expand on it.

The pieces of evidence we may use to describe past events are still more or less what they were before Edison and Lumière began their film shows. "Facts" remain what they were then, and there are few (if any) novelties to be dug up regarding Cromwell's policy or Custer's political ambitions. But cinema is a means of expression different from written accounts. Some specialists say it is a new language, and we can accept this word if we consider that any set of signs that allows people to communicate is a language. The variety of materials used to communicate and the way in which these materials can be arranged characterize a language. In this respect cinema contrasts obviously with books or talks. The content of a historical film can be close or even similar to the content of a book but it is the cinematic treatment—in other words, the simultaneous use of pictures, sounds, and words—that gives films their singularity.

TONY BARTA   I certainly agree with you about that, but to what extent is it possible to assume that cinema has changed our vision of the past?

PIERRE SORLIN   "Natural" languages are very good at explaining, at showing causes and consequences, but they do not go in for sophisticated conceptual descriptions. Take two cases: on the one hand, space, which is a determining factor in the evolution of societies; on the other hand, emotions and feelings, which are always important, especially during the revolutionary periods. How many words can we use to describe the variety and diversity of landscapes? Very few. "Classical" historians, say Gibbon, Macaulay, or Treveleyan, were well aware of the importance of geography. Possibly because they lacked the verbal tools to analyze it, they considered it a stable element, established once and forever, an organic whole which, underlying the vagaries of human conducts, served as an arena for events. Treveleyan insisted that the main phases of British history could be "read upon the map"; he treated the natural features of Britain as living characters which had "opened" the country to the world and had defined its most salient attributes.[1] On the other hand, during the second third of the twentieth century, historians began to debate the significance of place in understanding social and economic processes. They stressed the fact that people's conception of the world, far from being defined by permanent geographical features, was shaped by their ability to move—for instance, in agricultural societies, by the distance farmworkers had to cover to reach their fields. More importantly, historians came to the conclusion that the soil, the rivers, and even the climate were in permanent interaction with mankind and that, on the basis of an initial set of possibilities, they were modified, damaged, and restored by human beings. There were many reasons for which historians changed their minds, be it simply the possibility offered by airline companies to move from one corner of the world to another. But the influence of movies must not be underrated. Consider the works of John Ford. By putting space at the center of many of his pictures, by confronting his characters with American nature, by making them fight with the mountains and rivers as well as with other men, Ford created a version of the American past centered on the notions of distance and mobility. Once novelists or historians have written "the hill was high and steep," they have done all they are able to do, whereas the film can *show* it, and it is the editing, the dynamic association of different aspects of the background, that gives the landscape a new, previously ignored importance.[2] It is not by chance that Braudel, criticizing the traditional geographical expositions in *The Mediterranean and the Mediterranean World in the Age of Philip II* (1949), stressed the essential relationship between bodies and space, or that Hobsbawm showed, in the opening section of *The Age of Revolution* (1962), how the patterns of human activity, in the eighteenth century, were related to milieu and horizon.

The connection between films and historical accounts of collective emotions and feelings is even more obvious than the association of movies with nature. Historians like Michelet knew what an important role "masses" had in revolutionary times, but they tended to treat the mass as an entity, one of the various agents struggling to control the situation. After the First World War, a series of filmmakers, notably Ernst Lubitsch (*Madame Dubarry*, 1919) and D. W. Griffith (*Orphans of the Storm*, 1921) introduced on the screen huge, roaring crowds, hundreds of people running from one side to the other, waving, stopping, starting again, filling the white surface of the screen and suddenly flying away, being literally washed out. Shortly after the release of these pictures, Georges Lefebvre began to publish his studies on the role of the crowd in revolutionary upheavals, opening a new field of research which was then developed by British historians such as George Rudé (*The Crowd in the French Revolution*, *The Crowd in History*) and Richard Cobb.

TONY BARTA   I do find it hard to attribute most of this to the movies. Marx could have mattered more than Gaumont.

PIERRE SORLIN   It would be pointless to wonder whether the historians mentioned above were used to going to the pictures, because what really matters is not the personal behavior of individuals but the concerns and curiosities shared by most people in a given period.[3] Films aroused interest in topics previously neglected and, wittingly or not, historians writing for their contemporaries had to care about the background against which events took place and about the emotions, hopes, angers that moved the historical agents, especially the mobs.

TONY BARTA   Did film art—notably montage—change the way historians wrote? It certainly influenced poets and novelists.

PIERRE SORLIN   Films prompted spectators to take a different look at the past, but they did not challenge the dominant conception of history because they continued to tell it in the most traditional way. Since the eighteenth century, historical discourse has been organized as a well-ordered, and finally moralizing discourse that uses narrative structures and literary devices.[4] Films, like historical novels and history books, concentrate upon a period, in other words a more or less defined time with its beginning and its end. They narrate and, in order to make the narrative more thrilling, they seize upon some sort of climax—the turning point of a war or the height of a crisis. Good history films, Griffith's *America*, Renoir's *Marseillaise*, Connie Field's *The Life and Times of Rosie the Riveter*, Ken Loach's *Land and Freedom*, exploit the expressive potential of the medium. By playing on quick movements and by editing contrasted pictures of different characters, they make us *feel* how people perceived the challenges they had to face and how they reacted. Nevertheless, these movies inevitably culminate with both a great historical event and a private affair—the death of one of the heros or the reunion of two lovers. Plots end once history and personal fate have joined.

Historical films seldom depart from the model long ago described by Aristotle: initial situation, crisis, and resolution. It is still effective in contemporary movies. A typical example is offered by Wajda's *Danton*. Before spectators enter the movie theater the title of the picture and the advertising material have already informed them that they are going to follow the political life of one of the leaders of the Revolution who failed and was beheaded. The script itself and the shooting have been calculated to make viewers understand that they have been introduced into the realm of "Great Men." The film opens with four short sequences which represent, successively:

• a mob queuing in the rain in front of a baker's shop filmed in medium shot;

• two close-ups of a woman and a man in a riding coach;

- again the mob, with people fighting to enter the now open baker's;
- the arrival of a coach taken in long shot; the queuing mob runs toward the coach; an obviously jealous, angry man is looking down to the street.

At this point, shortly after the beginning of the film, we can guess what is going to happen. The first and third sequences have told us that this is a very difficult period, a time of hunger and fear, and that the mob is looking for a leader. The second sequence has introduced a seeming suspense (Who is the man? Given the title, he should be Danton himself, but we are not sure it is him) and suggested that the man in the coach is too much involved in private affairs. (The film is able to let us know that he is in any case more important than the woman.) The fourth sequence has given the mob a chance to meet a potential leader and warned us that there are a few men who are not happy with this alliance.

TONY BARTA   I'm not sure how these conventions are different from television.

PIERRE SORLIN   The cinematic history is logical, dramatic, and it develops toward a conclusion. Far from being purely casual, this way of narrating the past like a continuous, end-oriented story is a basic form of apprehension and depiction of history that is being seriously challenged by television. However important historical pretexts have always been, history itself has never been a major field of exploration for the cinema—mostly because history films do not constitute a genre and have nothing in common, except reference to the past. On the other hand, television makes an extensive use of history, not only with movies and serials but also in documentaries and newscasts, when a look at the background seems necessary to understand the present. How many times have television channels lacking something to show about former Yugoslavia used archive footage and retold the whole chronicle of the region? Statistics must not be taken at face value, but it is worth noticing that, according to specialists, history in its different versions makes up about one-fifth of television programs.[5]

TONY BARTA   I'd go further: if we bring in advertising and sport, the historical references would make up an even greater proportion. Research can be reasonably thorough in sports stories. In advertising, the research has another focus—the ideological triggers that will work with the audience.

PIERRE SORLIN   Film studios have enough money to hire historical advisers who help them avoid too glaring mistakes and find a leading strand for their movies. Since television companies which work hurriedly do not care to spend money, the comments on their programs are written by journalists or simply told by witnesses. In an otherwise interesting program like *D-Day to Berlin* (BBC 1, 1987) the sound track is reduced to the most elementary noises—bombs, machine guns, military marches—and to casual remarks made by the members of the crew which shot the pictures. This program illustrates in a lively way the American campaign in Europe during the last period of World War II, but it does not relate the history of the campaign. Quite often, there is a discrepancy or a lack of consistency between the text and the pictures which have been edited separately and mixed up at the last minute. In this respect, television programs do not offer the perfect unfolding of events that characterizes cinematic productions.

TONY BARTA   I'm confused. First of all, these films you refer to are shown on television almost every day, and thus reassert the conventions of the "perfect unfolding" you've described. Second, even with the more fragmentary style of television, the speed of that style allows no time to question the version presented. It has the same effect of complete closure.

PIERRE SORLIN   Although united under the same label of "audiovisual media," cinema and television are significantly different from a technical point of view. Cinematic dialogue generally goes with pictures taken near the subject and thus big in scale. However, the commonest framing, in film, is the "from the knees up" one. Close-ups look uncanny because we are used to perceiving any form against a background and seldom see an object deprived of context. Close-ups are therefore exceptional in cinema; they are either a single vastly enlarged detail in which one face comes forward to underline a state of mind, or a magnified object that stresses the importance of one point in comparison with the rest. On the other hand, close-up is the standard format on television. It normally frames a part of the human body, head and shoulders or just a face, which introduces a radical change in the representation of living beings. This device is justified by the social use of television, the TV is a domestic appliance which, like radio, must be capable of being followed by people who cannot stay in front of it; it is conceived of as a talking medium, even in its most fictional programs. Television stories seem akin to cinematic fictions in which the meaning is conveyed by dialogue, but on close examination the difference becomes obvious.

TONY BARTA   Are you talking about talk shows? Even there I'd say people are lured by the visuals to watch the set, to remain "viewers."

PIERRE SORLIN   Many television programs are long-lasting dialogue; what people do while they are talking does not really matter. But when spectators take a glance at their receiver, it is essential to give them an impression of authenticity. For that purpose, camera operators do their best to catch a face and keep it within the frame. This kind of inquisitive glance gives spectators a special feeling; the larger the image, the more they believe themselves to be directly involved. Right from the beginning, history programs have exploited the intrusive and falsely confidential nature of close-ups on television. *You Are There*, a series concocted by CBS from 1950 onward, was a success because of its clever, challenging framing. Antique, medieval, or contemporary events were told alternately by announcers, speaking as they would have done it for a news bulletin, and pseudo-witnesses who, affecting worry or shyness, did not keep their visage in the center of the frame so that the ever-present flow of words appeared to be searching for the interviewee's unstable, vanishing mouth. The small screen became then what it has remained ever since, a surface of fragmentation and recomposition.

TONY BARTA   There I agree. Yet Balàsz or Pudovkin would tell us the same about film art.

PIERRE SORLIN   As its name makes it clear, the cinematograph is the art of writing with motions, of transcribing motions. Its narration puts together a series of gestures ordered according to a spatial and temporal logic. On the other hand, the small screen, because it is small, does not offer any depth of field. It is not fit for quick, extended action such as battles or horse pursuits which it tends to blur; it has neither amplitude nor volume. Classical films do not merely attempt to suggest distances by linking every shot to those that come before and after. They also create a mental, imaginary world that spectators accept during the few hours they spend in a movie theater where they expect to be immersed. Television networks cannot follow these patterns. Their most important categories are stories broadcast in parts that must be conceived to allow spectators to follow even if they switch on in the middle of the transmission of if they miss a few episodes.

TONY BARTA   Is that true of documentaries? Some are standard narratives, others more adventurous. Most of them require visual attention as well as listening.

PIERRE SORLIN   The first history serials, put to air in the 1960s, were already made for an unsettled, changeable public likely to move away from the set or to channel-hop. In *Combat* and *The Gallant Men* (ABC, 1962) which followed small squads of American soldiers during the war in Europe, there was practically no story. The different episodes, shot in open air and in natural light, offered a glance at the daily experience of humble, unknown men. There was no imaginary narrator to explain what was displayed on the screen because the series was supposed to embody what Francesco Casetti has called the "magnification of daily life."[6] By stressing the importance of small details, of surprises and routines, the programs built up the context that these soldiers had created around themselves and a sense of the permanent menace that enveloped them.

TONY BARTA   What distinguishes that from a film documentary? It must in fact have been made as a film.

PIERRE SORLIN   Ordinary people filmed in close-up: that is enough to define a medium on which real and contrived interviews, false and actual witnesses, are almost undistinguishable. In a history book, it is the historian who runs the game. In a history film the actor comes first, his face and body become Nelson's or Lenin's. On the small screen it is often difficult to know exactly who is uttering the words. However, words are the most important material of television. This, I think, is one of the most relevant discordances between cinema and television, and one whose effects are crucial for the communication of history: television does not rely on written sources. The cinema which uses pictures and sounds seems also very far from texts but, in fact, it is close to them. Since Griffith, who introduced quotations and erudite references in his captions, filmmakers have boasted about their knowledge of authentic documents. Kean Loach's *Land and Liberty* is archetypal in this respect. Without mentioning Orwell, the film relies heavily on the memory of *Homage to Catalonia* whose theses are visually illustrated. The plot develops on the basis of press clippings, leaflets, and letters that a young lady finds and reads after her grandad's death; it is the written pieces that give the movie its consistency. Written documents seldom come into view in television programs and the few cases in which they appear make it easy to understand why it is difficult to use them. Attempting to evoke the British home front between 1940 and 1945, the producers of *A People's War* (Channel 4, 1987) had recourse to the Mass-Observation reports established in the 1940s,[7] and had pieces of these texts recited by comedians who acted as if they had been interviewed during the war. The experiment was rather uninspiring, the texts sounded much too formal to give the illusion of real talks and made the whole program sound extremely artificial.

TONY BARTA   I can't say that the many references to newspaper headlines and recorded speeches in historical documentaries give me the sense that television neglects such materials. They are very common devices.

PIERRE SORLIN   Compared with films or books, television employs few texts, but they can be used effectively. Beside interviews, television tends to combine three kinds of visual data: still pictures, archive films, and newly shot material. Stills, be they paintings, drawings, maps, or photographs, are seldom inserted in movies, their fixedness and the time necessary to fully explore them are at odds with the permanent mobility characteristic of moving pictures. Many history books have illustrations, but few of them really manage to create a coherent whole in which images and text react upon each other, and too often the former are a mere supplement, an ornament that embellishes the discourse. Television programs can also misuse stills, for instance when the lack of relevant documents forces us to linger on blurred portraits. But photographs and drawings, when they are intelligently scrutinized, when details and general view alternate, may have a strong power of dramatization. Stills that spectators can examine at leisure provide an original kind of evidence that was never fully exploited in the previous forms of historical discourse.

TONY BARTA   Are you going to outline a typical form of television discourse? What about the "flow" of television as a whole, the welter of images and references?

PIERRE SORLIN   Television is self-referential and self-representative; it does not stop recalling its own past. History films often contain bits of ancient movies but they present them as quotations and the differences in style are so obvious that, in practice, there can be no confusion between the old and the new shots. Television history does not pretend to maintain any stylistical unity and easily jumps from films to stills and from immediate interviews to past conversations or speeches. There is, of course, a real danger: spectators do not know where the material comes from and to what extent it is genuine. For many young viewers all black and white is automatically old, hence authentic, so that sequences borrowed from black and white fictions made two or three decades after the events that they evoke are considered perfectly veracious. We could endlessly argue about the pros and cons in the use of film extracts on the small screen but I am not trying to assess the accuracy of television; I only want to suggest that it has brought dramatic changes in the use of historical documents. A debate on values would be pointless here. And the same could be assumed regarding the introduction of newly shot material. Is it irrelevant to follow with a camera the path leading from St. James's Palace in a program on the execution of Charles I? I do not know—but I am sure that this gives the event another dimension that could not be found in a written text.

So television history is original in many ways. Its narration is often chaotic and made of pieces, of segments or sequences of information loosely connected to each other. There are no guidelines, no interpretation likely to provide a truly comprehensive account. While history films take the events for granted, as having taken place somewhere, at a given time, and aim at showing *how* they happened, television programs merge *into* what was happening and do not try to offer an organic, coherent vision, let alone to explain anything.

TONY BARTA   I find television histories explain all sorts of things—not least the questions many viewers want answered. But I'm surprised at your emphasis on the old "organic, coherent vision." Should historians be encouraging this view of history at the end of the twentieth century?

PIERRE SORLIN   If we skim the long lists of historical transmissions already broadcast, we may be tempted to say that, however popular they have been, they do not seem to have deeply impressed professional historians. Are we not facing something very banal, a situation in which lay readers enjoy the fancies of television while historians keep walking on? Such would be the case if television had only produced fantasies. But it also offers stunningly creative programs that directly question our practices. Among many examples, I'm especially interested in Edgar Reitz's *Heimat* because it is a real challenge for professional historians.[8]

TONY BARTA I am too, though not, first of all, for its qualities as television. It provoked more debate about German history because of the large German television audience, but it was not made as television. Reitz wanted to bring back a remembered past which Germans rarely saw portrayed on their screens.

PIERRE SORLIN Reitz believes that the past, which is a fundamental reference for any human being, has been unduly confiscated by "scientists" who make it dull and colorless under the pretext that they will interpret what eludes all interpretation. Having long been interested in oral history and thinking that everybody can tell a simple, true story, the story of their life, which would be worth filming, he spent a year in the Hunsrück, a hilly district east of the Rhine, which was his own *Heimat*, the place where he grew up. He collected testimonies and locations and characters from the past. Although he had not yet worked for a television channel, his method was typical of television: no intervention of historical advisors, direct contact with inhabitants, careful notice of the smallest, seemingly unimportant details. Once he had finished his inquiry, Reitz took a film crew to the same region and, working for eighteen months with actors as well as with local people who were not professionals (one hundred and fifty of them were involved in the shooting, several in leading roles), he made a sixteen-hour program which, first broadcast in Germany, was soon exported to most foreign markets and won its director an international fame.

TONY BARTA Yes—starting with the Venice Film Festival. Reitz has never seen *Heimat* as a sixteen-hour *program* but as a sixteen-hour *film*. He wanted it screened first in cinemas. Surely it is exactly the wrong example for your purposes.

PIERRE SORLIN That may be: most people saw it on television. There were long controversies about Reitz's silence over racial persecutions and the concentration camps. Accused of too easily redeeming the Germans from war atrocities, the director answered that people in a remote village, beset by the difficulties of daily life, paid no attention to the talk about Jews and other victimized groups. They knew no more about the Holocaust than the film shows and what they knew at the time was probably less than what they remembered afterwards.[9] These issues are extremely important, notably the last, which raises the problem of memory, but I cannot go into them here since I am focusing on another aspect of the series, its significance for a study of the past.

TONY BARTA I have gone into those questions, and they keep returning to the point that this is not a researched history, dealing with the usual historical issues, but first of all an autobiographical story, remembered by Reitz from his childhood in the Hunsrück. That is his main resource and the source of his authority in portraying realities.

PIERRE SORLIN *Heimat* does not tell a story, it simply unfolds, or develops, from 1919 to 1982, in Schabbach, an imaginary village in the Hunsrück constructed from a combination of several actual places.[10] The general tone is clearly indicated by the first episode in which a young man, Paul Simon, having just been demobilized from World War I, returns home. There are a few temporal ellipses in this part of the serial but, as a whole, Paul's comeback coincides exactly with the duration of the program. *Heimat* is thus a representation of time, a reflection over the way in which people experience the continuity of days and years. The series evolves chronologically, with no flashbacks or anticipations. Sometimes it jumps over a long period; in other sequences it follows the slow pace of the first episode. However, the dilatory rhythm does not correspond to important happenings such as the advent of Nazism or the beginning of the war. "Manifest history," the history told in textbooks, is not absent but it merely interferes in a lateral manner, through verbal allusions, or through small hints: pictures of Nazi uniforms in the streets of Schabbach, of elderly people or women doing the work of young men. The villagers know about events but they do not seem to form a clear idea of what is happening around them and they seldom express an opinion or offer an interpretation.

TONY BARTA They do what people do in real life—and in screen drama. They express opinions, show reactions, argue with each other. The way big issues are encountered is again quite unlike a television serial. Bits of information are discovered but not followed up, people fall out politically but continue to interact within the family and the village. Wilfried, Maria's little brother in the SS, is abused as a coward by her mother-in-law during the war. That was both dangerous and not so dangerous. Life goes on.

PIERRE SORLIN Time and a changing sense of space are very important. Places and characters suggest, rather than represent, the passing of time. There are things that change with the years. The war memorial is one of the visual markers that operate in the first episodes, it is evoked in dialogue, then built, unveiled, and, finally, villagers pass by it without noticing its presence. The other main device is the permanence of one character, Maria, who is nineteen years of age when the series begins, in 1919, and dies at eighty-two, when *Heimat* ends—in 1982. The story is not just Maria's life story but she appears, in short or long sequences, in each episode. The choice of a linear narration, without return to the past, helps Reitz to avoid the emergence of a main character: when we see Ernst Simon we do not know what Maria is doing and vice versa, what is not shown on the screen is lost for spectators. Unlike most history films, *Heimat* has no narrator, there is no voice-over to introduce us to the village or to bridge the gap between two episodes. At times the film appears to be wandering at random; it tracks through the streets, discovers previously unknown corners and new silhouettes or catches figures already familiar because they have been seen in other episodes. People run this way and that, the camera occasionally follows them, but quite often, stays idle in a corner and just records what passes in front of the lens. Some stories are developed along several episodes, especially those which involve Maria; others are interrupted and remain open-ended.

TONY BARTA   I'm still having difficulty with your reference to *Heimat* as a "serial," somehow following the conventions developed in radio and television. It does in fact have a narrator linking each episode to all that has gone before but in a style of sound and camerawork again more like a film. Indeed, the cinematography throughout owes everything to cinema and almost nothing to television.

PIERRE SORLIN   The intricacies of plots and subplots, the variety of characters and extras, the difficulty viewers meet with when they try to decide who is doing what, are typical of serials that do not tell a story but set up both an atmosphere and an unsteady network of personal relationships. Reitz, it seems to me, has tried to make his audience perceive that *Heimat* is a television series, not a cinematic work, by intercuting brilliant, wordless sequences with scenes shot as if they were composed for dialogue alone. An interesting trick, which surprised almost everybody when the series was first broadcast, is the alternation from black and white to color or the other way round. The device is meant to blur all possible indicators and to prevent viewers from believing that some shots (for instance the black and white ones) are more "authentic" than the others. *Heimat* insists that it is a historical fiction which, being made for the small screen—certainly it needed television sales—follows the rules of the medium. As any other television program, it is resolutely self-referential: the characters leaf through photograph albums, watch movies, read newspapers. Paul Simon is hooked on the new medium of radio, and his brother is indefatigable as a photographer.

TONY BARTA   The intrusion of media into the village—the telephone, the motor car, the highway—is one of the many ways Reitz deals with the larger historical issues. The snapshot reviews at the beginning of each of the parts ("episodes" is definitely not the right word) are a brilliantly handled device that again suggest the changes in the larger world while they concentrate on the smaller one.

PIERRE SORLIN   Well, at least we agree on that. Humdrum tasks and feasts, birth and death, demobilization and war, *Heimat* is a program about social conventions and cultural perceptions, attitudes to love and marriage, kinship and patrimony, locality and nation, tradition and modernity, which follows the lives of ordinary people in an unsystematic way. The successive episodes (I think that *is* the right word) are filled with images of traditional activities, of women spinning in a corner, of craftsmen and farmers working, of small, dark houses, narrow workshops, cattle and horse carts. It is an introduction to another feeling of space and time and a perfect example of cultural history. But *Heimat* is also a history work which, on the basis of a minute description of quotidian concerns and activities, elaborates on a thesis very important to Reitz. He wants to show that the genuine Germany of the local community, united around those who never left, the women, was not deeply affected by Nazism or even war but was disrupted by Americanization in the second half of the century. This view is, of course, arguable, but it is an historical interpretation, supported by a close examination of tiny, almost trivial data, not by a large-scale analysis.

TONY BARTA   Because Reitz is so good at indicating the larger story that is always there, even if outside the frame, his ambition to tell a more genuinely experienced twentieth-century history doesn't, I think, conflict with history as a discipline. But it deserves to be seen as what it is: history as a dramatic art, told by cinematic means.

PIERRE SORLIN   Specialists may despise this kind of storytelling and consider Reitz an amateur historian, but they cannot ignore the fact that thousands of viewers have learned more about the twentieth century from this series than from textbooks of university lectures. Interviewed about the present state of history studies, one of the doyens of American history, Bernard Bailyn, confessed to being worried about the degree of sophistication and abstraction reached by scholarship. He encourages his graduate students to watch television serials where reality appears to be an indeterminate mirage of possibilities at odds with the world of well shaped, clearly defined objects like textbooks or technical monographs.[11] When he mentions television, I think that Bailyn has in mind microhistory, as it has been developed by Carlo Ginzburg, Eugen Genovese, Rhys Isaac, or Emmanuel Leroy-Ladurie, a kind of historical work that describes small events governed not by commonsensical laws of cause and effect, as wars or economic changes are often explained, but by a network of influences and reactions.

TONY BARTA   I'm not sure that historiography has followed other media developments very closely. Do you think that is beginning to change?

PIERRE SORLIN   It might be assumed that the popularity of books like *Montaillou* or *Roll Jordan Roll: The World the Slaves Made* is closely linked to the impact of television. At any rate, these two kinds of history must be referred to the same paradigm, loosely labeled postmodern, or deconstructionist. Born from the crisis of grand, all-encompassing theories, postmodernism postulates that it is the task of historians neither to "interpret" the past nor to explain how and why events occurred. Preoccupied with potential social signifiers, postmodernism looks for symbols, or representations that take place in the head of individuals but which, while being private thoughts or images, could also be common to many people. It starts from the fragmented, the very simple acts performed daily by the black servants that Eugene Genovese has encountered in archives, or by the inhabitants of Schabbach invented by Reitz.

TONY BARTA   There is a rather important, if venerable, issue there. You've already raised it. One history purports to be documented, a documentary, and the other is a story, a fiction.

PIERRE SORLIN   Many scholars feel uneasy with what Frederic Jameson has called the "relativism" of postmodern history.[12] They see a scattered vision of the past, which does not help understand the relationship between yesterday and today. Even the boundaries between nonfiction and fiction have become blurred, especially in the portrayal of historical characters. *The Birth of a Nation* and *Danton* allowed their characters to believe (and the viewers to suppose with them) that they lived their lives as well as the roles allotted them by "history." *Heimat* and other comparable television programs produce a sense of imprisonment abetted by the absence of any larger depiction of Germany or its "history." But we now don't need to be bound by the old collusion between general destiny and individual fate. Even if there is still some of this in *Heimat*, Reitz as historian and film artist has given it a quite different quality. He has brought something more to television: the representation of duration. Viewers who meet the people from Schabbach every week during four months experience a kind of long-lasting relationship fairly different from the short-lived liaison they form with a film character or a group described in a book. The slow transition from one day to another prevents the people and events depicted in the story from blending with historical currents. They are too individual to represent historical ideas. Television opens a window on latent history, on what human beings endure without knowing that their pain, their work and their tiredness are history. The understanding of the past that our contemporaries have now encountered on the small screen is a less literary, less "historical," more vivid and human one.

NOTES

1. G. M. Trevelyan, *History of England* (London: Longman Green, 1926), pp. xiii–xv.

2. On this question, see Derek Gregory, *Geographical Imaginations* (Oxford: Blackwell, 1994), and Anne Buttimer, *Geography and the Human Spirit* (Baltimore: Johns Hopkins University Press, 1994).

3. However, we can note that a French historian of the Revolution, Alphonse Aulard, who was Lefebvre's supervisor, saw *Orphans of the Storm* and reviewed it.

4. This is an idea that has become rather obvious since it was exposed by Hayden White in *Metahistory. The Historical Imagination in Nineteenth Century*

Europe (Baltimore: Johns Hopkins University Press, 1973). See also, from the same author, "The Value of Narrativity in the Representation of Reality," *Critical Inquiry*, Fall 1980.

5. Francesca Anania, *La storia sfugente. Una analisi dei programmi storici televisivi* (Rome: RAI, 1986).

6. *Tra me e te. Strategie di coinvolgimento della spettatore nei programmi della neotelevisione* (Rome: RAI, 1988), p. 24.

7. These reports, written by voluntary observers who freely noted what they found important about the evolution of public opinion, are kept in the archive of Sussex University.

8. On *Heimat* see Anton Kaes, *From Hitler to Heimat. The Return of History as Film* (Cambridge, Mass.: Harvard University Press, 1989), pp. 161 ff.

9. See Thomas Elsaesser, *New German Cinema: A History* (London: BFI/Macmillan, 1989) and Eric Santner, *Stranded Objects: Mourning, Memory and Film in Postwar Germany* (Ithaca: Cornell University Press, 1990).

10. A second series, *Die zweite Heimat. Chronik einer Jugend*, broadcast in 1993, which deals with inhabitants of Schabbach who have migrated to Munich, is not entirely based on original testimonies.

11. Bernard Bailyn, *On the Teaching and Writing of History. Responses to a Series of Questions* (Hanover, N.H.: University Press of New England, 1995).

12. "Figural Relativism or the Poetics of Historiography," *Diacritics* VI, no. 1, Spring 1976, p. 2 ff.

13

Letatlin and Ern Malley: History Refracted Through "Impossibility" and Hoax

David Perry

> Cinema has at its disposal powerful weapons for acting on "nature,"
> transforming it through purely creative possibilities in accordance with
> an aesthetic task. . . . The cinema possesses its own laws of geometry,
> mechanics, physics, under which the most impossible situations become
> possible.
>
> —B. Kazansky[1]

> Art has always been art and not nature.
>
> —Pablo Picasso[2]

The Russian formalist theoretician Kazansky was right enough, when—in
the unmistakable style of Bolshevik rhetoric—he wrote of the cinema's
transformative power. Picasso, with his opposition of "art" against "nature," put it far more succinctly; but whichever of those two ways above
it's looked at, whether it's agreed that the cinema is an art or "a lie"[3] or
whether every film, fiction or documentary, exemplifies the operation of
Kazansky's "impossible laws of geometry, mechanics, physics," in either
case there must be serious objections to any film's claim to historicity.

Yet my feature film *The Refracting Glasses*[4] does seem to claim historicity. At the same time its form quite openly embraces impossible laws, and
its story is riddled with impossibilities. The leading character, Constant
Malernik, a fictional Australian artist, is fascinated by political and per-

sonal histories as much as he is by the history of art. In the beginning Constant is making a film, and his backyard studio pulsates with unnatural light. He tells us that he dreams of other films made in the Soviet Union and tries to emulate images from these films. His partner Lydia is more pragmatic, not sure that people want to see what he does. He has already painted a series of portraits of the Bolshevik leadership from the time of the 1917 revolution; images of these paintings recur throughout the film. Constant travels to New York to see an exhibition of early Cubist paintings; while there he makes pictures with his hand-held clockwork camera. He travels to the countryside of his youth, where again he makes pictures, and in his imagination he visits the Soviet Union soon after the revolution, creating animated images of the visionary art works of V. E. Tatlin.

An uncertain idealist about the Soviet Union, Constant eventually finds himself with Lydia in that place at the very moment of its dissolution. There he tries to be most often a simple observer, depicting Lydia's first meeting with many of her family and her aunt's revelation of awful experiences. He shows anecdotes about an empire in collapse, while also tracking down Tatlin's experimental flying machine, a relic of the optimism that the Soviet Union inspired in many people in its earliest days. Until the very end, Constant's attitude to all this remains ambiguous.

The film's styles change depending on which part of the story Constant is telling. Although he frequently refers to historical figures, and interviews and depicts real people from the contemporary world in "his" film(s), Constant also depicts himself as meeting two people from Australian art history who never existed except as figures in a literary hoax. That hoax is little known outside Australian literary and art circles, so an account of what became known as the "Ern Malley Affair" follows.[5] It plays an important part in the story of *The Refracting Glasses*.

In 1943/1944 two conservative poets, James McAuley and Harold Stewart, were unhappy with a perceived lack of literary craft in modern poetry. They wrote a number of verses "without intention of poetic meaning,"[6] then ascribed these works to a fictitious poet they named Ern Malley, who, as McAuley and Stewart constructed him, was haphazardly self-educated, and already dead. They then sent "Ern's" poems to *Angry Penguins*, an Australian literary journal of the time. A covering letter, in the name of Ern's equally fictitious sister, Ethel, said in part: "I'm not a judge of [the work] myself, but a friend who I showed it to said it's very good, and should be published."[7] The outcome was that in 1944 *Angry Penguins* published an edition "commemorating" Ern Malley, in which all "his" poems were printed. Max Harris, co-editor of *Angry Penguins*, wrote to Ethel that Ern "was one of the most remarkable and important poetic figures of this country."[8] Very soon, however, the actual poets' methods of assemblage, pastiche, and apparently random association were revealed in the popular press. The derision this provoked in many circles, and the discomfiture of the *Angry Penguins*, reverberates to the present day.

Among those who know of this storm in a literary teacup, opinions seem still to be polarized for and against the artistic merit of the poems. Those in favor, notwithstanding the intentions of McAuley and Stewart, believe there is merit in the fragmenting, freely-associative methods those two talented writers used so derisively. During the production of *The Refracting Glasses*, Ern Malley's poems formed at least one of the models guiding its structure. Thus the film embodies (as well as obliquely describes) an art history of mid-twentieth-century Australia.

The Refracting Glasses does not hide its structure under the "Hollywood style."[9] Its real author (not Constant Malernik, the ostensible "author" of its fragmentary parts) is enamored of Picasso's maxim about art being "a lie" (see note 3). Kazansky's "laws" and Picasso's dialectics are used in this film to fragment history, to refract it through several different lives—at least two of which are patently false (Ern and Ethel Malley)—while the artist with the highly unlikely name is a fairly transparent alter ego for the film's "real" author. Constant says near the beginning of the film, about films: "The only things that are real are the material facts of film itself; the dyes, the light on the screen: everything else is open to interpretation." Over the opening shots he shouts, as if through a megaphone, in emulation of revolutionary orators: "Kino—which contains *The Refracting Glasses* of time, distance, narrative, technology—the very grains of our materials!"

No claims there, clearly, to objectivity or truthfulness. And yet *The Refracting Glasses* has other models of creative method that laid claims to intentions of cinematic truthfulness: Dziga Vertov's *kino pravda*, and its more modern French development *cinéma vérité*. Both these approaches to film making were described by Erik Barnouw as being "committed to a paradox: that artificial circumstances could bring hidden truth to the surface."[10] In *The Refracting Glasses* there is something of an homage to kino pravda (as well as to the the films of Jean Cocteau) in the mixing of corny "magic" (a camera leaps into Constant's hands) with documentary-style images, grainy black-and-white images, a semi-abstract animated drawing, and a parody of Hollywood transitional devices (whirling headlines) all within one short scene, to encapsulate Constant's interests and establish the narrative detail of his forthcoming trip to New York.

Many such devices in *The Refracting Glasses* attempt to pose (if not to answer) questions about the truthfulness of photography and sound recording. Underlying all the tricks and style reversals in *The Refracting Glasses* is a denial of the cliché "a picture is worth a thousand words." The tricks and so on contradict that truism and assert that photography and filmmaking are simply other ways of drawing, or writing; that the truthfulness of the pictures and sounds that are the building blocks of all

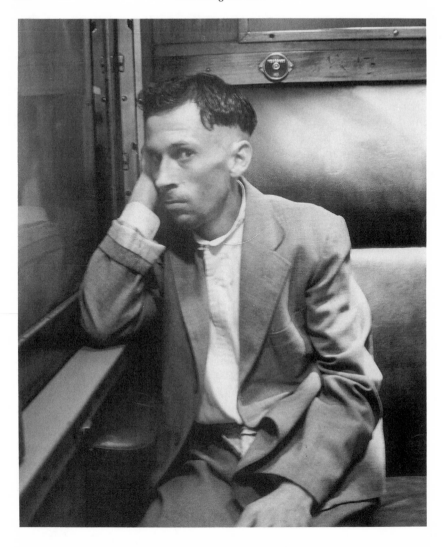

Iain Gardiner as *Ern Malley* in *The Refracting Glasses*: artists cannot prescribe the ways audiences should respond to their work. (Reprinted by permission of David Perry. Photo by Penny Glencross.)

films does not come from the fact that those building blocks are machine made; that those images are no more "objective" than handmade images of paint or ink, or the mental images we make from words read or heard.

Every photograph is made by various chemical and physical interactions combined with many peoples' skills and talents; it cannot be argued too strongly that they are made objects no less than paintings or texts, and do not have any special status as reproductions of the real world. Apart from the mechanical contraptions of the Lumières, Edison and all the others, what has made the cinema so ubiquitous in all its forms is photography's ability to reproduce itself—not the outside world—and thus to blanket the world with its images. The "naturalism" or truthfulness of those images is created in our minds as, transfixed by the conjuring tricks of our technology, we gaze at the images (as Constant put it, the "refractions" of our technology).

This is not to say that the truth is unknowable: it is not cause for despair. If photography is fallible, it is only as fallible as words or painted images, and truth and history are found, as always, not in a single image or statement, but in a process of constant dialogue and cross-referencing of images or statements. The starting point, as Daniel Walkowitz has said, is always "We know that 'something' happened."[11] It is just that "something"—or rather "somethings"—that *The Refracting Glasses* aimed to explore.

Two aspects of the film that are seemingly incompatible, and represented in such different styles that they shatter any possibility of conventional continuity, are those parts that, on the one hand, deal with McAuley and Stewart's literary construction, Ern Malley, while on the other hand, in other parts, the idealistic works of V. E. Tatlin are treated with due reverence.

Tatlin built several prototypes of a human-powered flying machine, which he called the Letatlin,[12] and as Constant Malernik quoted him, Tatlin hoped, with his machine, to "liberate all of us from the confines of gravity, allowing each to fly and move freely in space, and [to] relieve the towns of noise and overcrowding and cleanse the air of petrol fumes."[13] Several times in *The Refracting Glasses* the Letatlin is depicted, first as animated drawings in which it appears that Constant is attempting to give substance to something he has never seen, then later, while the Soviet Union is coming to an end, he finds and photographs one of the prototypes in Russia. Another equally visionary project by Tatlin was the Monument to the Third International, a massive steel and glass construction, never realized but depicted in *The Refracting Glasses* through computer animation, as if being built. Since this sequence too is represented as one of Constant's films-within-the-film, we can hardly doubt that Constant has immense admiration for Tatlin and his works.

Compared to those dreams Ern Malley's entire output might be said to describe a nightmare. He certainly became a nightmare for the Angry Penguins although for Constant Ern was exemplary: he was decidedly lower middle-class; he left school at fourteen, and when it came to poetry he was entirely self-taught. As he said in his first poem, he "had read in books that art was not easy."[14] Constant's unresolved struggles to complete any of the fragments that together make up *The Refracting Glasses* might suggest that

Leon Teague as *Young Constant Malernik* in *The Refracting Glasses*. The image seen through the train window is a part of V.E. Tatlin's *Monument to the Third International*. During this sequence of the film the interiors of the train are seen in black-and-white, while scenes outside the windows appear in full color. (© 1992 David Perry. Reprinted by permission of David Perry.)

he identified fully with Ern; yet we have seen, too, that he has unqualified admiration for the Letatlin and the Monument.

It is, of course, difficult to find anything in common between Ern Malley and the works of Tatlin. It must seem perverse to even suggest any kind of connection between the idealistic Constructivism of the Soviet Union in the late 1920s and the deeply traumatized individualism of the fictitious Ern Malley. When they were made, the Letatlin and Malley's poetry were no doubt utterly incompatible, but now firmly in the past they are both vivid illustrations of how intentions can lead to results undreamed of, not just in art but in real life also.

What an artist intends is usually to do first of all with structural or stylistic matters. One way or another these are practical things, vessels into which meaning flows as if by intention. Unless an artist scrupulously avoids any suggestion of imagery, meanings will almost certainly arise. Meaning is, of course, what readers extract when they read, viewers when they view; it could even be argued that humans will read meaning into anything. The Rorschach blots so popular with some psychologists exploit precisely that tendency, and some people would say that Ern Malley's work does the same.

But of course, things are rarely that simple. Looking at the poems from their makers' viewpoint they are not genuine poems, but to make their hoax explicit McAuley and Stewart had to lace Ern's work with passages that were coded clues to their intention. In other words, far from being meaningless, the poems are at times passionately meaningful about that most modern difficulty, in the absence of guidance from Church or Party, the impossibility of pinning down any kind of fixed and unchanging meaning in the products of human imagination. There is no suggestion that McAuley and Stewart misunderstood their own intentions, far from it, but when those intentions are acknowledged they give an added edge of bitter cynicism to the character of their amazing creation, Ern himself.

What McAuley and Stewart never seemed able to accept was that Ern Malley revealed to at least some artists in the forties and early fifties the idea that artists cannot prescribe the ways that audiences should respond to their work. For very different reasons it can also be said about the Letatlin that its present meaning is only remotely connected to its original intention. It is now possible to see that those historic incompatibles, the Letatlin and Malley's poems, have acquired over time layers of meaning that are firmly anchored to the real structures of the works themselves but were literally invisible to their makers.

It might be said that if the intended function of the Letatlin was human flight powered by human muscles, indeed nothing less than the "liberation of us all," then the Letatlin, like the revolution, must be called a failure. There is no doubt that Tatlin saw the Letatlin as a practical device,[15] although most of his contemporaries saw it as a foolish and foredoomed failure. (Notably, a famous Soviet glider pilot, K. K. Artseulov, did believe that it had possibilities.[16]) But it can now be said that its metaphorical connection with an heroic revolutionary dream—fallen, like Icarus, into a sea of oblivion—has entered into our knowledge of the Letatlin, truly become part of it, so that we can look at it now as neither Tatlin nor his contemporaries did.

It is, of course, the failure of the dreams—the undelivered intentions of the revolutionary period—that inform the melancholy mood of the end of *The Refracting Glasses*. Through his kino-eye, his hand-held Bolex,[17] Constant makes some efforts to show us images that depict that failure. Lydia's relating of her Aunt Iya's story tells of it. Constant's Russian teacher warned him of it unequivocally long before he went to Russia. In fact, virtually everything he's ever seen or read has warned him of it. The ghost of Ern Malley even, in its own hysterical way, attempted to warn him.

All of this, of course, cries out for interpretation. One of the commonest ways of developing that interpretation is to ask the author, "What did you mean?" in regard either to such and such an image or phrase, or to the work as a whole. Most authors will attempt to give an answer—of course, they always have intentions, intended forms, intended meanings—for their work; and depending on how articulate they are their answers will be more or less illuminating, or at least persuasive. In the case of *The Refracting Glasses*, however, can it be that the author's intentions about meaning should be discounted, if not entirely ignored? Fictional figures—Ern and Ethel Malley, and Constant—are given the same credibility as characters as are the entire Bolshevik leadership of 1917 ("bit players" who only ever appear as painted images). Equal credibility is given as well as to the author's real-life partner, Lydia, and to Constant's hired narrator, Voice-of-God, who seems to veer between having fictional arguments with Constant and reading straight narrations. Much the same confusion of fact and fiction (or dream and reality) seems to occur in relation to stories told about Tatlin's projects.

In attempting to interpret all these narrative events, all these incompatibilities, it must be obvious that *The Refracting Glasses*, although it continually refers to historical events, is in fact not primarily a history. The film plainly aspires to be art, but being a film it can hardly avoid also aspiring to be popular art, even if it scrupulously avoids using the "Hollywood style" in most of its parts. There are aspects of several documentary styles to the film—in fact, notwithstanding its elements of cartoon style animation and fantasy, and the meetings between Constant and Ern and Ethel Malley, there might be a case for calling the whole film a documentary, or more likely a pseudo-documentary like Woody Allen's *Zelig*. An audience could interpret all these events—inconsistencies, impossiblities, the hoax—as warnings to believe nothing seen, heard, or read—or at least, nothing seen or heard in *The Refracting Glasses*. Or an audience could see the whole film as a collection of devices of art designed to draw attention to the constructedness of this film—and by extension, all other films.

When we try to deal with photography, cinematography, the "Hollywood style"—all of those things loosely collected under the term "The Media"—our greatest difficulty actually had its origins long before anyone ever heard of "The Media," almost at the very origin of photography, the eerie verisimilitude of which gave rise to a belief that photography was more truthful than, fundamentally different from, all earlier forms of depiction, testimony, reportage. If *The Refracting Glasses* does have a coherent thesis, at least in the author's view, it is simply that the almost mystical belief about photography, and other more modern forms of recording, is entirely wrong, and that all those ways of opto-electro-mechanical recording can be equally truthful (or untruthful), as is every other form of depiction or description.

Of course, the author might be wrong. Just as the intentions of Tatlin and his contemporaries' interpretations of the formal results of his work are quite unlike the author's interpretations, and the intentions of McAuley and Stewart did not and do not deter people from finding meaning in Ern Malley's poems, it has to be allowed that audiences will find altogether other meanings in *The Refracting Glasses* than the author does.

This does not mean that any particular view is wrong, but that the dialogue between those views is a process, a spiraling-in that gets ever closer to defining Daniel Walkowitz's "something." That process might sometimes, at least, be historical. Thus the author likes to think that his film, even when it is plainly fantastical, is about history, which after all only exists in images and texts in some material form.

NOTES

1. B. Kazansky, *The Nature of Cinema* (1927), quoted in Herbert Eagle (ed.), *Russian Formalist Film Theory* (Department of Slavic Languages, University of Michigan, 1981).

2. Pablo Picasso, quoted in Alfred H. Barr, *Picasso, 50 Years of His Art* (New York, 1946) in Christopher Green, *Cubism and its Enemies* (New Haven and London: Yale University Press, 1987), footnote 58, p. 166.

3. Pablo Picasso: "Art is a lie that teaches us to see the truth." This maxim has been quoted so often that the present author cannot say what its source is.

4. David Perry, *The Refracting Glasses* (1992), 16mm film distributed by AFI Distribution Ltd., Melbourne.

5. For a complete account see Michael Heyward, *The Ern Malley Affair* (Brisbane: University of Queensland Press, 1993).

6. Ibid.

7. From "Ethel Malley's" letter to *Angry Penguins*, used as part of Ethel's lines in *The Refracting Glasses*. (The writings of "Ern" and "Ethel Malley," and the appearance of those personages, were used in the film with the express permission of the co-editor of *Angry Penguins* and publisher of the poems of "Ern Malley," Max Harris, to whom rights were assigned by McAuley and Stewart over the pseudonym "Ethel Malley.")

8. Heyward, *The Ern Malley Affair*, quoted in Robert Hughes's introduction.

9. The "Hollywood style" was accurately described in the *Sydney Morning Herald* (of all places!) as "making the camera work, direction and editing seamless, so as not to dilute the strength of the narrative" in the "TV" section (September 22, 1995).

10. Erik Barnouw, *Documentary: A History of the Non-Fiction Film* (New York: Oxford University Press, 1974).

11. Daniel Walkowitz, comment during discussion of these ideas at the Sixth History and Film Conference, La Trobe University, Melbourne, 1993.

12. This word was made by joining Tatlin's name with the Russian verb, letat (to fly).

13. Dr. Christina Lodder, *Russian Constructivism* (New Haven, Conn.: Yale University Press, 1983), quoted by permission in *The Refracting Glasses*.

14. "Ern Malley," poems "Dürer: Innsbruck, 1495," first published in *Angry Penguins* (Autumn 1944), reprinted in Heyward, *The Ern Malley Affair*.

15. In Moscow in 1953 Tatlin gave a lecture in which he outlined the history of the planning (1921) and construction of three Letatlins (1930–1933). This author was shown, and allowed to copy, a transcript of that lecture held in the Museum of the Air Forces of [the old Soviet Union] at Monino, outside Moscow. In his lecture Tatlin described a tethered test of the Letatlin "in a strong wind." He stated unequivocally that the machine lifted five meters above the ground, but in a melancholy conclusion states that the tests were "discontinued because the winter was fast approaching," a statement that is associated in *The Refracting Glasses* with Constant's painting of Stalin.

16. Artseulov's reasons for his support are given in a second document, copied with the Museum's permission, at the same time as the one above.

17. Brand-name of 16mm. cameras, usually spring-driven, especially popular with avant-garde "underground" or "alternative" filmmakers.

14

Projected Lives: A Meditation on Biography and Cinematic Space

Kathryn Millard

I've always been an avid reader of biographies. As a filmmaker, I'm particularly attracted to the large canvas that biographies offer. Biographies seem to me to be about repetitions, gaps, silences, absences, patterns revealed over long periods of time, lives that don't steadily progress but unfold at times slowly and at times in a rush. Over the last ten years, I've worked on several film biographies. Some have been made: *Point Of Departure*, about the life of writer Jean Devanny, *Light Years*, an exploration of place, memory, and the photographs of Olive Cotton, *Parklands*, a fictional biography of my father. And one has not yet been made: *Interior in Yellow*, about the Australian painter Grace Cossington Smith.

The South Australian Film Corporation, Tapley's Hill Road, Hendon, Adelaide. Interior. Day. In a building that housed a munitions factory during the Second World War and is now a film studio, I speak with a film marketing executive about the script I'm developing. This meeting has been suggested by the funding body providing script development funds. I have all kinds of ideas about interior landscapes and a painter who presents the world as an intensely ordered yet fragmented whole. Explaining this to the marketing executive is not easy. He offers some suggestions. "Look, a painter who paints wardrobes—now that's not interesting. But, if you tell me that the painter is young, struggling for recognition. She rejects the young man courting her; her painting must come first. For years she struggles to develop her art. A new exhibition opens, a mystery man buys one of her paintings for an unheard-of sum. Her career takes off. We find out that the mystery buyer is her rejected suitor. . . . Mind you, you're the writer, I'm not telling you what happened, but I am telling you that you have to take a little dramatic license to tell a good story."

With a few notable exceptions, film biography in Australia has been dominated by the heroic linear narrative, chronicling the lives of "great Australians"—cinematic projections of lives moving forward inevitably, overcoming obstacles that stand in the way of clearly signposted destinations. Biographies construct subjects that fit into fields of meaning that have already been mapped. The questions most often asked of those proposing film biographies are, first, "How important is this person?" and second, "How will we really get to know them?" These questions don't acknowledge that there might not be definitive answers, that biographies inevitably raise questions about our ability to know about the meaning of other lives—that biographies are about negotiating complex relationships between subject, author, and reader.

The dominant approach to filmmaking has, like traditional history, primarily been concerned with events and "what happens." Conventional wisdom has it that the film medium is incapable of portraying interior lives, only exterior actions. "Central conflict theory" is the term filmmaker and critic Raul Ruiz uses to describe this method of organizing screen narratives. A story is thought to begin when someone (a protagonist) wants something and someone else (an antagonist) wishes to prevent him from having it. All the elements of the story are then arranged around this central conflict. Such a theory of screenwriting eliminates all stories that are not concerned with confrontation and assumes that drama is not possible without key moments of decision—a model that, Ruitz argues, privileges the culture of the United States, where the ability to make decisions and act on them quickly and decisively is particularly valued.[1]

Reflecting on some of the issues around cinema, history, and biography, I browse through novels, criticism, photographs, and films, marking my own pathways of thinking and remembering through images and texts that have particular resonances for me. Paul Carter writes of a "spatial history" that engages not with geographical space but with historical space. Carter's historical space is poetic in nature, and its history is about creating a dialogue, inscribing a space with historical meanings. He suggests that the literatures of spatial history—letters home, explorers' journals, unfinished maps—are not like novels and their narratives do not conform to the rules of cause and effect that have dominated empirical history. Instead they must be read as unfinished maps, and records of journeys. The literatures of spatial history are not about smooth progression but about fragmentary asides, observations, reminiscence, and scraps of dialogue. Above all, they make no claims for completeness but are—like journeys—exploratory: recordings of the search for a language.[2] Film, concerned with the organization of pictorial and narrative space, is a medium particularly suited to the exploration of "spatial histories"—in this case a recording not just of a search for language, but for a specifically filmic language.

Australian National Gallery, Canberra. Interior. Day. The gleaming surfaces of a workbench, a trolley laden with leather-bound volumes, a pair of white cotton gloves; the tools of the pictorial researcher. Behind the theatricality of the National Art Gallery's public spaces lies a maze of rooms where prints and paintings are stored, dissected, and analyzed. I begin researching *Interior in Yellow* by spending several weeks looking through Cossington Smith's sketch books; recipes for paint, exercises in perspective, quotes about light, watercolors from a journey to England and Europe, working drawings for paintings and prints now on display. A visual diary from childhood to old age, spanning more than eight decades of the painter's life. The Director of the Gallery strolls past and asks what I'm doing. "A film? I don't know how you'll manage that. Wonderful painter, terribly boring life." He shakes his head in disbelief.

Recent writings across history, literary theory, fiction and cultural geography have much to offer the filmmaker/biographer, looking toward new horizons, looking beyond the closed linear biography. Speaking from the boundaries and intersections of disciplines, a growing body of work challenges the cultural biases inherent in traditional stories and advocates more layered forms of address to deal with complex realities. Hayden White asks: "Does the world really present itself to perception in the form of well made stories, with central subjects, proper beginnings, middles and ends and a coherence that allows us to 'see the end' in every beginning?"[3]

Art Gallery of South Australia, North Terrace, Adelaide. Interior. Day. I walk through the rooms of the Art Gallery of South Australia, a place familiar since childhood. The histories of the paintings and art objects arranged spatially; rooms dedicated to the eras and movements in which the histories of the visual arts are usually narrated. I stop at the paintings of Grace Cossington Smith. Small blocks of brilliant color arranged against each other. Although many of the paintings are still lives or interiors, the blocks of vibrant color create a shimmering effect, a sense of movement. More and more people point me to the writings of a curator, acknowledged as "the authority" on Grace Cossington Smith. The curator was responsible for organizing a major retrospective of her work and, so it is claimed, securing her a place in Australian art history. His portrait is of a gentle, graceful woman, a woman full of light. A woman who steadily, unquestioningly realizes her vision. No false starts, no detours. I find this portrait dissatisfying, though I do not yet quite know why.

An account of a life that I keep returning to is Drusilla Modjeska's *Poppy*, an imaginary biography of the narrator's mother and an exploration of the limits of traditional history and biography. The starting points for Poppy's biographer are the visible, tangible evidence of a life. In this case, a ring, a string of pearls, a locket, a golden heart, and some papers. Modjeska's narrator soon finds these inadequate as historical evidence, asserting that: "History does not move in straight lines, it is fractured and uneven and runs off at tangents. The temptation is to talk as if the chronology went somewhere and changes have clear derivations and destinations."[4] In order to move beyond the available historical facts and evidence and to challenge linear chronologies, Modjeska's narrator is forced to move into the unfamiliar, and for some even taboo, territory of dreams, memories, imagined events, and conversations. The search to know about her mother's life becomes as much about silences, gaps, and absences as recorded events.

While writers like Drusilla Modjeska address issues of narrative space, cultural geographers and historians consider space as metaphor. Robert Harbison in his book *Eccentric Spaces* considers how maps, cities, gardens, and department stores are ways of ordering knowledge spatially.[5] Museums—like art galleries—arrange history spatially, so that walking through these spaces we can experiment with different sequences of remembering. Inevitably, a consideration of spatial patterns of ordering knowledge also brings up issues of scale. In his explorations of place, American essayist Barry Lopez argues for the local, the small scale; intimate places associated with human presence rather than the heroic myths of national geographies[6]—spaces from which it is possible to catch the movement of sun against skin, glimpses, shadows, impressions.

Spring Forest, Koorawatha, New South Wales. Exterior. Day. I walk through Spring Forest, with photographer Olive Cotton. Over a thousand acres that she has photographed for nearly fifty years. Olive points to the old Buick in which the family made their journey from Sydney, the garden bed where two of her photographs, "Dead Sunflowers" and "Cherokee Rose," were composed, a line of wattles in the distance. Together, we explore the sites of her photographs, and a form begins to emerge for the film. A film structured around the rhythms of walking and photographs composed like memories. As we walk home along the stretch of road with the avenue of gums and the white bridge, or clear the kitchen table for a bundle of Olive's photographs—these activities mirror the search for a space from which to speak. I come to see Spring Forest as landscape on an intimate scale, given form and order by the lives of the people who dwell there. There is a sense that the land has been walked over and over, is steeped in memories, stories, and photographs.

Silence. Expanses of blue white ice. Toward the horizon, a speck of black. Music begins. The black speck in the distance becomes a human figure walking slowly, deliberately, toward the camera. A tension builds between the stillness of the held frame, with its expanses of sculpted ice, and the movement of the figure. Shadows, black against white, the sound of wind. This is the opening sequence from *Thirty Two Short Films about*

Glen Gould, François Girard's film biography of the Canadian composer, musician, and radio producer who, by all accounts, was given to seeing issues in rather black and white terms. In Girard's film, the themes and preoccupations of Gould's life are played out in hotel rooms, recording studios, phone boxes, and diners. And against expanses of ice and water, besides lakes and beaches. The film's predominant hues are blue and grey, black and white, colors associated with coolness and definition. The biography is structured as thirty-two films, each with a title and divided by frames of black, and the phrases have a cumulative effect, like some musical compositions.

Toorak, Melbourne. Exterior. Day. I arrange to meet with a woman who collects Grace Cossington Smith paintings. My destination a leafy Melbourne suburb, littered with mansions and Volvos. A world totally unfamiliar to me. A chilly winter's day. The woman has a letter I might like to read. From the doorway, she directs me to a bench in the garden. Closing the door, she goes in search of the letter. As I wait in the garden, I pull my black coat tight against the wind. At another Toorak house, a woman inspects the label on my inexpensive coat as she takes it from me. "That will keep you warm, dear," she patronizes. Neither of these interview subjects has any particular insights to offer. It becomes clear that for some people, paintings—like silver and designer gardens—are the accessories of wealth, an attempt to buy a relationship to culture. This aspect of Cossington Smith's legacy is of little interest to me. Instead, I attempt to trace the artist's journey inward. The poet Gerard Manley Hopkins's term "inscape" is sometimes used to refer to Cossington Smith's still lives and interiors, illuminating the everyday.

From early forays into the city to paint the vast forms of crowds, buildings, and the incomplete Sydney Harbor Bridge—halves still straining to meet—Cossington Smith moves closer to home, painting the bush near Turramurra. In landscapes that are flowing and ordered, roads and land gently unfurl. Then she focuses more closely again, painting views of plants and flowers from her own studio. Her later works—the "golden interiors" for which she is best known—are of her own home. Brightly lit and framed by open doors and windows, they beckon us in.

In a series of black and white images, crowds make their way through city streets, car headlights are reflected onto wet roads, shadows fall onto pavements, emptying office blocks are lit. The archival montage from cities around the world that acts as a prologue to Lawrence Johnston's *Eternity*. *Eternity* intercuts archival film, interviews, and re-enactments as it follows the shadowy figure of Arthur Stace. Witnesses speak to camera, recalling Arthur Stace's writing of the word "eternity" across the length and breadth of Sydney for over forty years. The interview subjects are arranged against painted scenery—romanticized scenes of nature including woodlands, thunder-filled skies, and stormy seas, in shades of blue or gold. The colors are particularly prominent in contrast to the film's predominantly black and white tones. The film's performance style adds to the notion of "witnessing" Stace's life. Some particularly enthusiastic interview subjects speak as if from the pulpit on a Sunday evening, while others are more inquiring or reflective.

The frames of *Eternity* are carefully composed, and the camera is often still. Shadowy figures or lights move through the frame. Much of the imagery is concerned with day and night, light and dark. The black and white images give emphasis to the textures, surfaces, and forms of the city. From time to time, muted colors of archival films almost bleed into the black and white sequences. We follow Stace over bridges and rooftops, through train stations and subways as he seeks out and marks even the most inaccessible corners of the city. *Eternity* is just one of the many possible biographies of Sydney. The film's structure and aesthetic strategies are particularly resonant with its themes. In the film's closing sequence the figure of Arthur Stace is momentarily illuminated by a photographer's flashlight. Or is it streaks of lightning? Choral music builds and there is flash after flash of image, light against dark. Through the act of writing, a formerly homeless man transforms the city into an intimate space, challenging the myths of the supposed impersonality of the contemporary city.

Olive Cotton walks through the avenue of gums that mark the entrance to her home at Spring Forest. Reaching the end of the road, she checks the viewfinder of her Rolleiflex camera. Waits for white clouds to drift into position. Gums tower against the sky. Soft shadows fall onto the dirt road. A small figure against roads, sky, and trees; Cotton takes the photograph. The patterns of time burned into a black and white image. In my memory, this black and white image dissolves into a landscape painted in gold. As a child, my grandmother took me to the Art Gallery Of South Australia on North Terrace. This is where I first saw Grace Cossington Smith's painting "The Road To Turramurra," with its blocks of color and road and land gently unfurling into the distance. The painted landscape dissolves into an interior. To the center of the frame is a yellow standard lamp. As an adult, Cossington Smith's niece tells me about the painter's last years at Turramurra. Light fades, it is early evening. Grace Cossington Smith, now in her eighties, lives alone in the crumbling family house. Her eyesight is no longer the best. She takes hold of the standard lamp and slowly makes her way around the room, searching for a favored object, her pathway illuminated by the unwieldy lamp.

Reflecting back over the film biographies that I have made or begun to compose, their images offer a partial version of my own life. For the moment, I've consigned folders of notes and images about Cossington Smith to an archive box. My own interests have moved closer to home as I interrogate the spaces of my own family history and the places where I grew up. For me, Adelaide's streets and suburbs are layered with stories, images, fragments from generations of family life. Myself, my brother and sister line up in the front yard, in descending order of height. There's a square of lawn, a row of rose bushes. Dad peers through the viewfinder of his Brownie camera and lines up the shot. A photograph is taken, the shadows and memories of a place exposed. Later, the snapshot takes its place in the family photo album, alongside Dad at work—in his detective's suit, at the scene of the crime, pointing to the evidence.

Increasingly, as a filmmaker, I find myself outside the cultural institutions of art galleries, public libraries, and archives. Instead, I read the traces of people's lives from domestic interiors, front gardens, suburban streets, parks, city buildings, tracts of bush—and the spaces of the photographs, canvases, objects, poems, and stories that name those places and link them to lived experience.

NOTES

1. See Raul Ruiz, *Poetics of Cinema* (Paris: Editions des Voir, 1995), Chapter 1, "Central Conflict Theory," pp. 9–23.

2. See Paul Carter, *The Road to Botany Bay: An Exploration of Landscape and History* (New York: Knopf, 1988) and *Living in a New Country: History, Travelling and Language* (London: Faber and Faber, 1992).

3. Hayden White, *The Content of the Form* (Baltimore: Johns Hopkins University Press, 1987).

4. Drusilla Modjeska, *Poppy* (Melbourne: McPhee Gribble, 1990), p. 90.

5. See Robert Harbison, *Eccentric Spaces* (London: Secker and Warburg, 1977).

6. Barry Lopez, "The American Geographies," in *Writing Home: Writings on Nature and Culture from Orion Magazine* (Boston: Beacon Press, 1992).

15

Long Exposures: A Poetics of Film and History

Janet Sternburg

A young girl in a bright orange sweater and short black skirt iceskates alone on a frozen patch, rows of detention camp barracks behind her, slushy flat earth surrounding a bleak oblong on which her blades incise their strokes. For a brief moment, the soundtrack of voices ceases and the only sound is the swish of her skates across the glassy surface, arcing forward and backward within its small compass.

I am haunted by this image of the skater who appears in Rea Tajiri's *History and Memory*, of her white skates as the camera moves in closer to that upright and tender meeting of skate and bare leg, and to that blade below, scratchily carving its marks. In this image from and of the past, the filmmaker herself is evoked, a figure passing and repassing across patches of time, revisiting with keen perception a scarred site.

She is joined, I believe, by other contemporary film and video artists who are envisioning the past in new ways that break with traditional representations of history. Instead of telling history through conventional documentary means in which the narrative is structured from verifiable sources, these makers are creating poetic interpretations, associatively linking "evidence" drawn as well from personal experience, memories, dreams, and imagination. In so doing, they are implicitly proposing an alternative understanding of historical narrative in which the primacy of truths claimed by facticity yields to the equally pressing claims of interior life.

In three works that I find emblematic—Tajiri's, Peter Thompson's, Janice

Tanaka's—several different pasts are shaped by their tellers into those understandings of process, change, and meaning known as histories. This
transformation occurs because of (and not, as history is traditionally
taught, in spite of) the artists' rendering of gaps in knowledge; of their own
questions, especially as these interrogations butt against other people's secrets; of memory fragments that surface repeatedly to consciousness envi-
sioned only by acts of the imagination. These artists unveil the rough,
problematic contours of the past and, in so doing, give rise to an authentic
poetics that delineates the pressure exerted by that past, as well as the
imprint on those who live with its aftermath and search for its traces.

If history as described by Walter Benjamin is that angel who wants to
"go back and fix the things that have been broken," these film- and videomakers are the allies, cohort, and instruments of that angel. But Benjamin
warns that the storm of progress is inexorably blowing the angel backward,
away from the past's wreckage and into the future. Interpreting that image
freely, I believe it suggests a pervasive personal and cultural tension that is
itself being portrayed by these artists, situated between what might be reclaimed, mended, and perhaps redeemed, and what is unrecoverable. With
their moving images of this tension, film and video artists are reinvigorating
historical narrative as a living force, recast through the expressive forms of
contemporary culture.

Near the start of *History and Memory*,[1] there is an odd hokey moment
that suggests a way to being to think about these investigations. Tajiri
stages a scene from her family's past, in which her teenage sister wants to
take a snapshot of a boy on whom she has a crush. He is an unwilling
subject, squirming under her contradictory directions: "Look down . . .
look up . . . look a little happier, look dejected." When he impatiently urges
her to "Just take the picture," she replies, "This is a long exposure." Beyond her attempt to protract the encounter, the phrase "long exposure"
implies that events once hidden in the dark are now revealed and clarified
through the sustained light of inquiry. Further, it conveys the sense of an
artist's vision focused on the past with a willingness to keep the shutter of
one's attention open and suspended because, in this effort, there is no escaping the unblinking I.

December 7, 1961
View from 100 feet above
the ground . . .

•

The spirit of my grandfather witnesses
my father and mother as
they have an argument
over the unexplained
nightmares their daughter

has been having on the
20th anniversary of the
bombing of Pearl Harbor . . .

To date, as here at the beginning of *History and Memory*, is to place a marker pointing the way to the terrain of the past. The text continues scrolling, laid out on the surface of the screen in a way that is not literally a poem but has the movement, the breath between phrases, the breaking away of words from their anchor in conventional prose that is associated with poetic intent. The first image appears—a woman, her back turned from the camera, is hording a canteen into which water flows. "I don't know," Tajiri says voice-over, "where this came from. . . . I just had this fragment." The memory returns as a close-up of cupped hands, and later again simply as a shaft of water. This vision of a woman receiving liquid that pours from an unseen source is beautiful but also unsettling: just where is the scene occurring? Far indeed from the regular world of houses with readily available tap water. As the filmmaker later discloses, the house of her parents, classified as the property of enemy aliens, has vanished, stolen away by thieves. The site of this water is an internment camp in the Arizona desert; the woman is Tajiri's mother as she appears in her daughter's memory. But this image is not a memory in the usual sense in which previous experiences of the self lodge as residue in the mind. Here the experience belongs in fact to Tajiri's mother, who has banished it from recall. It has been deposited instead as shards in the consciousness of the daughter, who now must find a way to make the pieces fit together.

Water. A camp. Another continent, another history. The concentration camp at Dachau, seen briefly in *Universal Hotel*,[2] is a site empty of evidence of what has taken place there and thus drained of meaning, an expanse now of gravel bordered by trees, composed by Thompson's eye as formally as a Zen garden. This film also starts with a date, 1981, that marks the filmmaker's beginning attempts to locate a sequence of photographs whose existence is suggested by a single photograph that Thompson encounters in a book and cannot dislodge from his mind. Taken in 1942, "It records," Thompson says, "the freezing of a prisoner at Dachau. The prisoner is identified as 'test person.' " Throughout, Thompson speaks the narration flatly, pronouncing the article "a" as a long vowel, as though he were a student reading from a textbook. The sentences are declarative, neutrally descriptive, giving a sense that the filmmaker is treading warily and lightly, aware of the great distance, the space of suffering that separates him from the subject of these experiments. "The purpose of the test," he intones, "is to find the best methods for rewarming German pilots after they crash into Arctic seas." The filmmaker's intent is to discover surrounding images that, taken together, will reveal the step-by-step procedures of the test, recovering its narrative specificity and thus returning it to history.

The opening images of *Universal Hotel* look down from the filmmaker's hotel room at one of the great public spaces of Europe, the central plaza of Sienna. People stroll, crisscrossing its cupped ellipse. This field of vision carries historical resonances of the nearby fourteenth-century allegorical frescoes of Good and Bad Government, which depict the founding of Sienna's city-state and reflect on the twofold aspects of structures of power: order in the service of civic benevolence and harmony; order imposed for the purposes of oppression and death. Over the walking figures, Thompson is speaking on the telephone, making inquiries about the whereabouts of possibly remaining photographs. His own search for order, for evidence that could lead to understanding, is being met by those foes of coherence: ignorance, amnesia, denial.

Eleven photographs are eventually unearthed from archives scattered throughout Europe, and it is to them that Thompson returns, arranging them again and again in variant orderings that correspond to his looking more minutely, closer each time, seeing different details that suggest alternative sequences. No photographs are found of the women prostitutes who, in another aspect of the experiment, were brought to Dachau from the concentration camp at Ravensbrück and used to excite the subjects, warming them sexually through what the Nazi doctors termed "animal heat." What remains are images of one man, the "test person," clothed first in pants and shirt, then pictured dressed in the uniform of a flight pilot, then immersed inside a metal bin filled with iced water, then hauled from the water and, finally, standing to face the camera again.

During his journey, Thompson comes up against his own uncertainty. The film turns inward, to his dream in which the subject of the experiments stands behind a closed door in a mysterious building identified as the "unfamiliar hotel." This image is summoned against when Thompson acknowledges that what he says about these photographs cannot be verified. His thwarted search for proof leads to another kind of truth, born out of urgent desire to bring the past into present-tense encounter and rendered through a fictive dialogue in which the filmmaker places himself at the closed door of the resistant past. Speaking in a low tone over images of light moving on the surface of water, Thompson converses with the person behind that door:

> *Me*: Open it.
>
> *Him*: If you force it, I'll go behind
> another door and in another room . . .
>
> •
>
> *Me*: I'll be your witness.

Him: Don't dare to talk to me about that.
    I had enough of that.

Me: I want to talk with you.

Him: You might be talking to yourself.
    I might already have walked away.

Me: Go ahead. Walk. I might hear your footsteps.

The encounter is complex in its interplay of supplicating, demanding, taunt-ing, contestatory, unyielding, and empathetic elements. As invocation, it is reminiscent of Tajiri's summoning the ghost of her grandfather to help her imagine "things that have happened for which there are no observers except the spirits of the dead." As exemplar of daring artistic strategies, it suggests as well a rendering of history in which the difficulties of knowing and understanding the past are as important a subject as the passage of events. It serves, too, as an affirmation of the artist's intent to heed the still reso-nant past, even as it retreats. Filmmaking becomes, in the words of the narrator in Chris Marker's related film *Sans Soleil*, an attempt "to perform the rite that would repair the web of time when it had been broken." The filmmaker speaks from his own immersion in the waters of the problematic past; his own long exposure.

    A bicycle, riderless, careens around the aisles of a coffee shop in Tanaka's *Memories from the Department of Amnesia*,[3] a video structured like cham-ber music into a series of movements, intimate and distilled. This initial image-processed sequence carries a sense of loss, and, indeed, the tape is an elegy to Tanaka's then recently deceased mother. A viewer feels an al-most physically dizzying concern that the bicycle might at any moment topple, combined with a sense of marveling at the difficult maneuverings and precarious balances that convey a metaphor for survival within the constraints of her mother's life.

    That life as embedded in personal experience, as well as in history and in memory, is rendered through a complex final sequence in which the screen holds concurrent multiple images. On the right, Tanaka's camera moves across snapshots of her mother, sometimes with her family, at other times alone; in one especially memorable image, a portrait seems to come closer until the features virtually dissolve. These photographs blend, at the center of the frame, into another series of images moving along the left of the screen, also in stately procession of emergence and departure. Here, a hand arises from the bottom of the frame, lifting a photographic negative and displaying it in a gesture that suggests both holding it up for personal inspection, as though from a developing tray, and producing it as evidence for others to see. For a moment, the hand remains in the frame while another hand, white and light-filled (rather like a fern in a nineteenth-century botanical photograph), repeats the gesture. One image glides over the next, these hands and photographs in alternating exposures passing and repassing each other in a continual duet of light and dark, of lifting and leaving.

Toward the bottom of the frame, titles convey chronological events in Tanaka's mother's life. Between the dates of her birth and death is the record of hopeful beginnings and what Nadezhda Mandelstam has called "ordinary heartbreaks," intermingled with the impress of political matters upon her personal circumstances: "1st child born, Sept., 1940. . . . Divorce, 1948 . . . Released from Mazanar, 1943 . . . Uses Chinese surname to get a job, 1945 . . . ." Finally, to the visual litany of images and text, voices are added. Two women (Tanaka and her daughter) lightly and fondly reminisce: "She used to date and run around . . . I never knew that until after she had passed away . . . Remember, we went through her cedar chest and she had all those wild outfits she saved . . . ?" Yet another dimension of this life is revealed, contrapuntal with the others, affording a sense of how a life escapes from the margins of its telling.

The multilayered sequence of images and sound held together by formal design becomes, in its totality, a meta-image, by which I mean an amalgam so complex that it carries implications of process and change as well as its own explicit denotations. Viewing it, I am struck by its capacity to reveal the varieties of interplay among images as they appear and vanish, and thus by its resonance with Benjamin's description of historical origin as much more than "the process of becoming of that which has emerged," but rather "that which emerges out of *the process of becoming and disappearing*" (emphasis mine). In Tanaka's sequence, the moving image itself carries ideas about history, suggesting, too, how conceptual thought emerges from and is wafted on the flow and ebb of phenomena. Moreover, these capacities of the moving image implicitly extend Benjamin's notion that to grasp the rhythms of history, one must have a "double insight," that is, an understanding of the simultaneity, "as in a whirlpool," of the forces of becoming and disappearing. The same can be said about memory, which moves through consciousness in eddies of remembrance and forgetfulness, becoming comings. By complex concurrencies and simultaneities of imagery, text, and voice, the moving image interlaces history with memory, exponentially increasing "double insight," opening new relations and collapsing the distance between the vortex within and the vortex without.

Who then is the angel of history to these film- and videomakers?

It is the spirit of Tajiri's grandfather, hovering over and witnessing the past.

It is the test person, voicing his refusal to again be a subject.

It is the gesture of a hand that reaches down into a wellspring of images to draw forth another exposure.

But the dilemma of that angel, gusting away from the damages even as it wants to extend a restorative arm, requires a more inclusive account. To the litany, one must add that ghostly grandfather unable to descend to earth and soothe his granddaughter's troubled dreams. And to this company must be named, and admitted, Sigmund Rascher, the doctor who conducted the experiments at Dachau. The angel of history must incarnate, too, those officials who, with the sanction of government authority, interned Tanaka's mother, even as it must embody also her reserves of gaiety and unmarked happiness.

Earlier, I described these film- and videomakers as allies, cohort, and instruments of the angel. Not for a moment does this imply that they believe themselves to be that angel. Rather, as allies, they are friends to the angel, connected by mutual concerns and empathetic with its predicament. As cohort, their works signal the presence of a growing company of artists who are enlisting their gifts in the creation of new expressive approaches to the complexities of historical understandings. As instruments . . . Are these artists also stranded in longing, facing the past across a distance whose ever-expanding divide is itself the subject to which they are constrained? Or can works such as the ones that I am discussing repair the web of time, when historical wounds have damaged links that make continuity possible, when perpetrators of those wounds have encouraged the sundering of memory, and when the injured have sustained those ruptures so that ongoing life can be bearable? Can artists bring solace to those on whom such harm has been inflicted?

To these last questions, the answer is a provisional "yes," if these artists are understood as carriers of the pain. As in bodies, the wounds of history have layers, extending through generational strata. In *History and Memory*, Tajiri says, "I could remember a time of great sadness before I was born. We had been moved, uprooted. We had lived with a lot of pain. I had no idea where these memories came from, yet I know the place." The project of retrieval and healing belongs deeply then to second- or third- generation artists who themselves are scarred.

It is no accident that works such as the ones here are emerging at present. These later generations have come to artistic maturity in a time when it is broadly understood that knowledge is partial and contested, and thus they are willing and able to create from within that understanding rather than through the myths and comforts of omniscience. Then, too, these generations are in a complex temporal relationship to the events they evoke, both near enough to have access to first-person accounts, and their relationship to place; often the actual site, in which history has traditionally been sought, has altered so radically that its meanings have dispersed and are mediated by memory. These new works reconfigure time and place from the vantage point of a new "location," one that requires acknowledgment of its ambiguous and wrenched status. And, of course, these experiments that so advance the possibilities of historical narrative arrive at a technological moment when the language and tools of media have become sufficiently flexible to be at the disposal of multilayered inquiries.

This new work also appears in challenging relationship to the present cultural moment when the distinctiveness of specific histories has been explored as a means to understand the powerful idea of difference. Even as these histories remain integral, another impulse has equally strong implications. The desire to express the philosophical, personal, and metaphoric dimensions of history serves as a thread, wrapping itself loosely but cohesively around discrete histories. Work created from this desire is itself connective, crossing divisions to suggest shared concerns, and helping to heal the condition of long wounding through the making of long exposures.

Closer now, the woman who earlier was turned away from the camera is seen full face, her head bent slightly and receptively forward, eyes closed, a smile of great sweetness lighting the curve of her cheeks. The image of Tajiri's mother returns, her hands ceremoniously dipping below the frame. Rushing water pours again through the soundtrack as, in slow motion, she lifts her cupped hands to her face. Water, a luxury of water, anoints the desert of her temples, her brows. It streams down her cheeks and, as her parchedness is relieved by this gift, so too is her loss assuaged by her daughter's creation of an image.

NOTES

Reprinted from *Common Knowledge*, Vol. 3, no. 1, Spring 1994, by permission of the author.

1. *History and Memory*, a video by Rea Tajiri. Distributed by Electronic Arts Intermix, New York City.

2. *Universal Hotel*, a film by Peter Thompson. Distributed in 16mm by Drift Distribution, New York City, in video by Facets Multimedia, Chicago.

3. *Memories from the Department of Amnesia*, a video by Janice Tanaka. Distributed by Video Data Bank, Chicago, as well as NAATA, San Francisco, and Electronic Arts Intermix.

16

Enchanted Experience

Ross Gibson

I'm looking to get a feeling for a way of knowing, a *way of knowing with places and their pasts*. Let's call it research into the possibilities of a post-colonial culture. Such research seems increasingly necessary in a settler-society like Australia, where I choose to live, for it has become clear that we have not been served well by the philosophies of governance that were imported out of the eighteenth century and put in place here. So I want to get a feeling for some other ways of knowing an Australian's place in the world of time-and-space.

This process of "getting a feeling" is proposed here as a technical term rather than as an alibi for tentative beginnings or as a vague, "new age" appeal to instinct or *genius locus*. I will look for such an "integrated" way of knowing in a couple of places: the Pilliga Forest in northwest New South Wales; and the site of the first Government House where British colonialism was administered at Sydney Cove between 1788 and 1846, when the house was demolished. But before surveying these intensely significant precincts and the audiovisual portrayals that I have made of their histories, I need to spend some time puzzling through a larger question about time-and-space and historical knowledge.

What does it mean to know a place in the twentieth century, in a nation formed out of the second wave of European military imperialism? For European-Australians like myself, it means working with, around, and against a heritage of "psychological mapping" which causes experience to be ruled off into subjective and objective realms of sovereignty and challenge; it means being governed by the Cartesian compulsion to maintain one's sense of self by way of actions applied to a world of objects, a world in which space is believed to be a neutral stage where dramatic, self-definitive actions propel a person into the "new world" of the future.

However, living in the place called Australia also means being exposed to a web of alternative philosophies and land-cultures, those of Aborigines, Melanesians, Polynesians, Asian garden-farmers, European peasants, and others. And once the Western mentality begins to suspect that it is somewhat dysfunctional in its present context, the process of knowing a place begins to entail experimentation with adapted modes of being in the world of matter and meaning, the world of time-and-space, of past, present, and future.

As one way of commencing this groundwork, I want to retrace some strands of modernism, a movement which I take to be a radical response to a crisis in the conditions of Western presence-in-the-world at the end of the nineteenth century. Choosing from the myriad available definitions, I am calling modernism a means of constructing "worldviews" which presume a *profusion* (rather than a Cartesian *delimitation*) of spatial and temporal vantages on experience. In other words, I'm choosing to understand modernism as a process that disallows the tidy, stable placement of a subjectivity separate from, and in charge of, a world of experience and potential "out there" in the future, past the boundaries of the presently sovereign self. In this respect modernism is a set of attitudes and strategies formed to disallow the "imperialist" belief that the world can be organized as a resource for the affirmation and profit of an active, assertive self moving conclusively along a line of time. The Cubists' attempts to annihilate singular viewpoints in representational space-and-time; the Italian Futurists' celebration of an earth-scrambling technology of radio waves and electromagnetic energy; the Russian Futurists' dreams of accelerating existential time to a "voluminous" kind of chronic ubiquity that renders linear history obsolete: these are some of the more striking examples of modernist challenges to the conception of history as a positivist series of eventful subsumptions of the past.

Pondering these changes to our ways of "modeling" experience in time and space, I've been wondering about modernist geography and how it might inform the reimagining of post-settlement Australia. So I've gone back to Ellen Churchill Semple's *The Influences of Geographical Environment* (1911), a strange amalgam of evolutionary determinism and poetic speculation. Even as it tries to be strictly scientific and developmentalist, the book is also charged with an irrationalist attraction to "primitive" consciousness. Semple believes in a kind of spiritual telegraphy webbing the globe wherever human societies have managed to live. Consider the opening paragraph of the book:

Man is a product of the earth's surface. This means not merely that he is a child of the earth, dust of her dust; but that the earth has mothered him, fed him, set him tasks, directed his thoughts, confronted him with difficulties that have strengthened his body and sharpened his wits, given him his problems of navigation or irrigation, and at the same time whispered hints for their solution. She has entered into his bone and tissue, into his mind and soul.[1]

Semple starts from the proposition that mind and soul are integral to her science of geography, that they are the "object" of her investigation and that when she analyzes the geographical characteristics of the earth she is also examining the structure of human experience. A functional separation between human subjectivity and scientific objectivity seems untenable in Semple's scheme of things; the inner world of the subject and the outer world of objects are folded into each other. She looks for a way of knowing in a world where experience has become wider, faster, and more multifarious than any single, stable viewpoint or time-lined story can hold.

Like many early-modernist texts, *The Influences of Geographical Environment* is an attempt to register a verve that runs and rules the complexifying culture of the twentieth century. This verve, or energy, or mind-and-soul: how could you know it? Semple implies it might be caught with a rigorous intuition involving immersion in, and receptiveness to, the surging valency of experience and ecology. I suspect that this is how you start to know with a place. You begin with nothing more than a sense of an intricately charged, overall pattern in the material world in which you are implicated. You get a feeling. It's something like "knowing in your bones."

To draw this knowing into the realms of analysis and communality, we need words. (I'm trusting that language is the patterned material that makes our most complex and communicable models of being in the world of time-and-space.) What are some of the words we have for knowing the domains where colonialism has taken place? Land. Territory. Terrain. Earth. Real Estate. Space. Emptiness. Environment. Property. Realm. Stretch. Expanse. Reserve. Note how each word is toned with multiple connotations. Each warrants close analysis, but the one I want to work with is "tract." A tract is something you can read.[2] But let's not ignore the other nuances. A tract is also a region or area of indefinite extent; an anatomical term for a system of organs; a short discourse on a religious topic. These glossings are especially illuminating if we try to work with the Australian idea of a *tract in a colony*. "Colony" has a complex derivation stemming from the Greek *kolon* (limb or organ) and the Latin *colere* (to cultivate). The two nuances relate well enough in so far as each is concerned with *organization*, with integrating a body of constituent parts or organs so that a coordinated entity can function in the world.

This etymology suggests there is some sense in thinking about tracts of colonial land in bodily terms. The language we have inherited encourages us to know a place as a network of feelings and stimulated responses in much the same way that one can know the overall cohesion (or soul?) of one's own body precisely because one is immersed in it and neurologically mapped throughout it. Or to approach the idea from another direction: as far as I understand the systems, most hunter-gatherer societies organize feelings into crucial sites throughout their country so that the people and the country are intricate with mutual sentience. Such people ail when their tracts are abused. This should not be surprising. The country has entered the bone and tissue, the mind and soul. The country is a structure of feeling that is also a way of knowing, a way of being alive in one's place at all its times.

But what happens in a colony? How does a settler-society incorporate the new country once the multiple lesions of arrival, battle, and settlement have been endured? The place which newcomers deem to be devoid of meaning and intricacy, how can it be made "nervous" with deeply felt significance?

The organization of a colony happens through storytelling, through the application of intense emotions and ideas all over the country so that the feelings and memories of the citizenry are coordinated by the country. And it happens slowly. (One is tempted to say organically.) Eventually particular locations are charged with particular stories which overlay or occasionally intermingle with whatever stories were in place in the indigenous landscape (some history, some myths, some fantasies, some cautionary tales). The stories arrange ideas, fears, aspirations, pleasures, and pains spatially in geographical patterns and temporally in narrative rhythms that can be experienced and re-experienced by the people settling into (or being unsettled by) the country. Violence in the north can be felt as convalescence in the south. Fire in the present might be harvest in the future. Or, as Ranginui Walker has summarized a key aspect of Maori cosmology: one can only contemplate a future by keeping one's attention fixed on all the events of the past which are told and re-told assiduously so that they are available and informative *all at once* in the environment of time-and-space. Informed by the connection among all your human descendants, you back into the future, knowing how to move only because you never turn away from the time-and-place you have come from. A fool turns around to face the future, as if anything could be seen there once you took your eyes off the luminous, interrelated stories that are placed in the past.[3]

In northwest New South Wales, the forest called the Pilliga has a clumped and intricate past. Through violence, infection, and invasive systems of agriculture, the place has been organized out of its native corporation into something that is beginning to have a new comportment now that the marks and rhythms of colonization have been set down. How to know this torn tract? How to sense its patterns? One way is through *A*

Million Wild Acres, Eric Rolls's great literary account of the forest. In this tangle of local history plus Romantic tall-taling and auto-didact science, the Pilliga eventually gets represented with contentious, complex patterns of "liveness": plants and animals are described in terms of their breeding cycles and interdependencies; people of the forest, past and present, are characterized; events, such as the introduction of exotic species and the renegade turns of feral evolution, are narrated to show the ever-shifting imbrications of animals, vegetables, minerals, and signs that comprise human understanding of the country. The book is a litany of personae, morphologies, and stories that have occurred or are persisting in thousands of locations throughout the changeful system of timber and scrub called the Pilliga. Across 450 pages, Rolls treats the place as an integrated, sentient system; he attempts to divine the structure of its wonder.

But Rolls is not only attempting to assay the nervous system that is already in the Pilliga. He is also grafting meanings into it through the process of his own storytelling. He is looking for signs of life and he is organizing the country, galvanizing it with charges of his own choosing. With his array of histories and morphologies he is attempting to enchant the forest.

This idea of enchantment comes from Morris Berman's *The Reenchantment of the World*, which is in part an account of the European alchemical tradition. Berman analyzes an ancient scholarship founded on the premise that "matter possessed consciousness." In a the world that was preternaturally enchanted, the alchemist "did not *confront* matter; he *permeated* it."[4] Immersed in an enchanted world, the alchemist sought to become elementally knowledgeable.

One might argue that, in a *colonial* world, the settler is detached rather than immersed, initially perceiving absence rather than enchantment in the new location. (For example, in 1818 John Oxley was the first white man to see the Pilliga. He called it "forbidding," "miserable," and "desert."[5]) In the logic of colonialism, consciousness must be brought to the new world and ascribed to objects and places during the processes of naming and settlement. Colonial enchantment, therefore, would be the gradual orchestration of consciousness, the singing into place of meaning. And by galvanizing the country with stories, a narrator such as Rolls and the reader of a book such as *A Million Wild Acres* can eventually become both constitutive of and constituted by the enchantment. The people might permeate the country and get organized by it even as they array it. With time, as the history of a territory alters from its colonial status, the parvenu enchantments that have been put in place fuse with some of the native ones that have persisted through the turmoil. And in this jittery reanimation, a nervous system of meaning manages to prevail.[6] This is one way to understand the postcolonial condition.

The importance of *A Million Wild Acres* is that it facilitates such reorganization of country. It is a deliberately feral book that ranges across several modes of address, deploying legend, document-based historiography, zoological morphology, oral history, and autobiographical reminiscence in its processes of enchantment. Integrating a place that slowly coheres in the reader's consciousness, the book folds the reader and the Pilliga into each other.

Because this literally *sensitive* incorporation of country seems crucial to the reduction of alienation in the place I inhabit, I have been looking for ways of transforming Rolls's literary project in other media and constituencies. Hence my involvement recently in an essay-film called *Wild*[7] which is set in the Pilliga and which condenses, develops, and adapts many of Rolls's ideas while attempting to deploy film form to conjoin citizen and country ("subject" and "object") in a way that disallows our knowing these two entities as separate.

Film is well-suited to this task, particularly in the way it folds a spectator into a scene through the all-encompassing environment of sound and through editing sequences which array space over, around, and *in* a viewer whose vantage-point is being "shifted" constantly across a profusion of possible sites-of-being and sites-of-telling.

The film-theory term for this process is "suture."[8] A viewer is placed in a position. Then a cut occurs and a new placement is effected. With the next cut, the "wound" of the previous displacement is stitched insofar as the viewer's perturbance is allayed by a new move which "explains" retroactively the previous displacement. As this repeated process of cut-and-heal recurs, the film sends the viewer away from himself and all over the place. The viewer "becomes" an expansive, changeable "place" that is kept alive in an immediate, urgently remembered past wherein all the "places" of meaning course simultaneously through the viewer's consciousness.

Consider this hypothetical sequence as an example: a shot of a woman looking; a shot of a car approaching; a shot of a man at the wheel of the car; he is looking; a wide shot of the street, the car, the woman; an extreme close-up of the woman looking. Ponder the array of displacements and reconstructions that you as a viewer have undergone during this twenty-second encounter with a model of a world: you have "occupied" at least three different constructs of personality (in addition to whatever psychological configuration you brought into the theater!) in a "charged" universe, *and* you have moved all over and become the place itself.[9] Technically speaking, this has been an enchanting sequence. The spectator has been immersed in, or formed through, the locations of the film. The place of the film has entered the spectator's mind and soul. The viewer backs into the future of the film by concentrating on everything that is always becoming the ever-present past. With time, the spaces of the film pass through the spectator as all the shots are held in the memory so that the startling revelation of every new shot can continue to "heal" the viewer after the wrenching of each cut throws the world askew ever-again. The drama occurs in the modeled world of the film and simultaneously in the body of the person contemplating the world of meaning that arises.

So, hoping to fold a few more people into the Pilliga, we go into the forest with camera and microphone. We go to the locations and we cut-and-heal them so that the site-specific stories get evoked and enmeshed. We move viewers and forest characters around their particular locations. We take the viewer all over the Pilliga, with sound and stories accruing constantly, in an attempt to know a place that is charged with the significance of Aboriginal, colonial, and postcolonial Australia all contentiously incorporated in an urgently remembered present. With sounds, images, rhythms, and textures, *Wild* tells its history in the form of an audiovisual event.

As much as any written document, a sound, a gesture, or a way of walking might inform the present about how the past persists. Although verbal language may be our most complex and rule-governed way of representing the world to ourselves, it is also a censorious system, precisely because it is rule-governed. The past has vivacity and charge which has lodged not only in the words we can retrieve but also in maddeningly ephemeral events and pulses. How can the past be walked and glanced and breathed as well as talked?

We need film and video for such a question. We need the "convergence systems" of multimedia programs also, in order to imagine the past-in-the-present by thinking and feeling in response to sounds, textures, and choreographies all offered in various rhythms that propose traces of past consciousnesses to upbraid our common sense. The definitions you take for granted, the materials, gestures, and interpretations that you overlooked or presumed to be reliably settled, they can all get challenged as this extra-textual work proceeds.

In the convergence of all these traces, there's always the vivacious chance that the world you represent to *yourself* might undergo fascinating change; you might wander a little knowingly into what you don't know. This is how I'm understanding the work we've produced in digital media systems at the Museum of Sydney, which is a project dedicated to imagining and interpreting colonial history in the Sydney environs, 1788 to 1850.

Several terms require definition here, including "digital media." But first let's consider some other opportunities for doubt and redefinition: what is a "museum" nowadays, when so many electronic, *ethereal* presentations supplement (and sometimes even replace) the *material* culture that used to be the specialty of this kind of institution? And what is Sydney, once you concede that it is, and always has been, not only a place but also a receiver and transmitter of information from many times and spaces around the world? And what is "history" nowadays, particularly when you attempt to "tell" it with systems of documentation and narration that are highly manipulable and are thus ungoverned by a traditional reliance on the unim-

peachability of material "evidence"? In other words, what happens to the
status of a place over time when dubiety and negotiability irradiate the
matter that you invoke to define the place?

These questions have arisen in the Museum of Sydney mainly because
we have wanted them to be cardinal, but partly also because the digital
and multimedia resources that we have been working with have prompted
all kinds of redefinitions about the tasks now awaiting people who represent the past and the present to the present and the future.

In the case of the Museum, we are using digitized audiovisual systems
to deliver ever-reconfiguring "micro-narratives" about everyday life in the
Sydney environs. These are fictions "performed" by life-sized, computer-
rendered characters backgrounded by an "historical dreamscape" of images
and soundtracks that are all stored on laser discs. The stories and their
performances are based on historical research and are couched in a range
of generic-narrative conventions, from sailors' yarns and lovers' confessions
to surrealistic dream-movies. As viewers move throughout the meaning-full
space of the Museum, looking at objects and images of objects, looking at
people and images of people, dozens of questionable little histories get activated. The stories combine and recombine, over time, in a virtually lim-
itless "metanarrative" pattern. Objects, texts, stories and characters are
rucked and rubbed together so that little flames of fiction lick out pungently
from a tinder of records, rumors, and artifacts rummaged out of the everyday life of colonial Sydney, 1788 to 1850.

The Museum's "intertexts" do not present a conventional history. Nothing gets proved once and for all. No truths are established to put an end
to argument. Rather, the Museum spooks out some uncommon memories
and some wonderment from the tarnished old lamp of the past so that our
present lives might be visible anew in brief flickers of revelation. Therefore,
the Museum is a place for your imagining. It is designed to let you wonder
about some of the everyday experiences that have been overlooked in our
conventional histories. For example, you might like to imagine how you
could tell a history of Australian laughter. Or of Sydney sighs, groans, or
moans. Limps. Grunts. Agreements. Gestures of hello. Gestures of dismissal, seduction, or shame. We have to *imagine* these ordinary mysteries
now, because nobody thought to record them methodically in our past.
Except for occasional slips of the pen, or nonchalant sketches, private collections or archaeological lucky dips, there is little in the official records
that can help us catch fleeting experiences such as desire or repugnance.
The way the past breathed is rarely noted explicitly in the evidentiary systems that historians customarily go to.

In the Museum, the multimedia gallery called *The Bond Store* is designed
to help us muse up a better understanding of these everyday passions and
actions. It is a kind of warehouse and seance-room where we might attach
human character and voice to "dead" chattels that have been traded

through Sydney. It is a haunting-place where we might hear some of the stories embedded in commodities that have touched peoples' past lives. And in addition to the stories themselves, we might see and hear versions of the bodily comportments—the walks, gestures, vocal quavers, scars, and breathing patterns—that have been lodged in people in this place through time. Versions of these unquantifiable, always-questionable experiences are offered for consideration. As the sounds and images configure and reconfigure in the multimedia programs, fleeting minutiae of everyday life, pulsing rhythms, attractions and revulsions can be imagined, trusted, tested, or dismissed with reference to information that is accruing and potentially always available. Visitors wander curiously around *The Bond Store*, and the ethereal culture of the place "responds" by "embodying" and telling some of the stories that have arisen from research into the material culture. Depending on the chancy contiguity of story to story as the visitors snoop about, unstable larger histories get knitted together out of the microhistories. Therefore, during a thirty-minute period, let's say, a visitor can gather up a kind of demountable, questionable-yet-persuasive history, which is patently provisional and fleeting. The half-hour mesh of stories that you just "created" may not get constructed again. And if valuable meanings arose there for you, you must now be the custodian and communicator of them. In response to the slightly random, interactive space of the gallery, you become a provisional and sceptical historian.

Perhaps this sounds new and different. Actually, it is as old as communal narrative itself. As a friend quipped recently, an Aboriginal bark painting is as sophisticated a multimedia system as you could hope to find, with its spatially and temporally arrayed prompts (or "access windows") to hundreds of stories, songs, dances, gestures, paintings, journeys, and data.[10] What we're coordinating in the Museum is just another way to facilitate contentious communal interpretations of a habitable time-space. Deploying computational signals, the Museum is a series of sonic and imagistic prompts for remembering, imagining, and arguing.

Digital images and sounds are astonishingly manipulable—overlays, tonal changes, seamless reversals, and shape-shifting are all possible even as the results of the metamorphoses still look trustworthily photographic, despite the fact that they have been "written" not by light in the "real world" but by blips in mathematical systems. As digital audiovisual programs are becoming more common, it is ever more difficult to conceal the fact that photographic and cinematic realisms are not faithful indices or imprints of real events or objects. Representation professionals—photographers, cinematographers, sound-designers, layout artists—have known this for a long time. Lawyers have been disturbed to glimpse it for a decade or so. And now this fact is about to become popularly obvious: truth has always been a malleable set of contentions carefully administered by powerful classes of story-keepers. Because the systems for constructing the acceptance of truth are set to range about, truth is now poised to range about. "Validity in interpretation" (to borrow E. D. Hirsch's famous phrase) will be difficult to establish once the conventional documents of proof are no longer popularly believed to be inviolate.

This is causing both perturbation and celebration in the institutions that govern interpretation. Consider the ramifications for police work and criminal prosecution. Or take historians as another example. As a professional "class," academic historians have barely begun to know how to interpret the nineteenth-century photograph as a "document"; and now that large numbers of people are getting to manipulate digital information, it is becoming evident that the photorealist image (as well as the phonorealist sound) is principally a set of postures or propositions presented in a quaint style from the late nineteenth century. The impression of reality that realism used to support will soon begin to fade in front of us.

Is this a crisis? Well, it might be for people who need unimpeachable factuality. But it's also an *opportunity* for people interested in contending over interpretation. Here is the great challenge of digitization: suggestion and persuasion rather than unequivocal proof are now probably the best you can hope for when using imagistic and sonic "documentation" to present "truths" about the world. So, the items of evidence themselves are becoming more "corrupt." What of the processes of interpretation that happen around these items? What redefinitions of "narrative" and "history" are required now that the public sphere is adorned with the digitization and micronarrative patterning which is sometimes dubbed "interactivity"?

Let me declare immediately that interactivity is *not* inherently a libertine, democratic experience (despite the rhetoric that hucksters use to sell themselves in relation to it). Interactive systems are *pre-selected* systems. Someone or some organization has set the frames around carefully chosen data. Even so, the *negotiability* of the data and of the frame do get dramatized. One is still constrained by the chosen, available information, but one knows that the information is *relatively* unstable, *relatively* rearrangeable. Interactivity is thus *suggestive* of democratic procedures *relative* to the closed, directed, and overwhelmingly directive sets of propositions that usually get driven into line by standard authorial narratives.

This notion of relativity is crucial when interactivity is brought to historiography. And it is particularly germane in Australia, in this place and time where so many realities are attempting to relate on the contentious ground. With so much incontrovertible evidence of "otherness" in "our" midst now, and with so much evidence of the culpability of evidence, we are becoming more savvy about how relative differences are presently constitutive of everyday life in Australia. Moreover, it is increasingly apparent that the *past* everyday life in Australia must also be understood to be definitively unruly with relativity. One can see now that for hundreds of years, if not thousands, Australian realities have been contested and negotiated. And a digital, interactive museum, with its dubious evidentiary systems and its reconfigurable narratives, is well placed to prompt more of this "endemic" negotiability of meaning.

Such "historical volatility" has made me wonder about the *information* that is said to issue from the highways and byways of the digital world. It seems clear that once the binary blips are arranged into patterns of narration and speculation, they give rise not to information, but to *knowledge*. I take this distinction from Walter Benjamin's great essay on storytelling and tutelage in which he writes of the endlessly reorganizing system of awareness that gets developed in apprenticeship modes of learning.[11] This regime, where the master tells tutorial stories improvisationally in response to vocational puzzles and challenges, is contrasted with training routines that are "skills-based" and bolstered with written instruction manuals which assume (almost always wrongly) that the object to be learned is a static, inert thing. Benjamin implies that *information* is the mortar of immobile complacency in an unchanging system, whereas *knowledge* is a currency for inquiring and negotiating in an unpredictable world. Knowledge is the currency that gets generated out of experience remembered and proposed in myriad stories about fleeting versions of masterly activity in the changeable world-to-be-known. Knowledge never stops, whereas information gets poured out and then sets.

Accordingly, *historical* knowledge might propose a contentious set of feelings for the pulses of power and emotion that have shaped everyday life through the past. Historical knowledge might be an unstable, unending store of narratives that "ring true" occasionally and temporarily. Such shifty storytelling will never establish conclusive understanding. Nor does it aim to. Rather, narrated expertise—the enchantment of a place and it puzzles—is always looking and listening to stimulate an urgent, doubtful meditation on the unsettled status of the "audience." The people looking and listening then become aware of themselves as *somewhat* authorial in contention with the larger forces which also vie to arrange the experiential world, forces such as political power, climate, disease, economics, and the various configurations of yearning and revulsion that cause social action.

Historical knowledge prompted by digital and interactive systems cannot be classified as verifiable, reliable, or responsible. It does not accord well with the strictures of historical method. But as we learn more about the other past-stories—indigenous histories, criminal histories, outsiders' histories—that can still be imagined and retrieved and which were never documented for conventional historiographical purposes in Australia, we drift ever closer to declaring that orthodox history often gets in the way of the stories that really matter here and now. The more we learn about how dubious and open-ended our past-stories are, the more we are compelled to argue with the frames of realistic information that have been set as walls against our knowledge.

As always, our own liberties, thoughts, and feelings must be seized and tended for our own purposes. And even as governmental and commercial powers seek to commandeer the new audio-visual technologies, right now no one can tell anyone else exactly what is going on in the world of representation. And speaking historically, it is also increasingly difficult to prove what *was* going on in everyday lives of our past. For the moment, we're fortunate enough to have new ways of seeing and hearing that compel us to distrust our eyes and ears. This may be disenchanting to traditional historians, but it is also stimulating to our more changeful narrators of the past.

With contention and mutability in mind, therefore, I have been trying to make some sense of the Pilliga and Sydney Cove (and of Australia and postcolonialism, therefore), here in words and elsewhere in sounds and images. This will be an endless project, but in looking to conclude for the moment, I want to call up a very different tract of enchantment: the Alabama dust bowl of James Agee's *Let Us Now Praise Famous Men*. Agee's farmland is a long way from Rolls's timber country or the ghost-Sydney that the Museum conjures, but the quest-to-know is similar in each case, and Agee's words seem right for an ending which is restless enough also to be a beginning:

let me hope the whole of that landscape we shall essay to travel in is visible and may be known as there all at once; let this be borne in mind, in order that, when we descend among its windings and blockades, into examination of slender particulars, this its wholeness and simultaneous living map may not be neglected, however lost the breadth of the country may be in the winding walk of each sentence.[12]

So long as such uneasy, relational orienteering continues, the past will stay contentiously alive in the present. This is one way to enchant the present, to be immersed in the nervous system of meanings from all its times.

NOTES

A large portion of this chapter was first published by the journal *World Literature Today* in 1993. ©. It is reprinted with the permission of the editor.

1. Ellen Churchill Semple, *The Influences of Geographical Environment* (New York: Henry Holt and Co., 1911), p. 1.

2. See Krim Benterrak, Stephen Muecke, and Paddy Roe, *Reading the Country: Introduction to Nomadology* (Fremantle: Fremantle Arts Centre Press, 1984).

3. Ranginui Walker, *Ka Whawhai Tonu Matou: Struggle Without End* (Auckland: Penguin, 1990). See Chapter 1, "Mythology": 11–23.

4. Morris Berman, *The Reenchantment of the World* (Ithaca: Cornell University Press, 1981).

5. Eric Rolls, *A Million Wild Acres* (Ringwood, Australia: Penguin Books, 1984), p. 1.

6. After coming up with this analogy for the postcolonial condition, I discovered Michael Taussig's recent book, *The Nervous System* (New York: Routledge, 1992), which in some respects is about the gestalt of knowing.

7. John Cruthers, Ross Gibson, and James Manche, *Wild* (Sydney: Huzzah Productions, 54 mins, 16 mm, VHS, and U-matic). *Wild* is distributed by Ronin Films.

8. See Jean-Pierre Oudart, "Cinema and Suture," *Screen*, vol.18, no. 4 (Winter 1977/1978): 35–47; Daniel Dayan, "The Tutor-Code of Classical Cinema," *Film Quarterly* (Fall 1974): 22–31; and Stephen Heath, "On Suture" in his *Questions of Cinema* (Bloomington: Indiana University Press, 1981).

9. I recall attending a press conference for the director Nicolas Roeg in the early 1980s. In a revealing off-the-cuff remark, Roeg said that the great thing about working in the movies is that you get to move people. Knowing Roeg's predilection for a "wrenching" editing style, I take him to mean not only that viewer's emotions are activated, but that he gets to move people—characters and viewers—around, all over the spatial layout of the world represented in the film.

10. Thanks to Martin Harrison.

11. Walter Benjamin, "The Storyteller: Reflections on the Works of Nikolai Leskov," in his *Illuminations*, edited by Hannah Arendt (New York: Schocken Books, 1969).

12. James Agee, *Let Us Now Praise Famous Men*, first published 1941, reprinted (London: Picador Classic, 1988), p. 111.

Further Reading

Hospital Superintendent: It's alright. I'll tell them about your history.

Karl: You mean my past?

— Billy Bob Thornton, *Sling Blade*

Amidst so much written history, there are few stimulating books on how the past is turned into history by academic historians and other practitioners. Among many stimulating books on reading film, only a few deal directly with the problems of film as history. The following selection provides a variety of starting points: more are available in specialist databases. The more recent books also contain their own useful guides to further reading.

Benjamin, W. *Illuminations*. Edited by Hannah Arendt. New York: Shocken Books, 1969.

Burke, Peter. *History and Social Theory*. Cambridge: Polity Press, 1992.

Carnes, Mark C., ed. *Past Imperfect: History According to the Movies*. New York: Henry Holt, 1995.

Carr, E. H. *What is History?* Harmondsworth: Penguin, 1964.

Dening, Greg. *Performances*. Melbourne: University of Melbourne Press, 1996.

Jacobs, Lewis. *The Documentary Tradition*. New York: Norton, 1987.

Kaes, Anton. *From Hitler to Heimat: The Return of History as Film*. Cambridge, Mass.: Harvard University Press, 1989.

McArthur, Colin. *Television and History*. London: B.F.I., 1980.

McCann, Richard D., ed. *Film: a Montage of Theories*. New York: Dutton, 1966.

Mast, Gerald, and Marshall Cohen, with Leo Baudry, eds. *Film Theory and Criticism*. New York: Oxford University Press, 1992.

Nichols, Bill. *Blurred Boundaries: Questions of Meaning in Contemporary Culture*. Bloomington: Indiana University Press, 1994.

———. *Movies and Methods*. 2 vols. Berkeley: University of California Press, 1976, 1985.

———. *Representing Reality: Issues and Concepts in Documentary*. Bloomington: Indiana University Press, 1991.

O'Connor, John E., and Martin A. Jackson, eds. *American History/American Film*. New York: Frederick Ungar, 1979.

Renov, Michael, ed. *Theorizing Documentary*. New York: Routledge, 1993.

Rosenstone, Robert A., ed. *Revisioning History: Film and the Construction of a New Past*. Princeton, N.J.: Princeton University Press, 1995.

———. *Visions of the Past: The Challenge of Film to Our Idea of History*. Cambridge, Mass: Harvard University Press, 1995.

Sayles, John. *Thinking in Pictures: The Making of the Movie "Matewan."* Boston: Houghton Mifflin, 1987.

Sobchack, Vivien, ed. *The Persistence of History: Cinema, Television, and the Modern Event*. New York: Routledge, 1996.

Short, K.R.M., ed. *Feature Films as History*. Knoxville: University of Tennessee Press, 1980.

Sorlin, Pierre. *The Film in History*. Totowa, N.J.: Barnes and Noble, 1980.

Thompson, David. *The Aims of History*. London: Thames and Hudson, 1969.

Tulloch, John, ed. *Conflict and Control in the Cinema*. Melbourne: Macmillan, 1976.

Virilio, Paul. *War and Cinema: The Logistics of Perception*. London: Verso, 1989.

Warren, Charles, ed. *Beyond Document: Essays in Nonfiction Film*. Hanover, N.H.: Wesleyan University Press, 1996.

Williams, Linda, ed. *Viewing Positions: Ways of Seeing Film*. New Brunswick, N.J.: Rutgers University Press, 1995.

For current reviews and discussion consult the following journals:
Film and History
Film History
Historical Journal of Film, Radio and Television
Screening the Past: An International Electronic Journal of Visual Media and History
http://www.latrobe.edu.au/www/screeningthepast

Index

Contributors

TONY BARTA is a Visiting Research Fellow in the School of History at La Trobe University, where he founded the History and Film program in 1985. He has written on the role of screen media in historical understanding, on twentieth-century German history, and on genocide in Australia.

INA BERTRAND is an Associate Professor in the Department of Media Studies at La Trobe University, Bundoora, Australia. She has written extensively on both the history of Australian film and television, and the history which these media construct of Australia.

GREG DENING is Emeritus Professor of History at the University of Melbourne. He has a longstanding interest in different ways of representing the past. His books include *Islands and Beaches, The Death of William Gooch*, and *Mr. Bligh's Bad Language*.

ROSS GIBSON is a filmmaker and writer, whose films include *Camera Natura, Dead to the World* and *Wild*. He is the author of *The Diminishing Paradise, South of the West* and *The Bond Store Tales*. Half of every year, he teaches in the Media and Text Department at the University of Technology in Sydney.

SANDER L. GILMAN is Henry Luce Professor of the Liberal Arts in Human Biology at the University of Chicago. Among his books are *Jewish*

Self-Hatred: Anti-Semitism and the Hidden Language of the Jews; Picturing Health and Illness: Images of Identity and Difference; The Jew's Body; Freud, Race and Gender; and *The Case of Sigmund Freud.*

SUE HARPER is Reader in Film History at the University of Portsmouth, England. She has published widely in the area of British cinema. The British Film Institute published her book *Picturing the Past: the Rise and Fall of the British Costume Film* in 1994.

STAN JONES teaches German language, German film, and general film studies at the University of Waikato, Hamilton, New Zealand. He has a special interest in the films of Wim Wenders, in the reception of New Zealand film in Germany, and in film synchronization.

COLIN McARTHUR is a freelance writer and teacher. He was Head of the Distribution Division of the British Film Institute, and has written extensively on Hollywood cinema, British television, and Scottish culture. His publications include *Underworld USA; Television and History; Dialectic! Left Film Journalism from TRIBUNE; The Casablanca File; The Big Heat* and, as contributing editor, *Scotch Reels: Scotland in Cinema and Television.*

BRIAN McFARLANE is an Associate Professor in the English Department of Monash University, Melbourne, where he teaches film and literature. His most recent books are *Novel to Film: An Introduction to the Theory of Adaptation, Sixty Voices, The New Australian Cinema: Sources and Parallels in American and British Film* (co-authored with Geoff Mayer), and *An Autobiography of British Cinema: as told by the filmmakers and actors who made it.*

GEOFF MAYER is head of Cinema Studies at La Trobe University. His books include *The New Australian Cinema: Sources and Parallels in American and British Film* (with Brian McFarlane); *Film as Text; Media Studies: Narrative, Audience, Values and Process;* and *Movie Magic.* With Brian McFarlane and Ina Bertrand he is editor of the forthcoming *Oxford Companion to Australian Film.*

KATHRYN MILLARD is an Australian writer and filmmaker. Her films include *Light Years,* a biography of Australian photographer and writer Olive Cotton, and *Parklands,* an exploration of the dreamings of 1960s and 1990s Adelaide. She teaches in the Department of Media and Communication Studies at Macquarie University, Sydney.

DAVID PERRY is a Sydney-based painter and filmmaker who was a founding member of Ubu films and its successor, the Sydney Filmmakers' Cooperative. His experimental film and video work includes many shorter productions preceding *The Refracting Glasses.*

PIERRE SORLIN is Professor of Sociology of Cinema at the Sorbonne. Among his books are *The Film in History* , *European Cinemas, European Societies, Mass Media*, and *Italian National Cinema*. He has made documentaries (on urban landscapes and sites, and on the Portuguese community in France) and history films (on the French Revolution, the Dreyfus Affair, and the Popular Front).

JANET STERNBURG is an essayist and poet, as well as a writer for theater and film. Among the films she has written or produced are *Virginia Woolf: The Moment Whole* and *Thomas Eakins: A Motion Portrait*. She is editor of *The Writer on Her Work*, and a teacher of creative writing at the California Institute of the Arts.

DANIEL J. WALKOWITZ is a social historian and filmmaker. Director of the Metropolitan Studies Program and Professor of History at New York University, he is presently completing a book for the University of North Carolina Press on middle-class identity, *The Muddle of the Middle Class: New York Social Workers and the Politics of Identity in the Twentieth Century*. His most recent book, co-authored with Lewis Siegelbaum, *Workers of the Donbas Speak: Survival and Identity in the New Ukraine, 1989–1992*, is a sequel to his 1990 documentary on the 1989 miners' strike in Donetsk: *Perestroika from Below* (Barbara Abrash and Daniel Walkowitz, producers; Daniel Walkowitz, director; First Run Films, distributor).

ISBN 0-275-95402-1

90000>

HARDCOVER BAR CODE